STUDENT SUCCESSES With

THINKING MAPS®

SECOND EDITION

School-Based Research,
Results, and Models for
Achievement Using Visual Tools

DAVID N. HYERLE | LARRY ALPER

Foreword by Patricia Wolfe

CORWIN
A SAGE Company

CORWIN
A SAGE Company

FOR INFORMATION:

Corwin
A SAGE Company
2455 Teller Road
Thousand Oaks, California 91320
(800) 233-9936
Fax: (800) 417-2466
www.corwin.com

SAGE Ltd.
1 Oliver's Yard
55 City Road
London EC1Y 1SP
United Kingdom

SAGE India Pvt. Ltd.
B 1/I 1 Mohan Cooperative Industrial Area
Mathura Road, New Delhi 110 044
India

SAGE Asia-Pacific Pte. Ltd.
33 Pekin Street #02-01
Far East Square
Singapore 048763

Acquisitions Editor: Hudson Perigo
Associate Editor: Allison Scott
Editorial Assistant: Lisa Whitney
Production Editor: Cassandra Margaret Seibel
Copy Editor: Melinda Masson
Typesetter: C&M Digitals (P) Ltd.
Proofreader: Theresa Kay
Indexer: Jean Casalegno
Cover Designer: Scott Van Atta
Permissions Editor: Adele Hutchinson

Copyright © 2011 by Corwin

Printed in the United States of America

Library of Congress Cataloging-in-Publication Data

Student successes with thinking maps®: school-based research, results, and models for achievement using visual tools/ editors, David N. Hyerle and Larry Alper; foreword by Patricia Wolfe.—2nd ed.

p. cm.
Includes bibliographical references and index.

ISBN 978-1-4129-9089-9 (pbk.)

1. Visual learning—United States. 2. Learning, Psychology of. 3. Thought and thinking. I. Hyerle, David N. II. Alper, Larry.

371.33'5—dc22 2010041858

This book is printed on acid-free paper.

11 12 13 14 15 10 9 8 7 6 5 4 3 2 1

Contents

List of Figures and Tables

FIGURES

TABLES

Foreword

The brain remembers what it has seen because humans are intrinsically visual beings. The eyes contain almost 70% of the body's sensory receptors and send millions of signals every second along optic nerves to the visual processing centers of the brain. It is not surprising that the visual components of a memory are so robust. And it is not surprising that when teachers use visuals in the classroom to represent concepts, their students retain the concepts longer.

Visuals not only are powerful retention aids but also serve to increase understanding. Imagine trying to comprehend governmental structure or the operation of an internal combustion engine without an accompanying diagram. The ability to transform thoughts into images is often viewed as a test of true understanding.

Many studies have demonstrated the facilitating effect of visual representations on learning and memory. Bull and Wittrock (1973) reported a study examining sixth graders' understanding and recall of vocabulary words using two different strategies. One group memorized the dictionary definitions of the words, while a second group illustrated the meaning of the words. The second group's understanding and retention of the words were much higher. Another study, concerned with learning Spanish vocabulary words, taught students to use an imagery process that linked the sound of the word to an image of a concrete noun in English. The students' retention of the words increased from 28% to 88% (Atkinson & Raugh, 1975).

The Thinking Maps® program takes full advantage of the natural proclivity of the brain to think visually. The authors describe Thinking Maps as a language of visual tools grounded in the thinking process, a most neurally apt description. Neuroscientists tell us that the brain organizes information in networks and maps. What better way to teach students to think about ideas and organize and express their ideas than to use the very same method that the brain uses.

This book provides an invaluable way to help our students truly understand and retain the concepts behind the facts, and to do this in an exciting and motivating way.

Patricia Wolfe
Coauthor, *Building the Reading Brain*

REFERENCES

Atkinson, R., & Raugh, M. R. (1975). An application of the mnemonic keyword method to the acquisition of a Russian vocabulary. *Journal of Experimental Psychology: Human Learning and Memory, 104,* 126–133.

Bull, B. L., & Wittrock, M. C. (1973). Imagery in the learning of verbal definitions. *British Journal of Educational Psychology, 43,* 289–293.

Wolfe, P., & Nevills, P. (2004). *Building the reading brain.* Thousand Oaks, CA: Corwin.

Preface

RENOVATION IN PROCESS

I remember all too well when my wife and I were remodeling our small cabin in the woods of New Hampshire after we realized that our family, and our home offices, needed more space. We added two rooms, a home office, and a garage. The renovation was a difficult process as we lived in a reconstruction zone—*much* more difficult than building a new house—but in the end the core of our home and the feeling were very much the same and we adapted to our new life. The renovation analogy maps nicely onto this second edition of *Student Successes With Thinking Maps*®. We let go of very little, and many authors revised their chapters by adding significant new insights, data, and stories within the framework we had established. We also have added three new chapters with plenty of room for future growth: one on the deep connections between brain research and cognition, another focused on inquiry-based learning in science, and a closing chapter on "bifocal assessment" using Thinking Maps® for seeing the formative growth of cognitive development and content learning simultaneously.

Books offer an array of starting points for new discoveries, so we also have added virtual rooms for you to explore beyond this renovation. The first edition, which was published in 2004, and the expanding work with Thinking Maps around the world inspired me to start up a nonprofit foundation—the Thinking Foundation—that supports continuing research, social networking, and broadcasting of results within and beyond the educational community. Many of the authors within this book have continuing updates, video clips, and even complete case studies placed on our website (www.thinkingfoundation .org). New research from Ethiopia, Brazil, and England is being added as we go to press. One of our most exciting projects is a series of film documentaries, the first of which, *The Minds of Mississippi* (set for release in January 2011), is about the Pass Christian School District on the Gulf Coast of the United States. The town of Pass Christian was landfall for Hurricane Katrina in 2005, wiping out homes, businesses, and school buildings and taking lives. The story of how this school system was rebuilt from the ground up, with Thinking Maps as a common ground for learning, is presented through this film documentary. The hard work by educators and the results by students resulted in the school district becoming the top-performing district in the state, leading to federal Blue Ribbon status. This story, along with the successes with Thinking Maps across the state, is introduced in Chapter 14 of this book by Marjann Ball. Sometimes we must renovate, and sometimes we need to start anew in the way we work; the transformative story of Pass Christian is written by Suzanne Ishee. A teacher in Pass Christian, Suzanne tells of amazing educators who moved quickly to fully reengage the "minds of Mississippi" in their classrooms.

Of course, when any kind of renovation or revision is being contemplated, you have to take into account that the world around you has also changed and, thus, so has your vision of what is possible. The results and research included in this book seem even more relevant now that the educational community is responding to the needs of our time: Since 2004 when the first edition was published, the educational community has been using the symbolic power and realities of "the 21st century" to see stark problems. Educators still haven't fully escaped and shifted the early-20th-century paradigm dominated by rote learning and teaching, closed-ended standardized testing, and classroom inequities that act to lessen the chances of successful school and work experiences for our children of color, those who come to school with the need to learn English, and those in poverty.

Our world *has* changed in significant ways over the last decade. In fact, since the turn of the 21st century, technologies have taken our children from passive viewers of static TV screens in the living rooms of most homes to handheld devices through which information is streamed to and from almost anywhere in the world. The guiding metaphor for this new world is "flat world," meaning, as Thomas Friedman (2005) describes, that technologies will ultimately connect all of us around the world—from developing to "first world" peoples—to wide-open opportunities in the global marketplace of ideas and products. Linda Darling-Hammond, a policy expert and leader in the field of promoting equity in classrooms through the improvement of teacher quality based on transformational standards, draws Friedman's metaphor into the title of her comprehensive analysis of the data in *The Flat World and Education* (2010). Darling-Hammond does not focus on technology as much as she does on the international data showing that thinking and problem solving must become the focus for learning. The 2006 report by the Program for International Student Assessment (PISA; National Center for Education Statistics, n.d.) is a linchpin for her argument:

> Importantly, the PISA assessments require more advanced analysis and knowledge use than most U.S. tests, going beyond the question "Did students learn specific facts?" to ask, "What can students do with what they have learned?" PISA defines literacy in mathematics, science, and reading as students' ability to apply what they know to new problems. It is focused on the kind of learning for transfer that is increasingly emphasized in other nations' curriculum and assessment systems, but often discouraged by the kind of textbooks and testing most often used in the United States. Indeed, U.S. students fall furthest behind on PISA tasks that require complex problem solving.

If we are using macrodata-based decision making on a student, classroom, school-wide, school system, and nation-wide basis, we will systemically shift our focus to the explicit nurturing of cognitive and critical skills development and rigorous training for transfer of these skills into content-based and interdisciplinary problem solving. Actually, this is exactly what the authors of *Teaching the Digital Generation* (Kelly, McCain, & Jukes, 2009) state: "Learning must focus on 21st century thinking skills," and "Assessment must encompass both knowledge skills and higher order thinking skills . . . assessment of higher order thinking skills must be an integral part of the teaching and learning process." Leaders of the "21st century learning" movement are now demanding a focus on critical thinking, communication, innovation, problem solving, and entrepreneurial thinking.

As you will find in this new edition of 19 chapters, Thinking Maps are a transformational language for directly putting into students' hands eight visuals tools that are based on eight fundamental cognitive processes for moving students, teachers, and administrators to deeper, collaborative thinking. This integrative language becomes a nexus across whole schools for inspiring and improving teacher performance, high-quality professional development, and coaching and leadership, as well as for engaging all students in deepening their abilities to think deeply within *and* across disciplines, and improving their performance on gate-keeping tests.

Linda Darling-Hammond (2010) offers that there is no greater challenge we now have as educators than to bring these kinds of tools to those with the greatest needs. We as a people are slipping behind in our educational performance in international assessments, and when we look inside our own house, we are resegregating some of our family members into rooms without windows and doors, as the prison population grows for young African American men and boys and for the vibrant Hispanic population. It is time for a transformation in how we perceive teaching and learning, and in the tools we deliver to *explicitly* facilitate students' thinking in the 21st century.

FLOW OF THE BOOK: THE BIG PICTURE

Here is a big-picture overview of how the wide-ranging stories across the 19 chapters weave together to create a unified theme of Thinking Maps as a transformational language for learning. From the authors of these chapters, you will learn about school-wide changes in teachers' effectiveness and student performance in an inner-city elementary school in Long Beach, California, where 85% of the students entering classrooms speak Spanish as their first language; students with special needs in a middle school in North Carolina making performance leaps of over three years' growth in mathematics; girls from a single-sex, independent, K–12 school in New Zealand rising over four years to the top of that nation's educational ladder; and entering junior college students in Mississippi significantly shifting reading comprehension scores, while those in the nursing program dramatically outperform their peers of previous years. As noted above, you will also hear about the Pass Christian School District, landfall for Hurricane Katrina, rising over the years to become the top-performing school system in Louisiana.

The authors of the chapters before you bring forth insights grounded in practical examples and experiences from their work to transform teaching and learning. Together, their work creates a compelling display of what can happen when Thinking Maps are used as a language for learning by students across different cultures and languages, for deepening instruction by teachers in classrooms, and for raising the quality of professional development and change processes within whole schools. Together, the authors share wide-ranging outcomes including *significant* quantitative performance shifts by students and qualitative changes in instruction from schools within cityscapes and sprawling new suburban neighborhoods to rural landscapes and into multiple countries. The chapters come together under four major sections, as shown in the table of contents Flow Map (see Figure 0.1) and descriptions below.

After an introduction to Thinking Maps as a language in Chapter 1, Section 1 integrates brain research and a range of other models such as Habits of Mind, multiple intelligences, and learning styles with practical examples of how Thinking Maps mediate students' thinking, learning, and metacognitive behaviors. The background offered in the first section lays the foundation for showing how Thinking Maps are used for content-specific learning in Section 2. Applications in the areas of reading comprehension, writing processes, mathematics, inquiry-based science, and technology offer a view of how thinking skills may be taught directly to students for independent transfer across the disciplines, while directly meeting state standards. This focus on content learning leads to Section 3, which shows how Thinking Maps work across whole schools for improving teaching and learning, from descriptions of elementary, middle, and K–12 schools that have implemented the tools for multiple years, to research from a junior college revealing significant results, to direct training of students in Singapore. The fourth and final section broadens the focus to look at Thinking Maps as tools that simultaneously support students as well as organizational learning. Thinking Maps facilitate the transformation of professional development within schools by "inviting explicit thinking" by teachers, in the coaching and supervision processes with teachers, and by uniting whole school faculties around a common visual language for "constructivist conversations." The last chapter is a synthesis of what many of the authors state in different ways throughout the book: Thinking Maps are effective and efficient representations of students' content knowledge *and* thinking processes, and thus become an additional set of tools for formative assessment.

TREE OF TRANSFORMATIONS

From a big-picture point of view, the successes that shine through the research and results discussed in this book reveal the development of rich content knowledge and, more important, reflections on the continuous cognitive development of *every* learner—student, teacher, and

Figure 0.1 Flow Map of Book

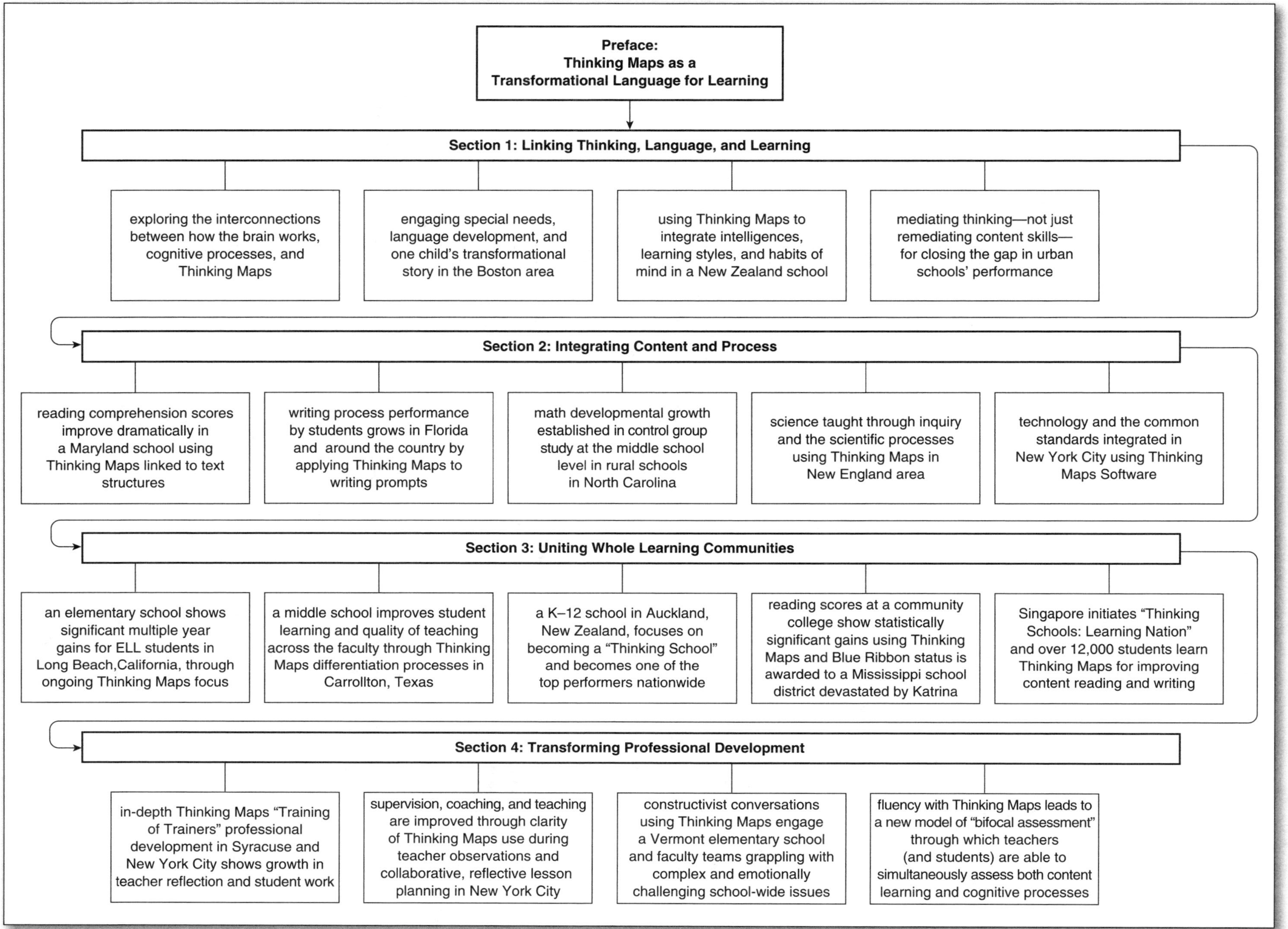

Preface:
Thinking Maps as a
Transformational Language for Learning

Section 1: Linking Thinking, Language, and Learning

- exploring the interconnections between how the brain works, cognitive processes, and Thinking Maps
- engaging special needs, language development, and one child's transformational story in the Boston area
- using Thinking Maps to integrate intelligences, learning styles, and habits of mind in a New Zealand school
- mediating thinking—not just remediating content skills—for closing the gap in urban schools' performance

Section 2: Integrating Content and Process

- reading comprehension scores improve dramatically in a Maryland school using Thinking Maps linked to text structures
- writing process performance by students grows in Florida and around the country by applying Thinking Maps to writing prompts
- math developmental growth established in control group study at the middle school level in rural schools in North Carolina
- science taught through inquiry and the scientific processes using Thinking Maps in New England area
- technology and the common standards integrated in New York City using Thinking Maps Software

Section 3: Uniting Whole Learning Communities

- an elementary school shows significant multiple year gains for ELL students in Long Beach, California, through ongoing Thinking Maps focus
- a middle school improves student learning and quality of teaching across the faculty through Thinking Maps differentiation processes in Carrollton, Texas
- a K–12 school in Auckland, New Zealand, focuses on becoming a "Thinking School" and becomes one of the top performers nationwide
- reading scores at a community college show statistically significant gains using Thinking Maps and Blue Ribbon status is awarded to a Mississippi school district devastated by Katrina
- Singapore initiates "Thinking Schools: Learning Nation" and over 12,000 students learn Thinking Maps for improving content reading and writing

Section 4: Transforming Professional Development

- in-depth Thinking Maps "Training of Trainers" professional development in Syracuse and New York City shows growth in teacher reflection and student work
- supervision, coaching, and teaching are improved through clarity of Thinking Maps use during teacher observations and collaborative, reflective lesson planning in New York City
- constructivist conversations using Thinking Maps engage a Vermont elementary school and faculty teams grappling with complex and emotionally challenging school-wide issues
- fluency with Thinking Maps leads to a new model of "bifocal assessment" through which teachers (and students) are able to simultaneously assess both content learning and cognitive processes

administrator—in a school. Many educators, as described in this book, brought Thinking Maps into their schools because they believed that there would be an impact on teacher instruction and student performance. They were proven right. Yet many of these teachers and administrators did not foresee that Thinking Maps would also transform the culture of learning across the whole school.

As you read the book, no doubt you will begin to create in your mind an evolving picture of the association of ideas, applications, and results presented. With each chapter you read, this picture may shift as you interpret the findings. This certainly happened with me as I read, reread, and began editing these chapters. The themes, on large and small scales, began to emerge in my mind, and I could not keep track of all of the information and concepts, finally leading me to create a Tree Map as one expression of the complex, overlapping discoveries made by the authors (see Figure 0.2).

On a blank piece of paper, starting at the bottom of the page, I began associating details that kept growing in clusters, like leaves on a tree, from across chapters. These informal groupings drew me inductively up to the lower branches, revealing seven basic categories near the middle of the page. I finally reached a new layer of limbs: four generalizations that for me most clearly represented a more expansive view. This structure enabled me to think about and summarize what I interpreted as key concepts: integrating teaching, learning, and assessment; displayed metacognition; tools for equity; and whole-school growth.

Integrating Teaching, Learning, and Assessment. One of the greatest concerns in schools today is how teachers can bring together curriculum and instruction in a way that is meaningful for student learning, while focusing on content standards and assessments. Almost every author in this book addresses this issue in some way, investigating how Thinking Maps become an integration point for these areas, especially across the most crucial areas of performance: reading, writing across disciplines, mathematics, and inquiry science (Chapters, 6, 7, 8, and 9, respectively). For example, in Chapter 7, Jane Buckner shows how the maps support the development of writing processes across disciplines and all grade levels, from emergent writers to high school levels, by providing clear "structures for organization." She emphasizes the need for teachers to model the integrated use of the maps across writing prompts and links this work to specific state assessments. In a different vein, in a new Chapter 9, Lou-Anne Conroy explains with great detail how inquiry-based learning in high school science classrooms engages students in independent and collaborative processes and thus heightens their awareness of their own thinking. In Chapter 19 on "bifocal assessment" I worked with Kim Williams to describe and refine a pragmatic sequence of activities for moving students to high levels of fluency with the maps, which, in turn, enables formative assessments of content concepts and cognitive processes.

Displayed Metacognition. This term was coined by Dr. Art Costa as a description of the power of visual tools, because these tools display before the learner a range of cognitive patterns of thinking, thus enabling richer reflections. This phrase also captures a central point made by many authors: When using Thinking Maps, students, teachers, and administrators become self-reflective, looking into their own thinking, and become self-regulated learners. These patterns, as Kim Williams discusses in Chapter 2, are extensions of how the brain works. The brain actively binds data together through neural patterns and networks information, pruning as needed, chunking information, grasping bits of linked information in working memory, and then holding onto them in long-term memory. Kim goes deeper in a provocative essay that actually shows that the cognitive processes grounding Thinking Maps are *directly* related to the unconscious patterning happening within the complex neural functioning of the brain. Bonnie Singer follows in the next chapter by telling "The Story of David," a boy with severe learning disabilities who,

Figure 0.2 Thinking Maps as a Transformational Language

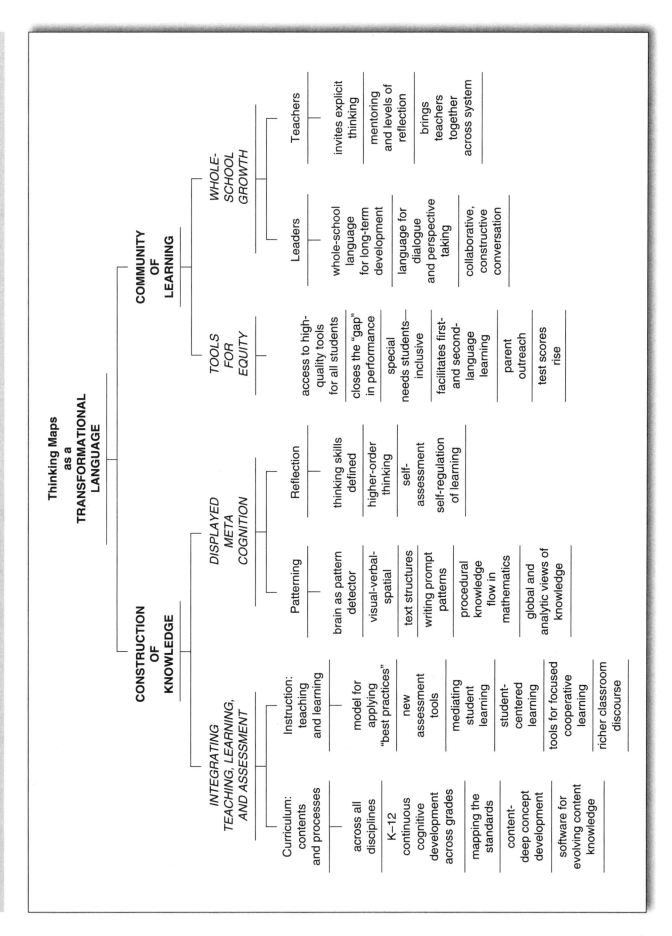

through the use of these tools over two years, was transformed from being a student with low performance to a self-regulated learner.

Tools for Equity. While the idea of facilitating cognitive and metacognitive development has been central to the past 50 years of educational psychology and neuroscience, often the promise of thinking skills instruction has remained elusive and inaccessible to those in the greatest need. Another theme that arises from this book is an understanding that the maps directly support teachers in mediating students' thinking. In Chapter 5, Yvette Jackson discusses how the maps become tools for mediating thinking and literacy development, especially when supporting children of color who are struggling to learn in underachieving, inner-city schools. As Yvette points out, these children are often merely remediated through repetitive cycles of content learning but not deeply mediated through their thinking abilities.

Ultimately, the issue here is about equal access to high-quality tools for thinking and instruction that support *all* students' thinking abilities, across languages and cultures at the highest level. This call for equity is answered throughout the book, most clearly in the stories by Stefanie Holzman in Chapter 11 from a school in California and by Marjann Ball in Chapter 14 from a junior college in Mississippi. Both of these chapters present research and results showing significant gains for closing the achievement gap.

Whole-School Growth. The field of education is now faced with the complex problem of teaching to the "whole child" while also attempting to transform "whole schools." We are moving away from seeing students as individual learners in straight rows of desks to a model of learning based on a circle of learning. Many schools are directly teaching to the social and emotional needs of all children, understanding that these are not just pathways to learning content, but are important in and of themselves. This involves consciously integrating conflict resolution and cooperative and social-emotional learning into the classroom context.

A similar shift is now occurring in the area of organizational change across whole schools as educators are becoming aware of how learning and leadership are intimately connected. An undercurrent of every chapter in this book is the depth of self-learning attained by students, teachers, and administrators *in the context of working across whole schools.* In Chapters 11–13, we are offered detailed histories of how three very different schools across the K–12 spectrum implemented Thinking Maps as a language in their whole schools, clearly demonstrating how learning, teaching, and leadership are united through these common tools. In Chapters 16–18, the authors focus on how educators learn to work together by visually surfacing perceptions and ideas through their interactions with each other. Sarah Curtis details the implementation process in Chapter 16 by looking at how high-quality professional development in Thinking Maps proceeds from novice to expert levels. In a revised Chapter 17, Kathy Ernst nicely balances Sarah's focus on professional development by showing explicitly how coaching and supervision are deepened by using the maps as tools in lesson observations and the pre- and postconference sessions to support teachers in becoming more self-reflective in the practice of teaching.

So often the conversations that happen in meetings in schools become procedural rather than reflective, sometimes combative rather than constructive. Larry Alper brings to us in his revised Chapter 18 an offering of new research on Thinking Maps as a language for leadership. Within this new research, he engages us with the term *constructivist conversations* as an expression of how Thinking Maps become a new language for deepening conversations so that people come together through the maps, facing their own and each other's thinking, "opening the space" for problem solving, and transforming the quality of thinking and learning across the whole school.

The four central ideas discussed above joined together for me as two major themes: "construction of knowledge" as a framework for learning and "communities of learning" expressing the communal quality of the educational experience. I finally reached the top of the tree, discovering the overarching view from which I could see and make sense of the details within the whole of the book *Student Successes With Thinking Maps*. The authors show us that Thinking Maps are a transformative language for learning, for personal growth and self-assessment, for collaborative work across complex and increasingly "virtual" technological organizations and societies, and as common pathways for communicating across diverse languages and cultures. As you may see in the written and graphic forms throughout this book, these maps have simple starting points and spread organically as a seed maturing to full growth, providing for the creation of infinitely complex patterns of knowledge for every child, drawing out our multiple frames of reference, and mirroring the richly textured landscape of our lives.

David Hyerle, Ed.D.

REFERENCES

Darling-Hammond, L. (2010). *The flat world and education.* New York: Teachers College Press.

Friedman, T. L. (2005). *The world is flat: A brief history of the 21st century.* New York: Farrar, Strauss & Giroux.

Kelly, F. S., McCain, T., & Jukes, I. (2009). *Teaching the digital generation.* Thousand Oaks, CA: Corwin.

National Center for Education Statistics. (n.d.). *A summary of findings from PISA 2006.* Retrieved November 8, 2010, from http://nces.ed.gov/surveys/pisa/pisa2006highlights.asp

Appreciations

It has been a delight working on this second edition with the folks at Corwin and all of the authors who added to their original thinking. Importantly, Sarah Curtis, now an elementary school assistant principal, was an editor of the first edition of this book, and her hard work still shines through these pages. With this edition, many thanks go to Lou-Anne Conroy, who helped bring this edition together by reorganizing chapters, figures, and flights of mind as we struggled to the finish line!

Our deepest appreciations go to all of the authors who have contributed to the work and research over the years as well as to the teachers, administrators, and students who continue to inspire us as they use Thinking Maps®. Many of the authors in this book and teachers and administrators in the field were initially inspired to bring the maps into classrooms by the hardworking consultants and representatives from Thinking Maps, Inc., who work their hearts out and stretch their minds across several countries and across most of the United States. We thank them for their passionate and determined efforts to bring their wide-ranging knowledge to educators and students every day.

We also thank those students quoted in this book who offered their applications of Thinking Maps and their profound, magical insights such as these:

"The maps are like a brain."

"Thinking Maps are the paper of my mind."

"While I am reading, my mind adds to my Thinking Maps all by itself, and suddenly I know more than I knew!"

About the Editors

David Hyerle, Ed.D., is an independent researcher, author, and consultant focused on literacy, thinking-process instruction, and whole-school change. He is the developer of the Thinking Maps® language and is presently codirector of Designs for Thinking, a consulting and research group based in New England. He is also founding director of the Thinking Foundation (www .thinkingfoundation.org), a nonprofit organization funding research and development on Thinking Maps and other approaches that make thinking a foundation for learning in schools for those with the greatest need.

Larry Alper, M.S.Ed., a former elementary school principal, is codirector of Designs for Thinking, an educational consulting group focused on research, literacy, and whole-school improvement nationally and internationally. Larry facilitates professional development seminars on Thinking Maps® in the Northeast and is the lead author for the seminar guide *Thinking Maps: A Language for Leadership.* Larry is presently focused on research and development for the use of Thinking Maps as a language for leadership across whole schools and school systems.

For contacting the editors or contributors:
David Hyerle, Ed.D., www.mapthemind.com

About the Contributors

Marjann Kalehoff Ball, Ed.D., is an independent consultant working in pre-K to college level across Mississippi and Louisiana. Formerly a professor of English and Development of Critical Thinking and Study Skills at Jones County Junior College in Mississippi, Marjann now works with Thinking Maps, Inc. and focuses on implementing and supporting schools to bring Thinking Maps into the daily life of the classroom. Believing that learning is a continuing process that can be fostered across all levels of education, she is convinced that Thinking Maps are an indispensable tool of learning for age or ability differentiations.

Jane Buckner, Ed.S., is a national educational consultant and author of works focused on developing writing proficiency in students from kindergarten through high school. She is presently a lead consultant with Thinking Maps, Inc. and working with whole-school implementation of *Write . . . from the Beginning* and *Write . . . for the Future.* Jane most recently authored a comprehensive teachers' and facilitators' guides to second language acquisition, titled "Path to Proficiency" (Thinking Maps, Inc., 2009). These guides integrate "thought and language" using Thinking Maps to scaffold language learning for students.

Daniel Cherry, M.Ed., is currently bringing his knowledge of Thinking Maps and other approaches to engaging learning and thinking at the highest levels to his sixth-grade students of Towle Elementary School in the town of Newport, New Hampshire. Before returning to the classroom Dan directed the New Hampshire School Administrators Leading with Technology (NHSALT) program as part of a Gates grant for the New Hampshire State Department of Education. He was also a former technology coordinator in the Lebanon, New Hampshire, school district.

Edward V. Chevallier, M.Ed., is currently serving as Assistant Superintendent for Curriculum & Instruction in the Northwest Independent School District, north of Fort Worth, Texas. Previously, he has served as a principal, teacher, and educational consultant and Thinking Maps trainer. As a middle school principal, Mr. Chevallier led his campus to make achievement gains by helping students use Thinking Maps as learning, thinking, and assessment tools. Upon leaving the principalship, he moved into district work in the area of curriculum and staff development. In that role, he was able to apply Thinking Maps to organizational planning and development. His work in public education began at the elementary school level as a teacher and principal. Mr. Chevallier is an experienced trainer in topics that include school leadership, instructional strategies, and brain-based learning.

Ho Po Chun, M.Ed., is a former teacher and elementary principal in the Singapore schools. Presently she leads the implementation of Thinking Maps for the Innovative Learning Circle in Singapore and is dedicated to developing the thinking abilities of students across Singapore.

Lou-Anne Conroy, M.A., has taught high school science for over 25 years. Presently she is an instructor for Teaching Science through the Inquiry Process (TSIP) sponsored by Massachusetts Science and Engineering Fair, Inc. and Gelfand Endeavor in Massachusetts Schools (GEMS). She facilitates the implementation of inquiry-based teaching and learning for education interns and works directly with classroom teachers to support sustainable science, technology, engineering and math (STEM) education for all children. Through her work as a consultant for Designs for Thinking and Thinking Foundation, she is convinced of the power of Thinking Maps to help children of all academic abilities learn science as well as function as a very compelling tool for the mentoring of education interns and lesson planning. In addition to her work with science education, she is actively involved in current scientific research institutions.

Alan Cooper, B.A., B.Ed. Dip Tchng. ANZIM, is a New Zealand independent consultant specializing in thinking skills and how learning occurs. As Headmaster of St. George's School (now a part of Collegiate School) for 17 years, he was known for taking responsible risks in educational innovation, including the first implementations of Thinking Maps, Habits of Mind, Multiple Intelligences, and the Dunn and Dunn Learning Styles models in New Zealand.

Sarah Curtis, M.Ed., is now assistant principal of the Bernice A. Ray Elementary School in Hanover, New Hampshire, a school that is part of the SAU 70 school system. She is passionate about enhancing student and teacher performance by supporting educational discourse through teacher reflection. Sarah was a co-editor of the first edition of *Student Successes With Thinking Maps* (Corwin, 2004) and conducted her master's level research on Thinking Maps and teacher reflection.

Kathy Ernst, M.S.Ed., is a national education consultant who has taught children and teachers for over 30 years. At Bank Street College of Education she taught online mathematics courses and served on the faculty of the Leadership in Mathematics Education Program. She is currently using Thinking Maps to develop visible processes of coaching, supervision, and professional development.

Stefanie R. Holzman, Ed.D., is the Co-Director and Internal Evaluator of the Charter and Autonomous Schools Leadership Academy—a federal grant at California State University, Dominguez Hills, in Southern California. She is also an adjunct professor at CSUDH where she teaches in the Education Administration Department. Prior to that she was Director of Curriculum, Standards and Instruction for the Orange County Department of Education in Costa Mesa, California. Formerly, she was the principal of Roosevelt Elementary School in Long Beach, California, a California Distinguished School and California Title I Academic Achievement Award Winning School with 100% of students receiving free lunch, 85% ELLs, and 99% minority. It was at Roosevelt that Stefanie found strategies to embed Thinking Maps© into all aspects of the curriculum, in all subject areas across all grade levels. She believed that despite demographics, all Roosevelt students were capable of personal and academic excellence. Of her other professional endeavors, none was as fulfilling as when she was encouraging the daily empowerment of Roosevelt students to become life-long learners!

Gill Hubble, M.A., LTCL Dip Tchng, is an independent international consultant on teaching thinking strategies, the design of whole-school thinking and learning programs, and organizational change. Associate Principal of St. Cuthbert's College for 16 years, she has also been a researcher and consultant to the Advanced Learning Center and Centre for Excellence at the college's Collegiate Centre. Presently, Gill is doing international consulting and giving keynote addresses on how places of learning may also become "Thinking Schools."

Yvette Jackson, Ed.D., is the Chief Executive Officer for the National Urban Alliance for Effective Education. In this capacity, she works with school district leaders and teachers across the country to customize and deliver systemic approaches to elicit high intellectual performances from all students. She is the author of *Pedagogy of Confidence,* which is the cornerstone of the design she oversees of tailored courses of study in cognitive strategies and instructional practices that focus on identifying and amplifying the intellectual potential of school dependent urban students.

Janie B. MacIntyre, M.Ed., is a middle school teacher, researcher, and educational consultant who was named as a *USA Today* Teacher Team member and a Christa McAuliffe Scholar. As a trainer with Innovative Learning Group, she has facilitated Thinking Maps training with over 3,000 teachers in multiple states.

Thomasina DePinto Piercy, Ph.D., is a former principal with 18 years of K–5 teaching experience. As a collaborative writer about data-driven, whole-school student performance change, she provides support for colleagues looking for similar significant and lasting results as have occurred at her former school, Mt. Airy Elementary. Thommie is the Director of Elementary Instruction for the Carroll Country Office of Education in Maryland and is author of the book *Compelling Conversations: Connecting Leadership to Achievement* (Lead and Learn Press, 2010).

Bonnie Singer, Ph.D., is the president/CEO of Architects For Learning, where she provides professional development for schools nationwide in instructional methods for teaching writing and literacy, and she directs a staff that provides academic assessment and intervention services. In partnership with Dr. Anthony Bashir, she developed the EmPOWER™ method for teaching expository writing. Dr. Singer received her doctorate from Emerson College, where she was also an instructor and clinical supervisor in the department of Communication Sciences and Disorders for many years. Currently, she holds an adjunct teaching appointment in Graduate and Professional Studies at Endicott College.

Kimberly M. Williams, Ph.D., is currently a school professional development and assessment consultant. She also serves on the graduate faculty of Plymouth State University in New Hampshire. She has previous taught at Hobart and William Smith Colleges in Geneva, New York, Dartmouth College in Hanover, New Hampshire, and Plymouth State University. Dr. Williams's research and publications have focused on cognition and tools for improving thinking in the classroom and she has two books forthcoming on assessment strategies for assessing thinking and learning. She also writes and teaches about topics related to education policy (specifically policies related to school security, students' rights, and funding), cognitive neuroscience and learning, and foundations of education. Her most recent book was co-authored with Dr. Marcel Lebrun entitled *Keeping Kids Safe, Healthy and Smart* by Rowan Littlefield Publishers released in early 2009.

1

Thinking Maps as a Transformational Language for Learning

David Hyerle, Ed.D.

KEY CONCEPTS

- A common visual language for thinking and learning
- Visible learning, best practices, and brain research
- Describing five essential characteristics of Thinking Maps® using a Bubble Map

INTRODUCING A PATTERN LANGUAGE

Thinking Maps are a *language.* I have used the words *model, approach,* and *tools* to name and define the maps, but these are inadequate placeholders for what is really a new language for thinking and communicating. First and foremost, this language is grounded in and defined by eight everyday, *interdependent* cognitive processes we use as human beings to make sense of our world and through which we survive. The second key dimension of this language is the eight visual starting points, or graphic primitives, from which emerge unique patterns that are congruent, respectively, with each of the cognitive processes. For example, a simple box of the Flow Map is drawn as a starting point for visually showing highly complex story narratives or parallel processes on a computer. It is clear that human beings are uniquely metacognitive, meaning that we can consciously reflect on *what* we are thinking and on *how* we are thinking. With Thinking Maps, all learners have a visual-verbal language of cognition, thus enabling a deeper capacity to see, transfer, reflect upon, and improve their thinking abilities.

Thinking Maps, in a nutshell, are a *pattern language.* Almost all languages (except spoken-only languages) have graphic primitives: 0–9 (plus operations such as +, –, and =) in mathematics, alphabetic systems such as the 27 letters of English (plus punctuation), and musical notation. Each of these languages is based on *unique graphic primitives* that are interdependent and combined in simple ways to create complex representations of ideas, emotions, analytic arguments, discoveries, and works of art. These symbols are arbitrary; they don't *mean* anything in how they look other than what *we* ascribe to them in our language community.

Thinking Maps (see Figure 1.1) are no different from other languages that have been developed within or across cultures: Languages are inherently *made* by humans and thus are arbitrary and incomplete, and have grey areas and ambiguous "rules" that sometimes govern strange usage. Yet, we agree as communities to use these imperfect languages because we find them useful for communication in our daily lives. But we have never had, as far as I know, a language of cognition, or, more specifically, a language for generating patterns of thinking based on human cognitive structures. Certainly, our spoken and written and mathematical languages are all based on being able to represent our thinking, ideas, and concepts but *not* for explicitly representing thinking as patterns. One would be hard pressed to argue that the words set in linear sequence found on this page actually *display* thinking patterns such as comparisons or categories, metaphors, or complex causal relationships. Our written languages have embedded within them all of these cognitive patterns, but they do not appear before your eyes right now on this page. The thinking patterns are embedded in the linearity of text, and you need to work a bit to dig them out. For example, in the Preface, you can see my conceptual understanding of the themes of the book in a Tree Map that would not be as easily represented in linear text. The most obvious example is this: When we Google directions to a place we are going, we can get both the linear, line-by-line directions and a visual map showing the network of back roads and major highways offering a multitude of options. Thinking Maps offer mental maps of how we are thinking and new routes for understanding.

Figure 1.1   Introducing the Thinking Maps Language

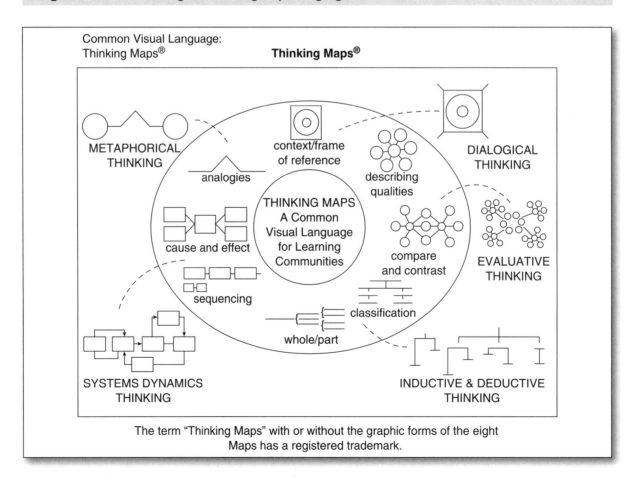

Thinking Maps complement and support the integration of all the languages we use in school, around the house, or at the workplace. As shown in this book, the maps directly support language acquisition, reading comprehension, writing processes, mathematics problem solving, and inquiry-based science. Thinking Maps offer a language that combines symbols: All other symbols and pictorial representations may be used within each of the maps. Maybe the most obvious link to other languages is in how Thinking Maps function. From a blank page or computer screen, we can map iterations of basic cognitive patterns starting with simple graphics, much like we write out sentences on a blank tablet. In Figure 1.2 you can view the graphic primitives on the left side, the corresponding definition of each cognitive process in the middle, and the depiction of an expanded map on the right side.

Psychologists, cognitive scientists, and educators have richly researched the eight fundamental cognitive processes, as described in more detail below, reaching far back into the early history of modern education. These eight structures were identified by Jean Piaget as "mental operations" that are foundational: These cognitive processes are used in isolation and in combination as we assimilate and accommodate new content and concepts. They are with us as we shift from concrete to abstract thinking. Mental operations such as comparisons, categorization, seriation, causality, and whole-part reasoning are with us our entire lives and develop as "content knowledge" and conceptual understandings become more complex. Try *not* using these patterns of thinking!

Thinking Maps, as a pattern language of cognitive processes, are a way for learners to become conscious of and transfer these mental operations into any learning environment, from early childhood to the adult workplace. Teachers use the maps to convey, facilitate, and mediate thinking and learning as every student becomes more fluent with the maps as a language. In single classrooms and across whole schools over multiple years, students are generating ever more complex applications of single maps by their own hands and creating unique configurations of multiple maps together in response to the content and concepts they are learning. Of course, several of the graphic primitives have been used for a long time to help generate and communicate processes, such as the Flow Map (or flowchart) for sequencing and cycles, the Tree Map for conceptualizing hierarchies and taxonomies, and the Brace Map for diagramming the anatomy of the major and minor parts of the human body. What is *new* about Thinking Maps is not the idea of dynamic graphic primitives (all languages are built on this premise), but that there is a coherent, interdependent, and universal array of thinking processes that are used in orchestration by students and teachers as a common visual language for learning.

From the early 1990s, our focus has been on *all* teachers immediately training *all* of their students across their *whole* school to become fluent with the tools. As you will read below, I first developed Thinking Maps after teaching in the Oakland Unified School District in Northern California in the mid-1980s. Over the years, thousands of whole-school faculties have implemented the maps, thus representing a great multiplier effect as large numbers of students from prekindergarten to college have become fluent in Thinking Maps. From first introductions to complex applications over time, students, teachers, and administrators move from novice to expert use in these tools, using maps independently, in cooperative groups, and as participants in schools for visually sharing ideas and for creating final products. Thinking Maps, introduced as *a common visual language* for thinking and learning across whole learning communities, are taught to students in order for them to improve their unique cognitive abilities and to transfer these processes deeply into academic fields. Thinking Maps are also used as a set of visible tools for interdisciplinary problem solving and decision making—not for a year or so, or just across a few classrooms, but as a systemic language for change across whole school communities, across school districts, and into the college level and workplace. Ultimately, within the networks of these cognitive processes are found our capacities to reflect on and improve our thinking,

Figure 1.2 Thinking Maps Graphic Primitives and Definitions of Cognitive Processes

Graphic Primitives and Definitions

primitives	Thinking Maps and the Frame	expanded maps

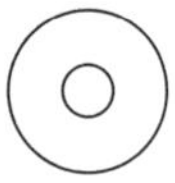

The Circle Map is used for seeking context. This tool enables students to generate relevant information about a topic as represented in the center of the circle. This map is often used for brainstorming.

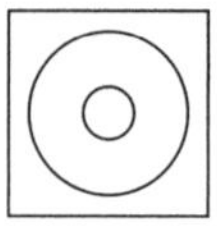

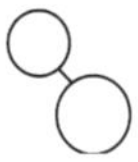

The Bubble Map is designed for the process of describing attributes. This map is used to identify character traits (language arts), cultural traits (social studies), properties (sciences), or attributes (mathematics).

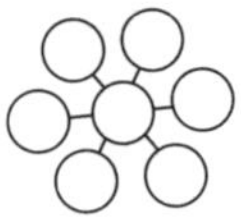

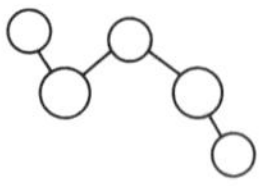

The Double Bubble Map is used for comparing and contrasting two things, such as characters in a story, two historical figures, or two social systems. It is also used for prioritizing which information is most important within a comparison.

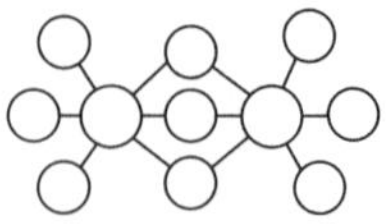

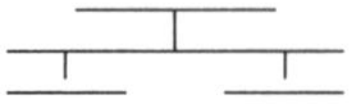

The Tree Map enables students to do both inductive and deductive classification. Students learn to create general concepts, (main) ideas, or category headings at the top of the tree, and supporting ideas and specific details in the branches below.

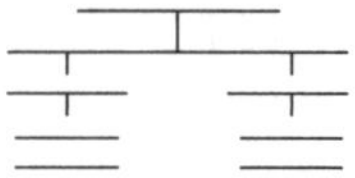

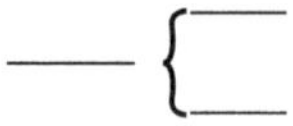

The Brace Map is used for identifying the part-whole, physical relationships of an object. By representing whole-part and part-subpart relationships, this map supports students' spatial reasoning and their understanding of how to determine physical boundaries.

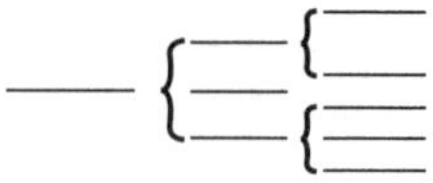

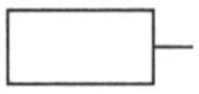

The Flow Map is based on the use of flowcharts. It is used by students for showing sequences, order, timelines, cycles, actions, steps, and directions. This map also focuses students on seeing the relationships between stages and substages of events.

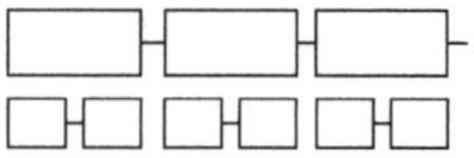

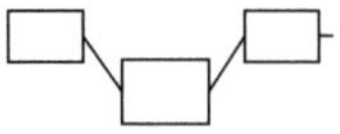

The Multi-Flow Map is a tool for seeking causes of events and the effects. The map expands when showing historical causes and predicting future events and outcomes. In its most complex form, it expands to show the interrelationships of feedback effects in a dynamic system.

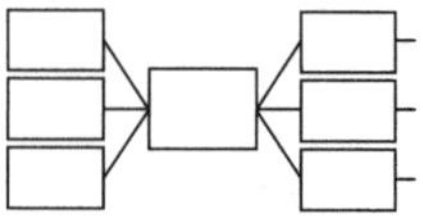

The Bridge Map provides a visual pathway for creating and interpreting analogies. Beyond the use of this map for solving analogies on standardized tests, this map is used for developing analogical reasoning and metaphorical concepts for deeper content learning.

The Frame

The "metacognitive" Frame is not one of the eight Thinking Maps. It may be drawn around any of the maps at any time as a "meta-tool" for identifying and sharing one's frame of reference for the information found within one of the Thinking Maps. These frames include personal histories, culture, belief systems, and influences such as peer groups and the media.

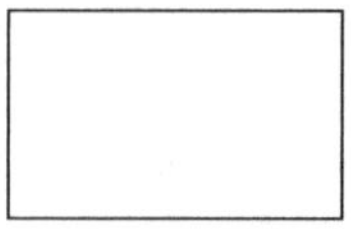

improve ourselves, support others to do the same, and hopefully improve the world around us.

VISIBLE LEARNING, "BEST PRACTICES," AND THE BRAIN

Before going deeper into refined definitions of the maps, let's ask a question that drives to the heart of how Thinking Maps work: What is the connection between thinking and learning? Is this a simple question? I don't think so; as a matter of fact, I believe we as an educational community had in our hands in the late 1970s and 1980s an answer to many of the dilemmas we face in classrooms today. Back then there was a "thinking skills" movement, and it was derailed for many different reasons but foremost because many of the leaders of the movement were in the discovery phase of a whole new paradigm for learning, exploring the possibilities and the ultimate effects of focusing on cognition, mediation of thinking, critical reflection, and metacognition. The "results" did not come soon enough, or the time was not ripe, or simply the idea of focusing systematically on thinking in the context of content learning was too big a shift. But now new research in the brain sciences (see Chapter 2) and comprehensive studies of the primary effects on learning are bringing us back to the future. Let's first take a look at some new research and then draw upon Robert Marzano's research on classroom strategies that work (Marzano, Pickering, & Pollock, 2001).

The most comprehensive synthesis of 800 meta-analyses ever completed on what drives high-quality student performance was recently published. The book is *Visible Learning* by John Hattie (2009), a professor of education at the University of Auckland, New Zealand. What is the overarching key to improving student learning? In the summary of the book, Hattie states,

> The story is about the visibility of teaching and learning: it is the power of passionate, accomplished teachers who focus on students' cognitive engagement with the content . . . developing a way of thinking, reasoning, and emphasizing problem solving and strategies in their teaching about the content they wish students to learn.

We all may say we do this, but let's be clear: Content has trumped process decade after decade. And our present assessment and evaluation instruments are mirrors for what we expect of children in the 21st century. Educators around the world really do not explicitly focus on thinking and cognitive development, even though we know that cognitive development is happening over the prekindergarten through college years in *every* child, *every* day. Why don't we directly tap these cognitive structures, make them visible, mediate them, assess them, enhance them, and give students the tools to consciously transfer these thinking processes beyond the classroom?

John Hattie (2009) identifies an array of factors that foster learning, but his in-depth analysis of data leads to a clear vision of the most influential foundations of learning: cognitive engagement, metacognition, and dynamic feedback between students and teachers. These focal points have the highest statistical "effects" on the lives of learners and teachers. Yet, Hattie is also clear-cut in his warning—this is an explanation of results from across a range of studies—and he does not pretend to suggest direct causality. This basically means these results should not be read as a list of "to-dos" for every teacher to write up on the whiteboard. His work gives us guidance and direction.

In another meta-analysis study more familiar to those in the United States, researchers at Mid-continent Research for Education and Learning, led by Dr. Robert Marzano, have identified nine essential areas that, when given systematic focus, have been shown to improve student achievement (see Figure 1.3).

Figure 1.3   Marzano's Nine Categories of Instructional Strategies

1. Identifying similarities and differences

2. Summarizing and note taking

3. Reinforcing effort

4. Homework and practice

5. Nonlinguistic representations

6. Cooperative learning

7. Setting objectives and providing feedback

8. Generating and testing hypotheses

9. Cues, questions, and advance organizers

To best understand how these research findings and John Hattie's (2009) new meta-analysis can immediately, effectively, and practically translate to teaching and learning, let's explore a classroom in which the use of Thinking Maps supported and connected the essential nine effective areas and Thinking Maps. This classroom experience occurred years ago in Jackson, Mississippi. In the 1990s, I was doing a lot of training in Mississippi, and after conducting in-depth training in transforming curriculum and assessment using Thinking Maps and cooperative learning techniques, I was invited into Norm Schuman's classroom. Norm had attended the seminar series, and I was sitting in at his request so that I could give him feedback on his integration processes.

Peek into Norm Schuman's sixth-grade social studies classroom in Jackson, Mississippi, and see groups of students huddled over books, working together, busily and intently sketching a picture of information, and drawing to the surface essential knowledge that was once bound by text. All groups use a common visual tool—a hierarchical structure reflected by a Tree Map—to collect, analyze, and synthesize the text into a clearly defined picture of a tribe as shown in Figure 1.4. Each group will also share this mental picture in an oral presentation, using the map as a visual guide on the overhead projector. The six cooperative learning groups have each been asked to read a passage from well-worn texts on a different Native American tribe in order to identify critical information about each Native American group: customs and celebrations, habitats, foods, gender roles and relationships among members, and spiritual beliefs. Norm emphasizes finding details about each of these topics, along with the fact that he will create the final test questions from the information each group presents. He methodically moves around the room and looks down at the developing Tree Maps, guiding here, scanning there, and nodding quietly in agreement at another table. The groups redraft these maps several times during two periods of instruction until only the most essential ideas have been distilled and organized from the text.

The following day, oral presentations begin. As each group member speaks about a key point of interest from one area on the map, his or her peers are busy at their seats, listening, sketching out the map, and making notes and comparisons to their own work.

Days after the presentations are over, Norm gives the students a test including questions based on text information they presented and questions that require them to have linked information from several of the Tree Maps. He also asks questions that involve the use of other thinking skills defined by the maps, such as the Double Bubble Map for comparing tribes, the Flow Map for showing the development of a culture, or the Multi-Flow Map for explaining the causes and effects of outside interventions. Students are ready for such questions because these tools have become a common way of communicating.

When asked about this process and, especially, about the level of his questions (answered by students who have come into his classroom as supposed underachievers from low socioeconomic neighborhoods), Norm responds, "I could never have asked these questions of my previous students, most of whom came into my class several years behind in grade-level reading. I hadn't given them the tools to make inferences like this. They didn't have the organizational abilities to work with so much information."

Figure 1.4   Native American Assignment Tree Map

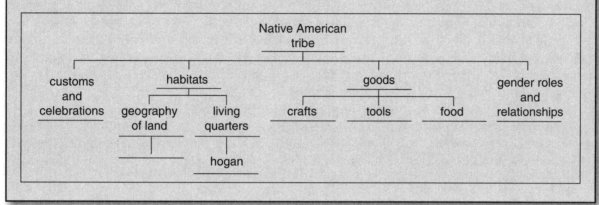

As you can see, Norm and his students apply and *unite* Marzano's effective strategy areas into fluid practice rather than interpret the nine areas as a "model" to be implemented. From the beginning of the assignment, through the presentations, and ending with the formal assessments, Norm and his students utilize Thinking Maps as tools to support processing, sharing, understanding, refining, presenting, and questioning information in order to transform information into knowledge. The clear categories of the Tree Map and the other thinking processes embedded in the visual tools provide clear objectives, feedback, and a set of cues, questions, and advanced organizers to direct and scaffold as students read for information. Cooperatively, using Thinking Maps as cues and questions, Norm's students are able to identify key similarities and differences and to synthesize chunks of information into meaningful learning during their note taking. During the presentations and assessments, the Thinking Maps continually provide the cues and questions to expand the learning, encouraging students to generate and test their hypotheses as they listen and link one tribe to the next. This Native American unit takes the list of nine essential classroom strategies, which could be interpreted as isolated practices, and explicitly and richly weaves them together into a multilayered, coherent learning experience.

Returning to John Hattie's (2009) research from *Visible Learning*, we can also *see* the thinking going on the classroom: Students are being cognitively engaged, they are reflecting on their thinking (metacognition), and they are getting direct feedback from their teacher, Norm Schuman, but also from their peers. This is because their thinking has become visible and they can share more easily what and how they are thinking together.

The link to "best practices" is apparent, and the link to present findings in brain research is even more obvious. Thinking Maps work precisely because they are fundamentally connected to how the brain thinks and learns. Just as the brain seeks patterns of information to network, Thinking Maps teach and supply an explicit visual language for students to find the patterns that exist and to construct their own networks of knowledge.

Long ago, most experts in brain-based research and learning agreed on two aspects of brain theory: The brain is a pattern seeker and is dominantly visual. According to Eric Jensen (1998), in his book *Brain-Based Teaching and Learning*, "Ninety percent of all information that comes into our brain is visual." The importance of the maps as concrete pictures of abstract concepts is linked to our ability to learn visually and the way the maps complement the complexity of the structure and processing of our visual cortex. Thinking Maps, which are visual patterns for thinking, are therefore well designed for teaching and learning. Because each map is a visual representation of a thinking process by way of a pattern, teachers can take advantage of a strategy that matches the natural learning tendencies of the brain. As we shall see in Chapter 2, the brain processes information from the senses and remembers information when it is meaningful and carries emotional value. When students "pay attention" using the maps, they are strengthening and building networks. Chris Yeager, director of consulting for Thinking Maps, Inc., has focused extensively on the linkages between what we know about the brain and why the maps work for students and teachers. She has drawn from the work of Pat Wolfe (Wolfe & Nevills, 2002), Robert Sylwester (1995), and David Sousa (2006) to create a Flow Map that shows these basic functions (see Figure 1.5). Thinking Maps are a "pattern-making language" that supports neural networking that is meaningful because the cognitive processes are fundamental to how the brain works through the neural processes of sequences, hierarchies, and causality. This is fully explored by Kim Williams in the next chapter.

Let's return to the classroom to reinforce this research in practice. Students in Norm's classroom working on the Native American units have the concrete visual tools to find the patterns embedded in reading and to see their own thinking emerge as they literally connect

Figure 1.5   How the Brain Processes Information Flow Map

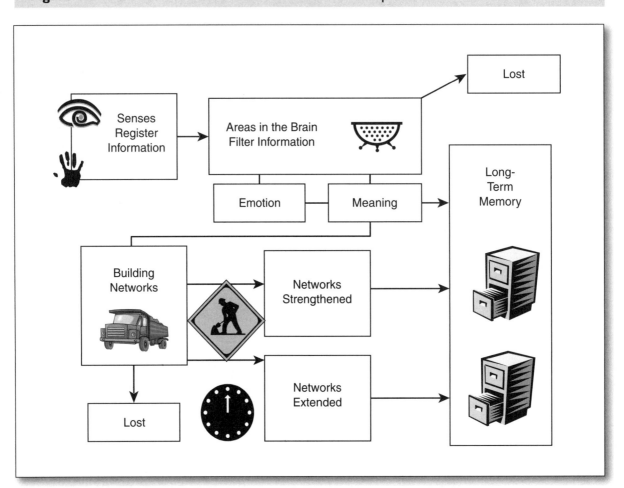

Source: Adapted by Chris Yeager from Wolfe & Nevills, 2002; Sylwester, 1995; and Sousa, 2006.

their ideas on the maps. They don't have to hold all of the information in their brains in short-term memory, or in repetitive, linear notes on a page. The students and teacher can understand each other from the note-making stage to the final presentations by way of the common visual language. When they present their material, students and teacher have a clear visual picture of their mental processes for understanding and for assessment.

When students repeatedly associate a concrete visual pattern with an abstract thought process, they learn patterns for what thinking looks like. These patterns then automatically signal the brain to recognize and even seek out thought processes in print, discussions, and assessments and across all of the amazing media sources they are now required to access for research purposes. In effect, students have wired together networks of neurons for metacognition. Like Norm's class, students become fluent with these patterns of thinking and begin to recognize them independently of teacher instruction, thus developing their own thinking and learning toward higher levels.

A BRIEF HISTORY OF THINKING MAPS IN DEVELOPMENT

Every one of the authors of this book has contributed in different ways over the years to the continuing evolution of Thinking Maps. The themes that emerge here go way beyond the first musings I had back in the spring of 1986. I remember a moment of clarity immediately followed by a humbling awareness. I was eagerly generating ideas for a workbook I was writing, meant for middle school students from underachieving schools. The focus was on the direct facilitation of their thinking skills abilities. I thought I knew what I was doing—and then *I realized what I didn't know.* Two core questions jumped from my mind, the first more theoretical, the second more practical:

What are fundamental thinking skills?

How do we support all learners to transfer these skills across disciplines?

These questions came directly from my frames of reference: I had been teaching in inner-city classrooms in Oakland, California, while studying the continuing underachievement in inner-city schools within low socioeconomic communities (serving mostly African American children). I was also becoming increasingly aware of the implications of the (still existing) inequalities of access to quality education and the systemic achievement gap. I was looking at the past research on cognition, cognitive styles, and mediation of thinking and learning, while trying to make sense of the array of new theories and practices of thinking skills instruction. During this time, the proponents of the nascent constructivist paradigm were challenging the strict behavioralist mind-set.

As these many frames of reference converged in my mind, another insight arose, first hurriedly scrawled across a paper napkin. My response was not a grand theory or model, nor was it a program of developmental lessons with a complex instrument for assessing thinking. As introduced above, it was a language called Thinking Maps. Defining Thinking Maps as a *language* was a clear expression of how these eight visual tools, each surrounded by a visual frame of reference, work in unison, enabling all learners to communicate what and how they are thinking. Through this language, we have found that all learners convey, negotiate, and evolve meanings with others, and within themselves, through visual patterns of thinking.

On a global level, Thinking Maps also may be defined as a synthesis of three types of visual tool that educators and businesspeople have used for generations: mind mapping/brainstorming webs, graphic organizers, and thinking-process tools such as concept mapping.

During my later research on Thinking Maps, I became intrigued by different types of visual tools, finally writing two comprehensive books on the theory, practice, and degree of effectiveness of these tools. Recently, I synthesized these books with current research in practice into a comprehensive text with a theme of 21st-century learning: *Visual Tools for Transforming Information Into Knowledge* (Hyerle, 2009). I have discovered through research, my own teaching, and experiences that each type of visual tool offers useful ways of visually accessing knowledge.

I also found that each kind of visual tool also has some weaknesses that cannot be overlooked. Mind-mapping techniques that surfaced in the early 1970s facilitate open-minded thinking yet lack the consistent structure and deeper levels of complexity required for today's classrooms. The now familiar "graphic organizers," which surfaced in the 1980s, help students organize large amounts of information and scaffold their thinking, but fail when they become static, blackline masters focused on isolated content tasks selected by the teacher, rather than initiated by the learner. These tools are task-specific organizers, because they usually focus on a specific content task and are often confined to the task at hand rather than easily transferable across disciplines.

A third kind of visual tool, "thinking-process" maps, is based on facilitating well-defined thinking processes. Two of these forms, concept mapping and systems diagramming, richly convey complex interdependencies in concepts and systems, respectively. Embedded in the strengths of these two models are also limitations: These models are each dependent on one form of visually structuring knowledge, hierarchical forms for concept mapping, and feedback loops for systems diagrams. This leads to an underrepresentation of other thinking processes. In addition, in practice, the translation of these complex models is often daunting to students and teachers alike.

The combined practical, theoretical, and critical attributes of these different types of visual tools have informed the continuing evolution of Thinking Maps into a 21st-century language for learning, synthesizing many of the best qualities of these other types of visual tools: an evolution from the generative quality of brainstorming webs, the organizing structure of graphic organizers, and the deep cognitive processing found in concept maps.

FIVE QUALITIES OF THINKING MAPS

The key characteristics of different types of visual tools led to Thinking Maps becoming a language of cognitive patterns that is analogous to the key or legend of symbols that you will find on *any* map. The graphic symbols are the simple visual starting points for generating complex maps for cognitive networks that link together content using a range of thinking processes. Each of the eight maps is theoretically grounded in a fundamental cognitive process or thinking skill. Awareness of five critical attributes of Thinking Maps (see Figure 1.6) and a close look at just one of the eight maps (the Flow Map) will clarify how all the maps work, and how they work together.

Consistent. The symbol grounding each map has a unique but consistent form that visually reflects the cognitive skill being defined. For example, the process of sequencing is represented by the Flow Map starting with one box and one arrow. This is the graphic primitive upon which the map is used to show linear concepts. Thus, a Flow Map might show just the three boxes, with key information written inside, showing the beginning, middle, and end of a story.

Flexible. The cognitive skill and the graphic primitive for each map lead to a flexibility in form and to the infinite number of ways the map can grow and be configured. So a Flow Map of a story may start at the beginning but grow in complexity to show many stages and substages of the story. This map could be drawn rising from the bottom left to top right of the page, reflecting the rising action of a story.

Figure 1.6 Qualities of Thinking Maps Bubble Map

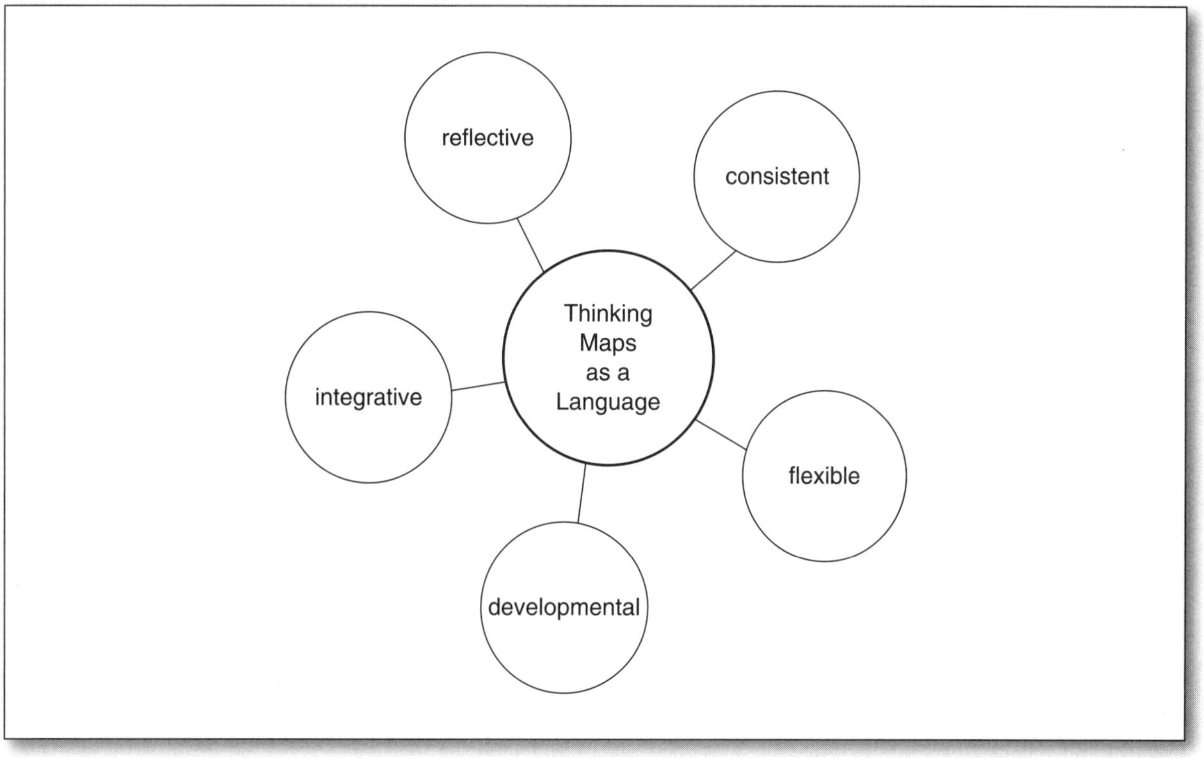

reflective

consistent

Thinking
Maps
as a
Language

integrative

flexible

developmental

Developmental. Because of the consistent graphic primitives and flexible use, any learner (of any age) may begin with a blank sheet of paper and expand the map to show his or her thinking. A Flow Map can be a few boxes long or evolve over time to fill a whole page. The learner—and the content of the learning—determines the complexity of the map. Every learner, from early childhood on, can use the Flow Map to show what he or she knows about a story and thus produce a different configuration of the content.

Integrative. There are two key dimensions of integration: thinking processes and content knowledge. First, all of the maps may be used and integrated together. Using the example of a story, a learner could use the Flow Map to show the plot, a Double Bubble Map to show a comparison of characters, and then a Tree Map to identify the main ideas and supporting details. Multiple Thinking Maps are used for solving multistep problems, for comprehending overlapping reading text structures, and for use during phases of the writing process. Second, the maps are used deeply within and across content areas. For example, the Flow Map is used for plot analysis in reading comprehension, order of operations in math, historical timelines in social studies, and studying recurring natural cycles in science.

Reflective. As a language, the maps unveil what and how one is thinking in patterns. Not only can the learner look down and reflect upon the pattern of content, but the teacher also reflects on and informally assesses the content learning and thinking processes of the learner. In addition, at any time and with every map, learners may draw a rectangular frame around a map. This represents one's frame of reference, or metacognitive frame. For example, a high school student may have sketched out a Flow Map and identified half a dozen turning points in the flow of a novel. By drawing the frame around the map, the student can jot down what influenced this analysis and the references in the text. The framing tool goes beyond merely referencing *what* one knows, to ask the learners *how* they know the information within each map.

INFINITE PATTERNS: BOUNDLESS THINKING

As human beings, we thrive, creatively and analytically, largely because of our innate capacities for communicating through languages: alphabets, numerical systems, scientific symbols, musical notation, software programs, international sign language, and Braille. Yet all of these languages have a foundation of fundamental cognitive structures such as sequencing, categorizing, comparing, and so on. Thinking Maps are really a metalanguage for learning, communicating, and synthesizing our thinking across the other languages we use every day.

Because of the universality of the cognitive skills upon which this language is based, and the visual-spatial, nonlinguistic form of the tools, the maps are used fluidly across content areas, languages, and cultures, as shown within this book. These cognitive processes conveyed through graphic primitives are used together, linked together, and visually scaffolded to create other products of learning, such as in a piece of writing, within the processes of second language acquisition, or for growth of academic language during an inquiry-based science unit. Learners and teachers transform what they are learning from various texts and media and use the maps to integrate what they know into conceptual understandings. They transfer and adapt the maps to shape and reform otherwise static content knowledge and enter interdisciplinary problem solving, knowing they have tools to organize their thinking and assess their content learning and thinking.

Maps are not closed systems. They are infinitely expandable and thus have no boundaries. They directly facilitate the Habits of Mind (Costa & Kallick, 2008) crucial to our engagement with each other and for facilitating an expansive openness of mind within ourselves. Ultimately, as the maps expand and integrate with words, numbers, and other symbols on a page, colorfully across a whiteboard, or on computer screens, learners and teachers face the stimulating, boundless nature of their own thinking.

REFERENCES

Costa, A. L., & Kallick, B. (2008). *Learning and leading with Habits of Mind.* Alexandria, VA: Association for Supervision and Curriculum Development.

Hattie, J. A. C. (2009). *Visible learning: A synthesis of over 800 meta-analyses relating to achievement.* New York: Routledge.

Hyerle, D. (1996). *Visual tools for constructing knowledge.* Alexandria, VA: Association for Supervision and Curriculum Development.

Hyerle, D. (2000). *A field guide to using visual tools.* Alexandria, VA: Association for Supervision and Curriculum Development.

Hyerle, D. (2009). *Visual tools for transforming information into knowledge.* Thousand Oaks, CA: Corwin.

Jensen, E. (1998). *Teaching with the brain in mind.* Alexandria, VA: Association for Supervision and Curriculum Development.

Marzano, R. J., Pickering, D. J., & Pollock, J. E. (2001). *Classroom instruction that works: Research-based strategies for increasing student achievement.* Alexandria, VA: Association for Supervision and Curriculum Development.

Ogle, D. (1988, December–1989, January). Implementing strategic teaching. *Educational Leadership, 46,* 47–60.

Sousa, D. A. (2006). *How the brain learns.* Thousand Oaks, CA: Corwin.

Sylwester, R. (1995). *A celebration of neurons: An educator's guide to the human brain.* Alexandria, VA: Association for Supervision and Curriculum Development.

Wolfe, P., & Nevills, P. (2004). *Building the reading brain.* Thousand Oaks, CA: Corwin.

Section 1

Linking Thinking, Language, and Learning

2

Why and How Thinking Maps Work

A Language of Brain and Mind

Kimberly M. Williams, Ph.D.

KEY CONCEPTS

- Cognition
- Learning brain
- Neural networks

Thinking Maps® are grounded in eight cognitive universals—thinking processes that our brains use every day: sequencing, hierarchical classification, part-to-whole, causation, comparing and contrasting, describing, analogies, and defining in context. While these processes work in unison, so too does our brain work in interrelated ways by patterning information. As Pat Wolfe states in the Foreword to this book, because maps network and plot information in patterns, "Thinking Maps are what the brain does."

With this macro view as a starting point, this chapter will drive deeper to the microprocesses of the brain at work by providing a brief look at how the structures of the brain—from the cellular level to the whole brain itself—actually engage in these same actions that are embodied in Thinking Maps. We will investigate how the brain is constantly activating processes such as sequences, hierarchies, and comparisons and is—in large part—based upon the continuous process of prediction, based on causal and analogical relationships. It is important to note that these functions are completely neuro*logical* and therefore unconscious, whereas the use of Thinking Maps in the classroom engages the conscious mind. These fundamental "process patterns" are, of course, only partially represented and activated by Thinking Maps. The benefit of making explicit patterns using graphic primitives such as the Thinking Maps is that all of us as learners become more aware of *what* we are thinking and also *how* we are thinking (metacognition). Providing tools that allow students to show what they know and also how they are thinking about it can be quite useful for assessing students' learning in the classroom. How intriguing: Thinking Maps used as visual patterning tools based on cognitive processes may express fundamental brain activity.

THE BRAIN AND THE MIND

This chapter will focus more on brain processes, but please keep in the foreground of your mind that while the thinking processes the brain uses are the same as the processes outlined in the Thinking Maps, most of us educators are more compelled by the use of the Thinking Maps at the level of "mind"—that is, the functional application and conscious experience of our day-to-day interactions in classrooms.

My dilemma in writing this chapter is that the brain does not work in discrete parts to create our conscious experiences of "mind": The mind works rather like an orchestra. While some instruments (such as flutes or violins) may be highlighted during some parts of a symphony, all members of an orchestra work together to produce a beautiful piece of music. The brain is the same—while there may be discrete parts of the brain that are highlighted during some types of cognition, these parts of the brain work together to produce beautiful thinking. And finally, we need different forms of cognition when we engage in a complex learning task, so much like our analogy of the orchestra and the brain, we need multiple, interrelated maps to produce beautiful learning outcomes.

THE BRAIN: PATTERN DETECTOR IN THE DARK

The brain is a pattern detector: It is constantly processing patterns . . . in the dark! The brain receives no information from the outside world directly, so it must rely on interpreting electrical impulses of neurons and patterns based on the input it receives from the senses. The algorithm that the brain uses to interpret the patterns of information coming in from the senses, Jeff Hawkins (2004) argues, is the same for all senses—sight, hearing, taste, touch, and smell. That is, the brain interprets the *pattern* of the electrical impulses in neuronal networks in the same way regardless of whether we see something, hear something, or touch, smell, or taste it.

While we do take in much of our information through our eyes, we also take in much information from our other senses. What the brain does with it, whether it comes in visually or not, is the same and consistent with the eight cognitive universals upon which the Thinking Maps are grounded. As it is an advanced organizer for linking each Thinking Map with a brain function, take a few moments to preview the Bridge Map (see Figure 2.1). As you read through each of the sections below relating neurological brain patterning to Thinking Maps as cognitive patterns, read with a critical eye: The ideas and propositions made herein are based upon a view that the underlying cognitive processes (thinking) such as hierarchies, comparisons, and causality exist in brain functioning and *not* that the brain actually makes physical "maps" such as Tree Maps, Double Bubble Maps, and Multi-Flow Maps.

THE FLOW OF SEQUENCING AND TREE HIERARCHIES

First, let's look closely at two prominent processes of brain functioning—sequential and hierarchical processing—and how they work in unison. The synaptic connections of the brain operate sequentially—that is, electrical impulses flow down one neuron to the next one to the next one and so on—stimulating each other and sending messages sequentially. New learning results when the creation of new patterns of firing results from the repeated sequential pattern of neuronal firing (see Figure 2.2).

Figure 2.1 Thinking Maps and the Brain Analogy Using the Bridge Map

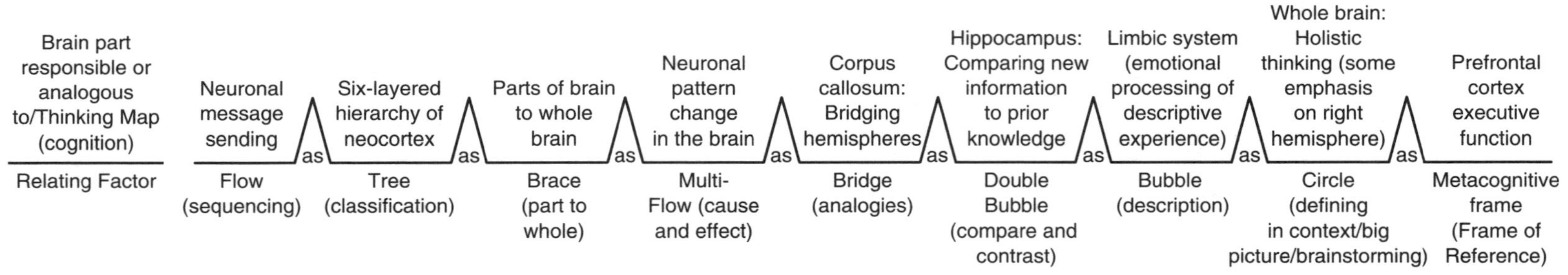

Brain part responsible or analogous to/Thinking Map (cognition)								
Neuronal message sending	Six-layered hierarchy of neocortex	Parts of brain to whole brain	Neuronal pattern change in the brain	Corpus callosum: Bridging hemispheres	Hippocampus: Comparing new information to prior knowledge	Limbic system (emotional processing of descriptive experience)	Whole brain: Holistic thinking (some emphasis on right hemisphere)	Prefrontal cortex executive function
Relating Factor								
Flow (sequencing)	Tree (classification)	Brace (part to whole)	Multi-Flow (cause and effect)	Bridge (analogies)	Double Bubble (compare and contrast)	Bubble (description)	Circle (defining in context/big picture/brainstorming)	Metacognitive frame (Frame of Reference)

Figure 2.2 Flow Map of Neuronal Sequencing

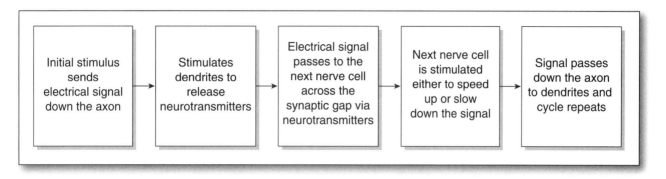

Jeff Hawkins, in his book *On Intelligence* (2004), explains how we can build intelligent machines based on what we know about how the cortex works and the importance of neuronal patterns. As he explains in the introduction to the book, his first interest in learning about the brain was during his time at the University of California–Berkeley in the mid-1980s and then at MIT, where he became entranced by the field of artificial intelligence. However, he ran into an interesting problem: There was no comprehensive theoretical model for the brain, so he began to study the neuroscience in search of the processes of the brain.

He argues that all areas of the cortex function largely the same way—they take signals from our senses and translate them into a series of electrical impulses that are stored in a series of sequential patterns.

> By design, every cortical region attempts to store and recall sequences. But this is still too simple a description of the brain . . . The bottom up inputs to a region of cortex are input patterns carried on thousands or millions of axons. These axons come from different regions and contain all sorts of patterns. The number of possible patterns that can exist on even one thousand axons is larger than the number of molecules in the universe. A region will only see a tiny fraction of these possible patterns in a lifetime. (Hawkins, 2004)

Thus, a primary process of the brain is to sequence information into patterns. Patterns are then stored and retrieved. This may seem obvious, but Hawkins then offers that the cortex functions hierarchically and sorts, filters, and classifies information by passing information both up and down the hierarchy. For example, if lower levels of the cortex receive new information through the senses (e.g., the eyes), and these lower levels do not recognize a given sequential pattern, they will send the pattern up the hierarchy until the pattern reaches a level of the cortex where it is recognized. Once the cortex recognizes a pattern, it sends signals back down the hierarchy. If the cortex receives a pattern it doesn't recognize, the pattern interpretation goes to the hippocampus where the pattern is either stored and remembered as a new pattern or forgotten if it is viewed as insignificant.

So our brains do not just send electrical impulses sequentially. Electrical impulses and synaptic/neuronal connections send messages up a hierarchy and back down. Neurons and neuronal connections are structured in a six-layered hierarchy where information flows up the hierarchy and back down as a pattern is translated and executed. How far up the hierarchy a signal travels depends on its complexity and novelty. This sounds relatively simple until we take into account what Robert Sylwester (1995) describes as the 30 *separate columnar subsystems* just for processing vision alone (see Figure 2.3).

Figure 2.3 Hierarchical Structures of the Brain

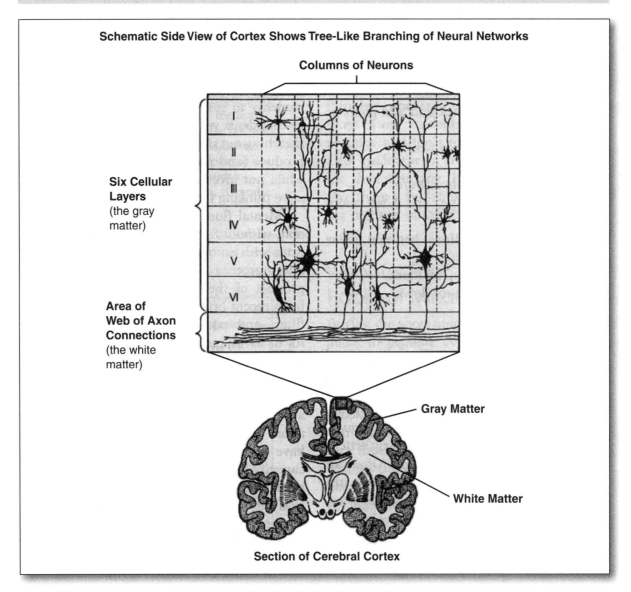

Source: Sylwester, R. (1995). *A celebration of neurons: An educator's guide to the human brain* (p. 46). Alexandria, VA: Association for Supervision and Curriculum Development.

Jeff Hawkins (2004), in his quest for a theory of the brain, then asks, "Why is the neocortex built as a hierarchy?" and offers this response:

> You can think about the world, move around in the world and make predictions of the future because your cortex has built a model of the world. One of the most important concepts in this book [*On Intelligence*] is that the cortex's hierarchical structure stores a model of the hierarchical structure of the real world. The real world's nested structure is mirrored by the nested structure of your cortex.

The words on this page are an example of hierarchical structure—letters make words, words make sentences, sentences make paragraphs, paragraphs make pages, and so on. The brain processes these patterns up the layers of the cortex.

These two fundamental brain processes, sequencing and hierarchical classification, which are physically activated by the structure of the brain, are, of course, two of the eight cognitive processes with the language of Thinking Maps. The Flow Map directly supports students in consciously constructing sequences, and the Tree Map is used to build hierarchical structures. It is interesting to note that these two processes are also the foundations, respectively, for fundamental text structures: narrative and main idea/supporting ideas/details.

THE PHYSICAL BRAIN AND THE BRACE MAP

Before we move too far along, let's remember that the brain is physical: It has what we describe as two halves, connected by the corpus callosum, with anatomical parts and hemispheres, regions, and subregions where certain activities occur. These regions are linked to each other and to our bodies in often mysterious ways that are being discovered daily through neuroscience research. Within the Thinking Maps language, the Brace Map is used to represent, in visual form, whole-to-part patterns. If you look back to *Gray's Anatomy*, you will find the exact graphic form of the Brace Map for showing these complex whole-to-part-to-subpart structures of the human body. The brain structure may be represented in its complexity by the Brace Map (see Figure 2.4).

One of the typical questions asked by teachers and students is this: *What is the difference between the Brace Map for showing whole-part patterns and the Tree Map for showing hierarchical patterns?* The Brace Map looks like a Tree Map on its side. There are similarities, but the *underlying cognitive process* of each is unique by definition and in how our minds structure the physical objects in our world. Traditionally, the Tree Map has been used to distinguish hierarchical, taxonomic, *abstract* category patterns such as the *types* of chairs and subgroups (rocking chair, desk chair, ski lift chair, beanbag chair, etc.) that may exist in this world. The Brace Map, in its traditional form used in anatomy classes, is used to show the physical, anatomical, concrete parts of a tangible, "touchable" object, such as the *parts* and subparts of a whole chair (back, seat, legs, cross braces). Simply put, you can't *touch* categories because all categories are abstractions created by human beings!

Why do these two processes get confused so often? The answer is partially in how the brain processes information on a most fundamental level. The brain as an unconscious operator, in the dark, relies on general to specific *scales* for both physical and abstract understandings of the world. The patterning of the "whole-to-part" processes of the Brace Map focuses on tangible, touchable, concrete objects (a general, whole object such as the "whole" chair and specific parts such as the legs, seat, and back). The hierarchical Tree Map suggests that each level "up" the hierarchy is more inclusive and ultimately more "abstract" and complex than the one below it (e.g., furniture as an overarching category, then chairs in general, then office chairs specifically). Thus the brain operates hierarchically all the time using the cortical hierarchy of the brain, *even when it is examining part-to-whole relationships of the objects that surround us.* This happens, remember, while the brain continues to use neuronal *sequencing* to transmit messages.

As Hawkins (2004) wrote of the hierarchical structure of the cortex and the part-to-whole relationship of the world,

> Every object in the world is composed of a collection of smaller objects and most objects are part of larger objects . . . in a very analogous way, your memories of things and the way your brain represents them are stored in the hierarchical structure of your cortex. Your memory of your home does not exist in one region of [your] cortex. It is stored over a hierarchy of cortical regions that reflect the hierarchical structure of the home. Large-scale relationships are stored at the top of the hierarchy and small-scale relationships are stored toward the bottom.

Figure 2.4   Brace Map of the Brain

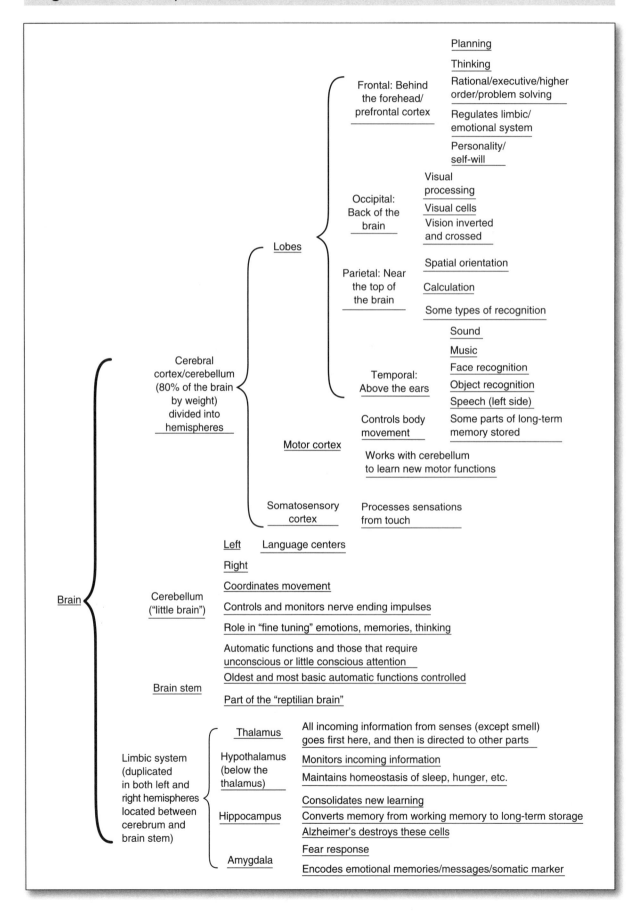

While this discussion may seem esoteric and disconnected from the learning that goes on in classrooms, it helps us realize that the spatial architecture and dynamics of the brain are processing the physical world in which we live, and with it whole-to-part relationships, as well as our perceptions of the abstract world of concepts often bound in the hierarchies we create.

THE MULTIPLE CAUSES AND EFFECTS IN FEEDBACK FLOWS

External events and experiences *cause* physical changes in the brain—by way of changes in electrical neuronal patterns. When patterns are reinforced over time (learned well), then the pattern of neuronal firing becomes more solidified. Once new learning is retained, it can be more easily used without consciously having to think about it. As a complex network of established patterns is created, expertise develops. For example, think about learning how to tie a shoe. Most of us adults are "experts" at shoe tying because we have repeated this sequence of behaviors thousands of times in our lifetimes—we can do it without thinking about it. When we first learn to tie our shoes, a weak pattern of neuronal patterns is mapped in our brains. Practicing this sequence over and over again causes our brains, through a feedback process, to actively change a neuronal firing sequence for shoe tying. Eventually, we become such experts we don't even have to think about it consciously. This is true for all learning—if we practice enough, the result is a permanent change in the brain. As the saying goes, "practice makes permanent." Rehearsal or repetition or practice *causes* changes in neuronal patterns, and the *effect* is the brain learning something new.

Consider, for example, learning the alphabet. Children learn to say or sing each letter without conceptualizing to the written word. Then children learn what each letter looks like. As they learn to read, they must sound out every letter to figure out what a word spells. Eventually, readers without reading difficulties will process entire words or even phrases as they become more fluent readers (expert). They no longer need to sound out each letter. Letter recognition becomes automatic and happens without much conscious thought. This change is a result of an actual synaptic change that happens in the brain. A pattern of firing in the brain is associated with the letter *a* and the letter *A*. In short, experiences *cause* changes in the brain at the synaptic and cortical levels. The *effect* is the brain learning (see Figure 2.5).

What do you think will happen next? We ask our students this question all the time. This thinking requires the brain to do cause-and-effect reasoning, and the Multi-Flow Map reflects these dynamics as a tool for predictive reading. The brain must process what came before, and consider similar situations and similar causes that have produced similar results. For example, a student might think, "The last time I read a book like this, the pigeon did not get his way, even when he begged, so I'm predicting that even though he is begging in the story now, he still will not get his way." A central strategy for improving reading comprehension (and what the brain is already doing when it is receiving inputs from reading!) is for a parent or teacher to stop reading the story and ask a child for multiple predictions, or the ripple effects of what has previously happened in the story. This *is not* just sequencing, because readers must often draw from different parts of the story, the temperament of characters, setting, author style, and a whole range of information that is not necessarily narrative in form.

We make causal predictions all day, every day. These predictions use cause-and-effect reasoning (e.g., "If *this* occurs, *this* will happen"). These predictions are often unconscious and essential to our survival. Our amygdala takes care of much of this beyond our awareness. Consider the following. I learned that when I raise my hand and get an answer correct, I feel smart and validated. I don't really think about this consciously, but it feels

Figure 2.5   Multi-Flow Map—Causes and Effects of Changing the Brain

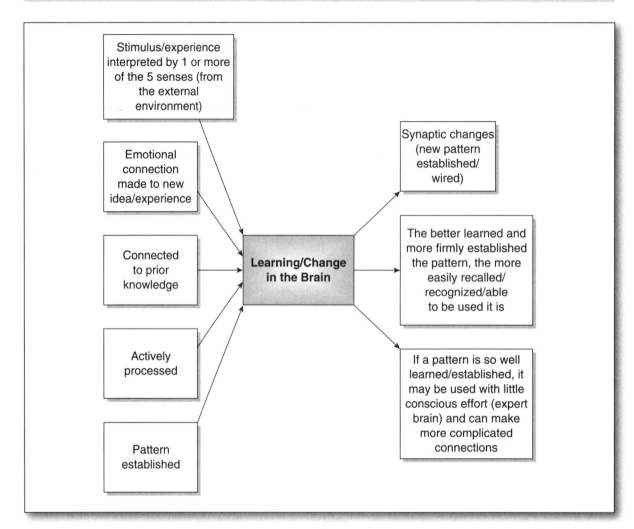

good, and I raise my hand and participate more in class. On the other hand, if I raise my hand, get the answer incorrect, and am made to feel stupid, I am not likely to raise my hand again. I feel unsafe and bad about myself, and I disengage. In the former example, my amygdala interprets safety and rewards and repeats. In the latter, my amygdala interprets harm and pain and avoids. None of this may be conscious at all. The brain is making causal inferences and adjusting behavior accordingly.

Prediction is an essential part of survival, learning, and creativity. While we might not see hand raising as essential to survival, it is certainly a key part of school engagement and success. We use cause-and-effect thinking to make predictions. The amygdala is responsible for keeping us alive—so if we encounter something dangerous, we learn to fear that thing (say, a tiger or a poisonous snake). Our brains use causal thinking in a conscious way to make predictions, but also the amygdala bypasses our conscious brain to make causal relationships about possible threats and dangers.

ON THE DOUBLE BUBBLE MAP: COMPARING AND CONTRASTING NEW INFORMATION

Once a concept is learned, the brain is wired to retain this prior knowledge as stored neuronal firing patterns (as described above). As it encounters new, but related, information, it maps this new information onto the existing neuronal patterns—thus modifying, expanding, and enhancing these patterns. To accomplish these enhanced networks or patterns or maps of associations that represent new learning building upon prior learning, the brain must constantly *compare and contrast* new information with what it already has stored. Within the language of Thinking Maps, the Double Bubble Map helps generate and represent on the surface a pattern that is occurring nonstop within neural networks. If we return to the fundamentals of cognitive science research—in Piagetian terms—the brain must either assimilate and/or accommodate the new information or discard it as unimportant or irrelevant to neural networks that already exist, and this takes constant comparisons.

The hippocampus (a structure shaped like a seahorse located in the older part of the brain's limbic system) is believed to bear primary responsibility for comparing and contrasting new incoming information with existing memories. Patients with severe damage to their hippocampus lose the ability to form new memories, but typically their long-term memories remain intact. Our hippocampus is believed to (among other things) compare and contrast new information entering the brain to establish neuronal patterns in the brain and revise and adjust these patterns accordingly (see Figure 2.6). Hence, this structure and this act of comparing and contrasting is central to our learning, remembering what we learn, and later recalling what we've learned.

DESCRIBING ATTRIBUTES: *MAKING SENSE* THROUGH EMOTIONAL AND SENSORY CONNECTIONS IN BUBBLE MAPS

How does the brain determine what information is worth storing into new neuronal firing patterns? Emotions. Emotions are the key to learning anything. Immordino-Yang and Damasio (2007) argued, "When we educators fail to appreciate the importance of students' emotions, we fail to appreciate a critical force in students' learning. One could argue, in fact, that we fail to appreciate the very reason students learn at all." Learning is emotional. If we have no emotional connection to an idea, the content of a class, a person, and so on, we likely will not remember it (or him or her).

The very use of Thinking Maps involves an emotional connection because learners make their own map meaningful: In so doing, they make the material their own, make a personal/emotional connection as they interact with the content, and will be better able to retain the information later. As Immordino-Yang and Damasio (2007) wrote in their examination of the research literature linking emotions and learning,

> First, because these findings underscore the critical role of emotion in bringing previously acquired knowledge to inform real world decision making in social contexts, they suggest the intriguing possibility that emotional processes are required for the skills and knowledge acquired in school to transfer to novel situations and to real life.

While I include emotions in this section on "describing attributes," they are implicated in the very use of the maps—and also, I would argue, emotions are strongly engaged when one ponders one's metacognitive reference points displayed in the frame used around each map.

So what happens when we are asked to describe attributes or engage in descriptive thinking as we use the Bubble Map? The very act of describing is emotional and based on making something meaningful. The brain must engage substructures of the limbic system (which

Figure 2.6   Double Bubble Learning

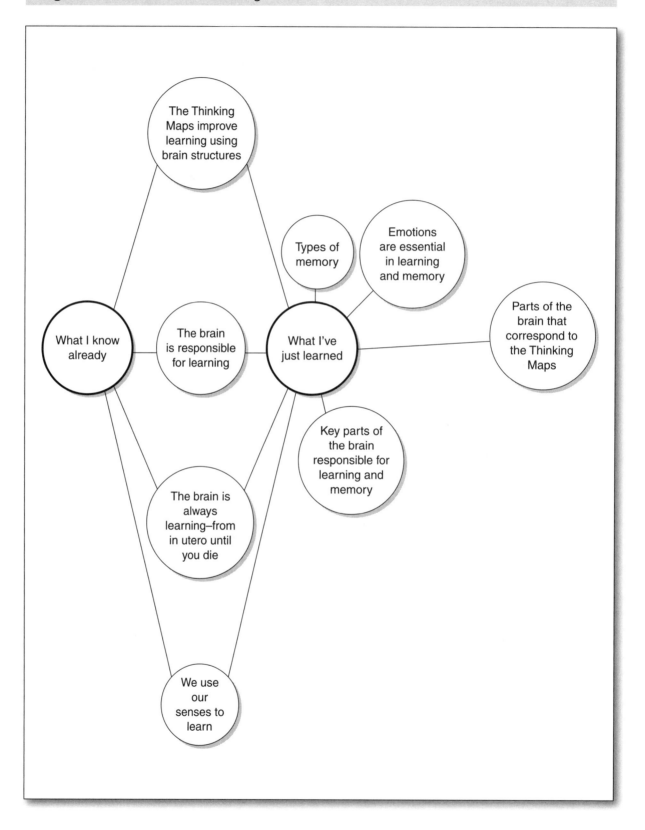

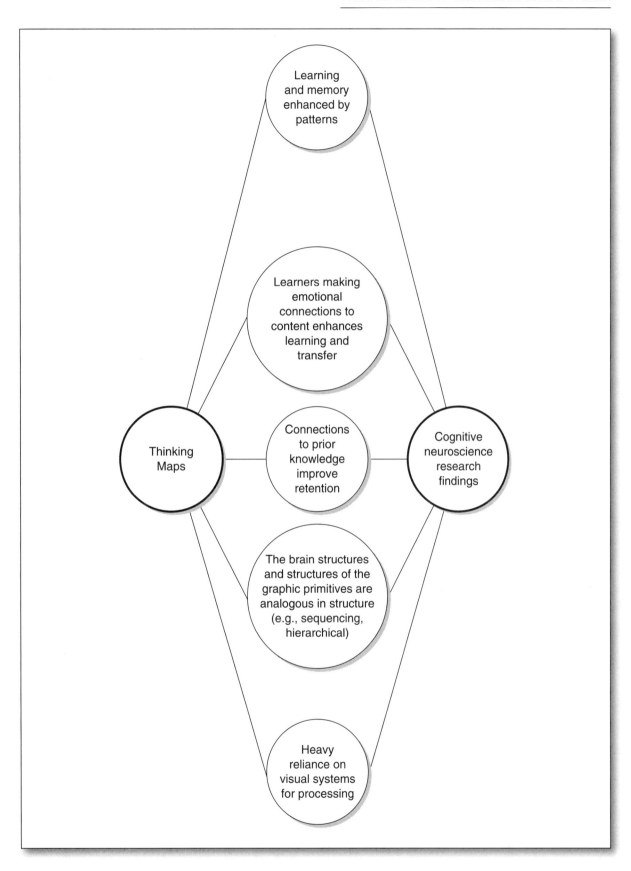

includes the amygdala, hippocampus, and basal ganglia). When we see the word *fear* flashed subliminally (beyond our conscious awareness), our brains evoke a mini fear response—activating the amygdala to trigger this fear response. When we experience pleasure when learning, the basal ganglia are stimulated, and pleasure chemicals such as dopamine are increased.

The actual structure of the nerve cell looks like a Bubble Map—with extensions coming off of the center. The brain makes connections this way—as Thinking Maps users have said of their use of the maps, "This is how my brain works!" Yes, it is! As Jeff Hawkins (2004) details, there are actually *centers* where the incoming sensory information comes together.

It makes sense, from a macro view, that creating a Bubble Map with descriptors, attributes, and properties is an emotional task because as one ponders descriptors of a particular object, one cannot help but respond to those descriptors emotionally: Connections to emotions enhance memory. Just think for a moment about the most emotional experiences in your own life—these memories (both positive and negative) are powerfully ingrained in your brain, and you will more than likely never forget them (e.g., failing your first test, falling in love, getting fired, getting married, having a baby). The more powerful the emotional connection, the more powerful the memory.

The brain, in the dark, is using sensory inputs from the body and always scanning for attributes or qualities to *make sense* of what it is learning—and to better understand its context. It must learn the attributes using the senses to be able to make meaningful connections to other networks that have already been created. When we first learn something new, we examine the attributes of it, and we assign our own attributes—many of which are emotionally grounded. For students it might be "This is too difficult" or "This smells good" or "She is really pretty" or "This book is really interesting" and so on. These emotional connections that the brain makes can either inhibit or enhance learning. The more positive the emotional connection to what is being learned—or the more significant the emotional connection to the attributes—the more likely the brain is to remember this information later.

As your eyes read this text, the limbic system of your brain is also engaging in a series of emotional reactions/responses that your cerebral cortex is interpreting into words. Hopefully, these represent some of the descriptions your limbic system is feeling as you read this book (see Figure 2.7).

Figure 2.7   Bubble Map of Text

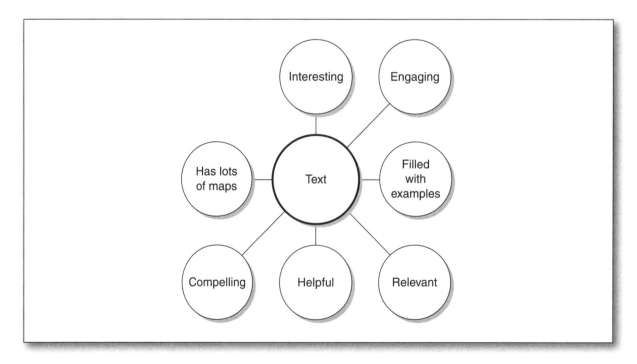

ANALOGIES: BRIDGE MAP AS THE CORPUS CALLOSUM?

The cognitive acts involved in the creation of analogies are complex and draw upon all of the other processes that ground each Thinking Map. For example, as the brain learns new information, compares and contrasts old to new, and creates new memories based on our emotional responses, we must make sense of ideas related to what we already know. The brain makes predictions (as we learn from causal reasoning)—it examines how one situation is similar to or different from (as we learn in comparative thinking) another situation. It attempts to make predictions based on current inputs that are based on previous experiences. Building upon these ideas, the conscious mind must deliberately examine *relationships* between and among ideas. This relationship when using the Bridge Map is called the *relating factor*. For example, let's look at this simple analogy: *Meow* "relates" to a cat as __?__ "relates" to a dog. What does the brain need to do to solve this analogy? First, it must know the qualities of a cat and a dog. Second, it must be able to compare and contrast cats and dogs. Third, it must be able to make some predictions about the behavior of cats and dogs—namely that dogs must make a sound if cats make a sound. In our culture we tend to think about analogies in this way. However, the cognitive road to analogies and metaphor is actually more direct than this in our everyday lives. Perhaps the input to the brain references a tree branch and its relationship to the tree trunk and makes an immediate mapping of the arm to the body, or compares the two headlights on a car with the eyes on a face. Stripped down, analogies often if not always represent cognitive relationships that are already identified in the brain and are essential to new learning.

According to Hawkins (2004), intelligence is the ability to make predictions using analogies. The more divergent or unusual or uncommon a prediction given the evidence available to the brain, the more creative the act. So, for example, learning how to type on a cell phone if you know how to type on a computer keyboard is a creative act according to Hawkins, but coming up with the notion of texting and the smartphone, many would argue (as Hawkins did), constitutes a much more intelligent or creative act.

But what does it mean to be intelligent or to have an intelligent brain? The notion of being able to measure one's *general intelligence* is a hotly contested one. Regardless of your philosophical beliefs about intelligence, one consistent way that general intelligence has been measured historically is through the use of analogies. Early experts in learning believed that we could measure intelligence through the use of analogies, such as through the Miller Analogies Test (at least in part). Analogies are standard fare in most testing regimens. Creating analogies involves complex thinking in the brain. It must first have learned ideas, but then it must take this knowledge a step further and make predictions and examine relationships between and among patterns of learned ideas.

In addition to the link between general intelligence and the ability of the brain to make predictions using analogies, the corpus callosum, which connects the two hemispheres, acts as a bridge between the left and right sides of the brain. The notion of a bridge is the graphic primitive for the creation of analogies within the Thinking Maps model. Bridging two complex ideas and making connections and predictions between and among them and others are what the corpus callosum does between the two hemispheres of the brain. We have learned from "split brain" patients (who have had their corpus callosum severed to prevent severe seizures) that certain important communication between these two hemispheres is profoundly affected. We need our two hemispheres to communicate, but, interestingly, our brain can function without this bridge—just not as well (see Figure 2.8).

I don't mean to suggest that the corpus callosum is responsible (exclusively) for the cognition that happens when the brain creates analogies. However, the hemispheres of the brain need to work together to do the kind of creative thinking required when using analogies—and the corpus callosum creates that bridge of communication between the two halves as the Bridge Map creates the connections between two analogous ideas.

DEFINING IN CONTEXT IN THE CIRCLE MAP: USING THE WHOLE BRAIN FOR HOLISTIC THINKING

Lastly, another form of cognition as related to brain structure and function is the way we function when we set out to make sense of anything: We must see the wider context of the situation from which we are gathering and processing information. When, for example, we enter a room such as a classroom, we are immediately immersed in the rich context of the people, the physical environment, the sounds, and all of the student work and teacher displays that give meaning to our visit. We can't help but sense the holism of the situation before focusing our attention on isolated people, interactions, and objects around the room.

What happens when we first set out to create a Circle Map and get all of our ideas down on paper (my students call this a "brain dump")? We are thinking about the big picture or doing what is called holistic thinking. Clearly in holistic thinking the whole brain is involved. We are pulling together all that we know about a topic or an idea. Returning to our classroom example, the associations we have with what a "classroom" means to us may be accessed. Our brain uses all kinds of thinking to accomplish this Herculean task of pondering "all that we know" about a topic. Evidence exists that the right side of the brain is working a bit harder during these kinds of holistic tasks, but the right side must work in concert with the left side. There has been some support, though, that while the left side is more seriously implicated in examining discrete parts, the right side focuses a bit more on holistic thinking (although some of these theories on hemispheric differences have been debunked, some still remain supported).

Figure 2.8   Corpus Callosum

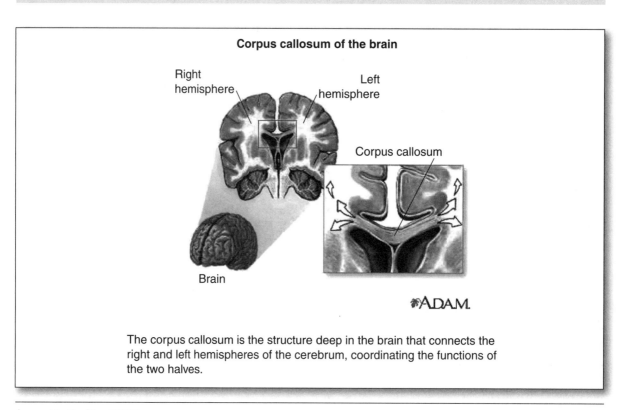

The corpus callosum is the structure deep in the brain that connects the right and left hemispheres of the cerebrum, coordinating the functions of the two halves.

Source: MedlinePlus (2010).

Figure 2.9 Circle Map Summary

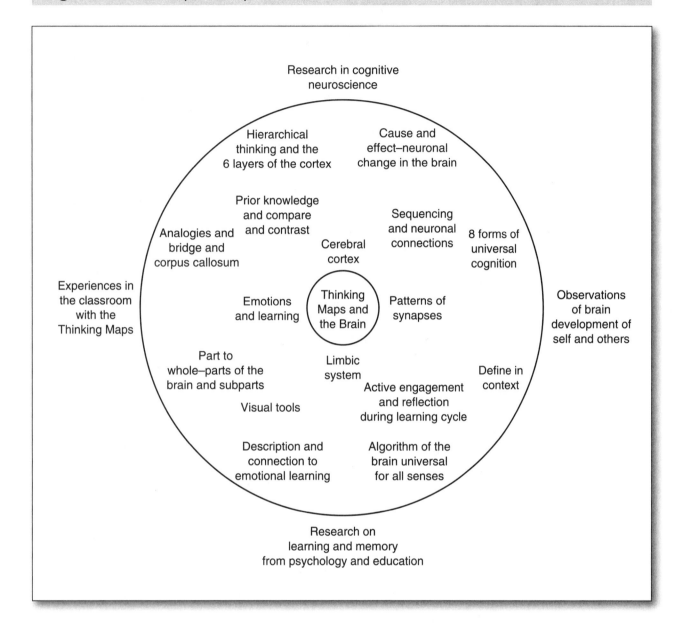

I think that the reason many of us who use Thinking Maps prefer to start a cognitive task with a Circle Map is that we use our whole brains to bring together everything that we know about something. We are not constrained by any other particular kind of cognitive strategy. We write down descriptive words and images, look at parts and the whole, ponder causation, and jot down members of categories. All of the ideas are put down to be sorted out later, and thus we are using the whole brain for holistic thinking.

In this Circle Map (see Figure 2.9), I put down the initial ideas I had for this chapter—drawing from the stored patterns in my cortex. I also have emotional connections to these ideas—triggering activation in the limbic structures of my brain. I type them out, using messages from my brain to my motor neurons to my muscles. Learning is a whole-brain activity. The Circle Map reflects this whole-brain activity, pulling everything together.

THE METACOGNITIVE FRAME: PULLING IT ALL TOGETHER

How do we know what we know? What influences our thinking? Put in the language of Thinking Maps, what is in our metacognitive frame? What is our brain doing when we ponder such a complex question? As discussed above with the Circle Map, the brain immediately identifies the context of an experience. At the same time, our brains are drawing on previous "frames" that are influencing how we perceive the context. If, for example, our experiences in school classrooms have been positive throughout our lives, our "frame of reference" will be more positive upon entering *any* classroom. These stored patterns, or *frames*, within our brains are retained as emotional latchkeys, and they drive our perceptions. In practice, it seems that many people seem to use the metacognitive frame more easily with the Circle Map (at least in my own observations and my own use). This may be because we are thinking about the big picture and using multiple forms of cognition. We are, on a basic level, engaging the whole brain and drawing from our vast storehouse of emotional frames that influence our perceptions of the immediate context for *whatever* we are experiencing.

When we draw the metacognitive frame around any of the maps, we are engaging the emotional structures of the limbic system as well as the more advanced cognitive structures of the cortex. Our senses examine new information within a context and send this information to the brain. The brain interprets the context as well as the new information. In the prefrontal cortex, our executive function allows us to make sense of the context or the big picture.

Why Metacognition Is So Important for Learning

Schooling should be all about *transfer*—that is, helping children learn content not only to do well on a given assessment but also to be able to apply the ideas to their lives outside the classroom. Students need help to see connections of content to their lives outside the classroom, and this needs to be done purposefully. We must be able to answer the age-old question that students ask: "Why do I need to know this?" Making connections is one of the many important uses of Thinking Maps. By allowing students the ability to create their own maps, and partially representing the connections their brains are making, they are personally invested in the content. They are better able to see the connections to their lives and to make an emotional connection, and are more likely to retain the information and be able to use it later. By using the Frame of Reference, we are giving students a visual tool that engages them in transferring the new knowledge into their own world of experiences and perceptions.

COOPERATIVE LEARNING, EMOTIONS, AND ASSESSING LEARNING

The relationships between brain structures and neural processes and the designs and cognitive processes we have briefly discussed above have implications for future research and development of deeper applications of the maps. Taken together, Thinking Maps as a language facilitate content learning and the development of language and cognitive abilities, and ultimately lead to richer patterning of experiences inside and outside of classrooms. While there are many ways that the maps support teachers and learners, two of the most significant areas are in how the maps are used for cooperative learning and for assessing student thinking and performance. These two areas are keys to facilitating both the creation of knowledge and reflection upon the processes and products of thinking.

Cooperative Learning and Emotions

Assumed in the use of the Thinking Maps is that their very use is collaborative. Individuals can and do create personal Thinking Maps that they might not share with others, but generally, for use in school, students, teachers, administrators, and others share their maps with each other to show and share their thinking. The brains of healthy humans are wired to be social and to connect. There are many brain parts that show this. For example, mirror neurons in the brain are activated when we see another person engage in an act—for instance, eating. If you watch a parent feed a young child with a spoon, she often moves her mouth unconsciously as she watches her baby eat from a spoon. Infants shortly after birth mimic their parents sticking out their tongues. As Sylwester (2005) writes,

> The remarkable mirror neuron system explains the modeling-mimicking process that is central to much human learning. Initial studies focused on a left hemisphere area that regulates speech production in humans (Broca's area). The discovery of mirror neurons might provide the same powerful unifying framework for our understanding of teaching and learning that the discovery of DNA did for our understanding of genetics.

Our brains are wired to connect to others. The Thinking Maps allow us to actually show a representation of our patterns of thinking to others, and in a collaborative or cooperative classroom students and teachers work together on maps and really *think together*—creating ideas and knowledge with each other.

Roger and David Johnson (1994)—the creators of a model of cooperative learning developed in the United States—write,

> It is only under certain conditions that cooperative efforts may be expected to be more productive than competitive and individualistic efforts. Those conditions are:
>
> 1. Clearly perceived positive interdependence
> 2. Considerable promotive (face-to-face) interaction
> 3. Clearly perceived individual accountability and personal responsibility to achieve the group's goals
> 4. Frequent use of the relevant interpersonal and small-group skills
> 5. Frequent and regular group processing of current functioning to improve the group's future effectiveness
>
> All healthy cooperative relationships have these five basic elements present. This is true of peer tutoring, partner learning, peer mediation, adult work groups, families, and other cooperative relationships. This conceptual "yardstick" should define any cooperative relationship.

As you read in this book about student successes with Thinking Maps, you will read some examples of students (and teachers and administrators) working collaboratively and cooperatively. When the Thinking Maps are used cooperatively, students can work toward meeting each of the above five goals by having a shared vision of their cooperative work that is tangible and representative of their collective thinking. These groups do need to be carefully managed, though. Students who feel left out have been shown in fMRI (functional magnetic resonance imaging) studies of the brain to activate the same parts of their brain that are activated when one experiences food poisoning. This kind of pain will make the brain try to avoid group work in the future—so it is important that all feel a part of the cooperative learning process.

Assessing Student Thinking Using Thinking Maps

One of the important uses of Thinking Maps for both students and teachers is as a tool to determine not only what one knows or has learned, but also how one is thinking about the information. In cooperative learning groups, one of the most difficult tasks is to assess individual participation within group work. When students in groups are creating their own maps, and then synthesizing multiple maps into "group" maps, it is a fluid process through which participants and the teacher can "see" the interdependent thinking across the group and "see" where the ideas came from.

In education, we say we want students to do more "critical thinking" and to "think at higher and more complex levels." Generally what we mean is that we want students to be able to engage in higher levels on Bloom's (1956) taxonomy. In Bloom's original taxonomy, lower levels of thinking were "understanding" and "comprehension"—the basic building blocks of more complex thinking. Bloom argued that cognitive tasks such as analysis, synthesis, and evaluation (in that order) were more complicated forms of cognition, and we should strive to engage learners at all levels as we design instruction. Bloom's revised taxonomy is quite similar, with the notable exception that the highest form of cognition is "creating." What do students do when they make a Thinking Map? They are "creating"—basically creating a visual to represent their thinking about the content.

As teachers and learners, we need to consider the important role of Thinking Maps in assessing not only the content but the cognition—how the brain is processing this content. As you read the many examples of student successes with the Thinking Maps in this book, think also about how useful having this information would be as a teacher, parent, or student as feedback about how the learner is thinking about the content. What a wonderful way to catch a glimpse into a student's brain processing. And isn't that exactly what good assessment should examine?

Assessment using the Thinking Maps allows us to see the brain in action—engaging in sequencing, hierarchical classification, causal reasoning, description, comparison, creating analogies, breaking complex items into parts, looking holistically at an idea or a topic in context, and then metacognition having an impact on the thinking. We can actually see the hierarchical structures (or how they are represented in one's mind), and we can see the sequences or patterns that students may have in their brains—the gaps in thinking and the brilliant connections. We need to see these universal forms of cognition in action. Thinking Maps, when used as a tool for assessment, will allow us such glimpses.

UNIFYING BRAIN AND MIND THROUGH MAPPING

As investigated in this chapter, the very function and structure of the brain seems to align with the eight universal forms of cognition proposed and supported in the theoretical framework of the Thinking Maps. This first look at the possible unification of the brain and cognitive patterns is exciting to consider. Basic brain structures work together to engage in more complex cognitive tasks—much in the same way that the basic graphic primitives of the Thinking Maps work together to engage in complex tasks. For example, one simple sequencing task, perhaps the basic sequence of a story, can be completed using a Flow Map. But completing a more complex task—say, critiquing a story—will involve identifying the main elements and categorizing them (in a Tree Map), describing the qualities of the main characters (in a Bubble Map), comparing and contrasting major ideas and themes (in a Double Bubble Map), and evaluating the qualities of the writing (for instance, what was "excellent" or "poor"—perhaps sorting in a Tree Map). As we see from each section above, each of the maps that represent eight cognitive universals connects to a brain part or brain function.

Our brains, like the Thinking Maps, do not operate in discrete isolated parts. The whole brain is at work when we use the maps. What I outline here are the areas of the brain that are most heavily implicated as they engage in the forms of cognition represented by each of the maps. The Thinking Maps must work together—much like the parts of the brain must work together—for good thinking to occur.

Once we see a person's Thinking Maps generated from a blank page or emerging in patterns on a computer screen, we have a chance to see the inner workings of the brain and cognition and use this information to give feedback. The use of the maps as an assessment tool to examine how the brain may be processing content can be very powerful—almost like seeing inside one's brain. As a teacher or learner, what could be more important than that?

REFERENCES

Bloom, B. S. (Ed.) (with Engelhart, M. D., Furst, E. J., Hill, W. H., & Krathwohl, D. R.). (1956). *Taxonomy of educational objectives: Handbook: Cognitive domain.* New York: David McKay.

Hawkins, J. (2004). *On intelligence.* New York: Holt.

Immordino-Yang, M. H., & Damasio, A. (2007). We feel therefore we learn: The relevance of affective and social neuroscience to education. In *The Jossey-Bass reader on the brain and learning.* San Francisco: John Wiley and Sons.

Johnson, D., & Johnson, R. (1994). An overview of cooperative learning. In J. S. Thousand, R. A. Villa, & A. I. Nevin (Eds.), *Creativity and collaborative learning.* Baltimore: Brookes Press.

Medline Plus. (2010). *Corpus callosum of the brain.* Retrieved November 19, 2010, from www.nlm.nih.gov/medlineplus/ency/imagepages/8753.htm

Sylwester, R. (2005). *How to explain a brain: An educator's handout of brain terms and cognitive processes.* Thousand Oaks: Corwin.

3

Leveling the Playing Field for All Students

Bonnie Singer, Ph.D.

KEY CONCEPTS

- Thinking Maps® as tools for developing students' executive functioning and metacognitive Habits of Mind
- A revealing story of the transformation in writing processes, executive functioning, and performance of one student with special needs
- Improving writing, oral language, and thinking processes in unison

Those of us who are fortunate enough to work with children often find ourselves forever changed by relationships with one or two of them. My life took a definite turn when I met David. He taught me that the mind of an eight-year-old is capable of much more than I had previously thought, and that even children with severe learning disabilities can learn to play the game of school as well as or better than their nondisabled classmates. Through David, I learned just how powerful Thinking Maps can be, and I saw how profoundly they can change a life. Thinking Maps not only got David back in the academic game; they also leveled the playing field so that he could emerge as a leader in his classroom.

As a speech-language pathologist in private practice, I have the luxury of being able to work with any student who struggles with language, literacy, or learning. In addition to David, I have had the opportunity to use maps with countless other children who are not diagnosed with learning disabilities but just have trouble learning—the so-called underachievers. Though each story is unique, similar themes emerge from the students and whole schools I have taught to use Thinking Maps. As a result, David's story is worth telling, for it offers us insight into many children who struggle with school and inspires new hope for their futures.

THE STORY OF DAVID

I remember vividly the day I met him. A small second grader with a chip on his shoulder, David sat down at my table, pulled a stack of crumpled papers from his backpack, and exclaimed with indignant exasperation, "Look at what she gives us!" He slapped a stack of graphic organizers on the table with a dramatic flair. "These are stupid," he declared, "and they don't help. I hate writing, and I'm not doing it!" On the table were five graphic organizers—variations on a typical web-style map. Although they had different shapes, they all depicted the same visual configuration: a circle centered on the page with ovals or lines radiating from it like spokes on a wheel.

This particular set of webs was given to David by his teacher with the intention that they would guide him with planning and writing a story. Attempting to use the only strategies available to him, he dutifully filled in each graphic. In the end, he had five webs on his desk. Rather than help him write his story, they overwhelmed him with information that neither looked like a story nor helped him order his thinking so that he could generate one. As a result, he gave up. This experience reinforced his already growing belief that he wasn't and would never be a good writer, and it strengthened the bad taste he had in his mouth for writing.

Historically, David had always had difficulty producing more than a sentence on his own. His motor skills were compromised, so handwriting was an arduous process for him. By second grade, he was identified as a child who wasn't making academic progress, so he was provided with support from the learning specialist in his school. Though he struggled academically, David was quite talented in some areas. His verbal IQ was 139—in the superior range, as measured by the third edition of the Wechsler Intelligence Scale for Children (WISC-III). But his visual-spatial skills were not nearly as well developed, as evidenced by his below-average WISC-III performance IQ of 86. Overall, his developmental profile, with a significant (53-point) discrepancy between verbal and visual-spatial abilities, indicated a nonverbal learning disability along with attention deficit hyperactivity disorder (ADHD), for which he took medication. The school psychologist who evaluated him reported that he had difficulty with visual discrimination, motor planning, attention to visual details, and visual-spatial construction. Further, he noted that it was particularly difficult for David to see the relationship of parts to the whole in nonverbal tasks and that he "may need help with sequencing, prioritizing information, and strategies to see the 'big picture' or how details relate to a bigger concept."

David could describe his problem with writing. He had trouble with handwriting, and he didn't know how to plan his ideas or start a piece of writing. Webbing strategies didn't help him, because he couldn't determine which idea on his web should go first. Nothing in the visual structure of a web suggested a good place to start. I suggested to David that his teachers were trying very hard to help him with writing but they weren't using a graphic that worked very well for his brain. Despite his vehement protests that "graphics don't work," I introduced him to the Flow Map, a Thinking Map for sequencing ideas. Together, we generated ideas for a story, while I modeled how to map them out sequentially. Afterward, I asked David if he thought he could write the story using the ideas on our map. "Sure," he quipped confidently, and he quickly drafted a lovely little story. The next week, I began to scaffold the use of the map, starting a new Flow Map, and he finished it and used it to write another story. Over the next few weeks, David practiced making Flow Maps with me before doing his story-writing homework. His attitude toward story writing slowly began to shift as he learned a simple technique that allowed him to see his thoughts before he wrote within a visual structure that looked like the discourse he was attempting to generate. After a break for summer vacation, I asked David if he remembered the Flow Map. He quickly drew a blank map, while cheerfully explaining what it was used for, how to make it, and how to use it for writing. With this visual image now rooted in his mind, narrative writing ceased to be a problem for him. So did his sour attitude about writing.

GAINING FLUENCY

Over time, as David became more fluent with the maps, his demeanor changed. Though his visual-spatial skills were indeed compromised, he was a quick study. With direct instruction and a good deal of guided practice, he learned the visual array of the maps and the pattern of thought each map represented. I realized we had turned a corner when his mother found him on the couch on a Saturday making a Flow Map of his day. The frustrated, angry, and resistant boy who had first walked into my office evolved into an enthusiastic, creative, and self-confident boy who was truly excited about learning and said "Thank you for teaching me" at the end of each session. David had learned a new language—a language of thinking. It was both a visual language and a verbal one. This language paved the way for explicit consideration of how, when, where, and why to apply specific thinking strategies to support his schoolwork.

In our second year of working together, David became so confident about his ability to think that when we had extra time in a session he began to make up Thinking Map games. We took turns creating problem scenarios and quizzing each other on how we would need to think to solve them. Here, he demonstrated that he had truly developed an awareness of his thinking and internalized the language of the maps, as he reported ways to use them that I had never taught him. The maps were now truly tools for thinking, learning, and problem solving, and these tools established a level of metacognition that I had never before seen in a child his age.

At the end of fourth grade, David had an updated neuropsychological evaluation before he moved away to another state. His WISC-III verbal IQ remained in the superior range (138), and his nonverbal IQ score rose 12 points (to a score of 98) from the below-average to the average range, as shown in Figure 3.1. Interestingly, significant gains were evident in some key areas of cognition—namely, his attention to visual detail and his ability to perceive part-whole relationships, integrate information, and plan and organize an approach to a task. In our two years of working together, we used Thinking Maps to develop each of these skills in natural and authentic learning contexts. When David moved and began to receive special education services, his learning-center teachers could not determine what was wrong with him. Despite significant cognitive discrepancies, he was metacognitively, motivationally, and behaviorally active in his own learning process, which masked the severity of his learning disability and allowed him to function on par with his peers.

At this point, David still had a significant discrepancy between his superior verbal skills and his average nonverbal abilities, but his presentation as a learner was dramatically different. First and foremost, he *knew* how he was thinking and could identify what kind of thinking any task demanded of him. As a result, he was highly self-regulated. He demonstrated the three defining features of self-regulated learning (Zimmerman, 1989): the ability to self-monitor, self-evaluate, and self-adjust. He had an arsenal of strategies that he could employ in any learning situation, and he readily employed them when tasks demanded complex thinking. Consequently, his self-efficacy for any learning task—even writing—was tremendously strong. David moved from being stuck on the bench to being a varsity player when it came to school.

WHAT CAN WE LEARN FROM DAVID?

What's interesting about David is that his story is representative of other students who learn Thinking Maps and who have special needs or are underachieving academically. This raises the question of what the maps do for children's minds. Clearly, the maps did not get rid of David's nonverbal learning disability or his attention deficit disorder. We know that such

Figure 3.1 David's WISC-III Scores Before and After Thinking Maps

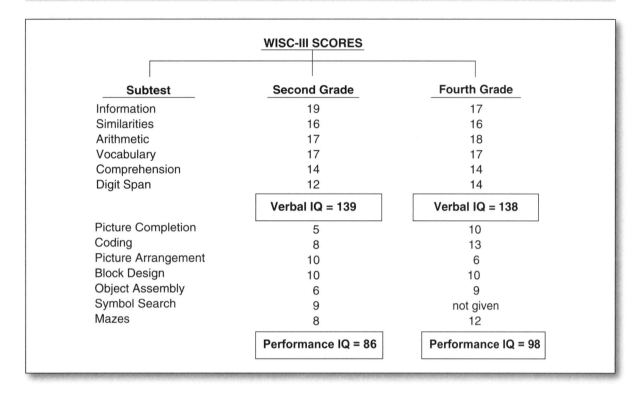

Subtest	Second Grade	Fourth Grade
Information	19	17
Similarities	16	16
Arithmetic	17	18
Vocabulary	17	17
Comprehension	14	14
Digit Span	12	14
	Verbal IQ = 139	**Verbal IQ = 138**
Picture Completion	5	10
Coding	8	13
Picture Arrangement	10	6
Block Design	10	10
Object Assembly	6	9
Symbol Search	9	not given
Mazes	8	12
	Performance IQ = 86	**Performance IQ = 98**

disabilities are lifelong, and his cognitive profile remained indicative of these disorders even after becoming proficient with the maps. However, the Thinking Maps did significantly affect his cognition as well as other things that aren't measured through standardized tests, namely his *meta*cognition and his day-to-day performance in school. Consequently, they affected his approach to problem solving, his enthusiasm for learning, his willingness to participate, and his beliefs about himself as a learner.

Over the years, I have used Thinking Maps with students who are underachieving academically and with those who have a wide range of disabilities (including cognitive deficits, language disorders, nonverbal learning disabilities, Asperger syndrome, high-functioning autism, and ADHD. I have yet to encounter a student who cannot learn the maps or use them in productive ways. The question remaining, then, is what exactly do the maps do for kids who struggle?

Seeing Patterns for Organization

First of all, the maps help kids see patterns. As Caine and Caine (1994) note, "The mind is a pattern detector." Many students who struggle in school do so because they fail to detect or intuit patterns. They don't see how what they did yesterday links to what they are doing today. They don't see the patterns of information that are laid out in a chapter or presented in a lecture. And, like David, though they may know a lot, they don't see how to pattern what they know in order to write or tell someone about it. Their failure in school, in part, stems from a fundamental difficulty with representing their thoughts.

Failure to invoke patterns for representing thought frequently results in disorganization. We see this very clearly in students who have ADHD. Individuals with ADHD have trouble with a range of abilities that are subsumed under the umbrella term *executive functions*. When we say someone has difficulty with executive functions, we mean he or she has difficulty planning an approach to a task, organizing a sequence of actions or series of data points, holding action sequences in working memory until they are executed, inhibiting actions that are irrelevant to the task at hand, deciding what to attend to and what to do, shifting when necessary, monitoring and evaluating his or her behavior, and adjusting his or her behavior and emotions in response to perceived success or failure (Denckla, 1998; Singer & Bashir, 1999, in press). In essence, these are the cognitive abilities CEOs tend to be good at.

Students with ADHD, by definition, have compromised executive functions, because attention and executive functions are governed by the same part of the brain. However, students *without* ADHD can also have executive function problems. As a result, disorganization is a common characteristic of a broad range of learning disabilities as well as general under-achievement. Thinking Maps allow students to see patterns that go beyond the word or sentence—patterns that capture the big picture. They offer students with varied learning abilities and learning styles a means for organizing their thinking and their understanding of the world. Further, they provide a vehicle for such students to represent and share what they know and understand.

Language for Learning: Supporting Oral Communication

In viewing how students represent what they know, the central role of language warrants consideration. Vygotsky (1962) asserts that language and cognition are inextricably intertwined (also see Chapter 6, "Maps for the Road to Reading Comprehension"). Cognition is limited by language, and vice versa. It is nearly impossible to solve a complex problem without an internal conversation—without talking your way through it. Educators want students to become better thinkers, and they depend upon listening, speaking, reading, and writing (to a far greater degree than other representational systems) for developing as well as assessing student knowledge and understanding. This puts students who struggle with language at a severe disadvantage when it comes to playing the game of school. Those who have strong linguistic abilities tend to do well overall, and those who don't tend to struggle inordinately in most academic subjects. Consequently, success or failure in education is largely dependent on language, as it is both the object of knowledge and one of the principal means through which new knowledge is acquired (Cazden, 1973).

As a speech-language pathologist, what has amazed me most about Thinking Maps is that they offer a milieu from which focused language can emerge. They scaffold and integrate multiple systems that support expression. Maps allow for interactions between listening, speaking, reading, and writing within a language of thinking that bridges visual-spatial and verbal representations. Consequently, they profoundly change both the language used *within* the classroom and the language demands *of* the classroom. This change allows students who struggle with listening, speaking, reading, or writing, or who previously could only stand on the sidelines, to get in the game.

Thinking Maps change the way teachers talk to students, which changes the way students talk to themselves and each other. We hear students and teachers use words such as *think, classify, sequence, analogy,* and *brainstorm.* These words represent cognitive processes—internal workings of the mind. In classrooms using Thinking Maps, such cognitive processes are taught to students directly, and the words that represent them are woven through an ongoing conversation about how to do the thinking that school requires. It is truly astounding to hear a first-grade teacher ask her class, "How are you thinking about this?" and have *all* of her students raise their hands confidently with an answer. No longer are students guessing blindly at how to approach a task, hoping they will stumble across a path that will lead to success. Now, they are asked to consider what cognitive route(s) they will take before they set out on their journey. That consideration takes place through language—through an explicit and constructive dialogue between teachers and students about what kind of thinking a task requires and which thinking tools will get the job done. This explicit conversation about thinking fosters the development of metacognition—the seed from which self-regulated learners grow.

Organized Thinking and Coherent Speaking

Thinking Maps explicitly promote student reflection, which is necessary for planning and organizing. In using the maps, students can develop the executive functions necessary to support language and scaffold social participation in a learning community. The maps store words and ideas until students decide what to do with them. Because they represent *specific* thought processes, and do so visually, they help students inhibit mental actions that are irrelevant to the task and decide what to attend to and what to do. They cue students to shift their approach when what they are mapping doesn't capture their thinking accurately, and they guide students to monitor and evaluate their behavior and make adjustments as necessary. As one student at the Learning Prep School in Massachusetts (a school for students with severe learning disabilities) once said to me, "The maps are like a brain."

I routinely ask students how the maps help them, and the number-one response I get is "They help me organize my ideas." Often, students and teachers mention the payoff this has with writing. What strikes me more is the payoff it has with talking. Thinking Maps change the way students talk to their teachers, their parents, and each other. Having a place to arrange and store their words helps them. What also helps them are the visual-spatial arrays that represent structured thought and discourse. The maps are devices that allow students to *see* what they think and find the language that will convey that knowledge to their teachers and each other in a clear and organized way. As one fifth-grade student told me, "The maps put my thoughts into action."

Nick, a sixth-grade student with a learning disability attending the Learning Prep School, shared a Double Bubble Map he made to compare and contrast the main characters in two books he read during independent reading (see Figure 3.2). He not only read the words and phrases on his map to his classmates; he also elaborated upon each idea by offering details and examples from the two books he read. For example, when discussing the similarities of the characters regarding the making of new friends, Nick explained that Robinson met a native person on his island, while Cody met a person in the woods. Both found new friends to help them survive while they were stranded in isolating environments—Robinson on an island and Cody in the arctic forest of Alaska. Nick recalled key facts about each character, and what is more impressive is that making the map helped him to remember, integrate, and understand the books at a very deep level. Talking *from* the map allowed him to share what he knew in nicely organized and coherent discourse. Nick noted that he never would have remembered all those details if he hadn't constructed that kind of map. He went on to explain that the Double Bubble and Tree Maps help him more than the other Thinking Maps because they depict ways of thinking he previously found difficult.

Having trained and mentored faculties of two schools that exclusively serve students with a broad range of learning disabilities (the Norman Howard School in Rochester, New York, and the Learning Prep School in Newton, Massachusetts), I have been struck time and time again by how oral communication in the classroom changes. Via the maps, communication literally takes on a whole new shape. Teachers and students have a means for integrating key concepts and conveying new understandings fluidly, grounding them in a spatial realm. It is fascinating to me to watch teachers and students talk about how they will use one map or another. They gesture as they talk; they make circles and boxes and lines in the air, and they plug their ideas into these imaginary spaces. Their spoken language piggybacks onto a spatial superstructure. Fluid classroom discourse, then, is born from the marriage of verbal and spatial realms—from the integrated workings of both the right and left hemispheres. I believe this has much to do with why the maps bring about such profound changes in classroom environments and student performance. They level the playing field for students who rely on relative strengths within either the verbal or the visual domain, bolstering whichever domain is weaker to bring about a more balanced learner.

Figure 3.2   Learning Prep Student Comparing and Contrasting Two Characters

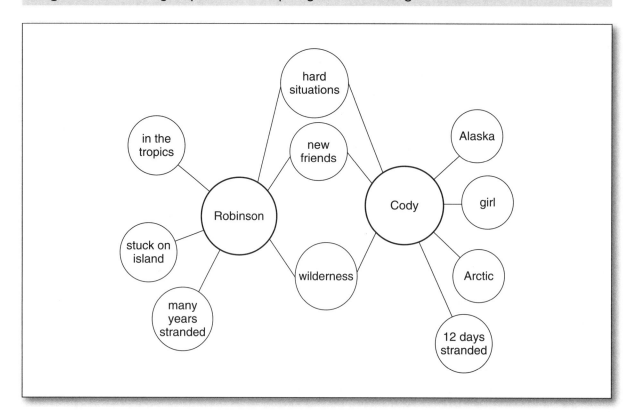

Not only does the nature of spoken communication change in classrooms using Thinking Maps, but the amount of spoken language changes. Discussion and debate become more elaborate when students have tools that allow them to see how all of the pieces of curriculum content go together. As their ability to show what they know improves, so does their motivation for and investment in learning. Often, reluctant or reticent students begin to take more risks and participate. After only six months of using Thinking Maps with students, many faculty members at the Learning Prep School reported that the students' spoken and written output at least doubled. Indeed, one sixth-grade teacher in Chicago noted that she used to do all the talking when she taught. Since teaching the maps to her students, she now talks far less often. Her students do the talking, and she helps them see where their learning conversation is going.

Closing the Gap for Underachievers

Though Thinking Maps have the potential to raise the performance of all learners, they are particularly powerful for students who are functioning in the bottom of the bell curve (i.e., students with identified special needs and those who are not coded but are struggling nonetheless, perhaps due to mild problems with executive functions). Who are these students, and what are the implications of using Thinking Maps with them?

In the lower quartile, we find three groups of students. One group has identified disabilities, but these students can function quite well when classroom instruction supports and accommodates their unique learning styles and needs. For them, the maps are strategies that bridge cognitive, visual, and verbal realms, perhaps providing a tool set that allows these students to manage mainstream curriculum demands. Another group has significant learning challenges that require special education services (e.g., students with language disorders, learning disabilities, perceptual disorders, motor disorders, or compromised cognition). The maps provide teachers of general and special education serving these students with a common language and tool set for teaching, thereby fostering collaboration and partnership among school faculty. Whereas these students generally lack flexibility in their learning styles and have difficulty transferring new learning from one context to another, the maps provide them with a set of tools they can use both in and out of the classroom. They form a bridge between general and special education.

A third group in the bottom quartile consists of students who are poor CEOs of their own learning. Lacking insight about how to meet academic task demands, they are underachieving relative to their potential. As a result, they aren't sure how to get from A to Z when given a task unless they are provided with explicit scaffolds. In some cases, such students fail to make progress in the general education curriculum and are referred for special education services. Too often, they don't qualify for extra support, and the gap between academic expectations and their achievement continues to widen. For all groups in the lower quartile, Thinking Maps can help students regulate their own learning and be more successful in the game of school because the maps serve as a device for mediating thinking, listening, talking, reading, writing, problem solving, and the acquisition of new knowledge and understanding. They can be used for universal instructional design and the successful inclusion of all learners.

The Thinking Maps, then, have the potential for reducing the number of students in special education and allowing more students not only to survive but to thrive in general education classrooms. Consequently, they have the potential to be a school's most powerful weapon when it comes to closing the achievement gap. As the Flow Map in Figure 3.3 shows, having a small set of flexible thinking tools lessens all students' anxiety and confusion about school work, which brings forth an increased sense of control and self-efficacy, which leads in turn to increased motivation to participate and learn as well as to greater academic success. Success further decreases anxiety and confusion, and the cycle continues. By leveling the playing field, Thinking Maps provide students who are not doing well with the tools they need to win at school.

Figure 3.3 Effects of Thinking Maps on Student Learning

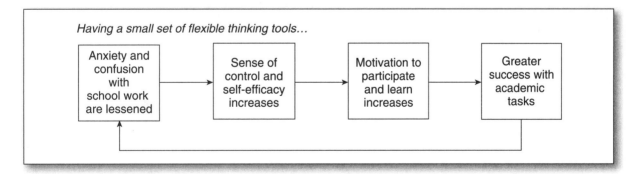

REFERENCES

Caine, R. N., & Caine, G. (1994). *Making connections: Teaching and the human brain.* Alexandria, VA: Association for Supervision and Curriculum Development.

Cazden, C. B. (1973). Problems for education: Language as curriculum and learning environment. *Daedalus, 102,* 135–148.

Denckla, M. (1998, November). *Understanding the role of executive functions in language, academics, and daily life.* Paper presented at American International College, Springfield, MA.

Singer, B. D., & Bashir, A. S. (1999). What are executive functions and self-regulation and what do they have to do with language learning disorders? *Language, Speech, and Hearing Services in Schools, 30,* 265–273.

Singer, B. D., & Bashir, A. S. (in press). Developmental variations in writing. In B. Schulman, K. Apel, B. Ehren, & E. Silliman (Eds.), *Handbook of language and literacy.* New York: Guilford Press.

Vygotsky, L. (1962). *Thought and language.* Cambridge, MA: MIT Press.

Zimmerman, B. J. (1989). A social cognitive view of self-regulated academic learning. *Journal of Educational Psychology, 81,* 329–339.

4

Tools for Integrating Theories and Differentiating Practice

Alan Cooper, B.Ed.

KEY CONCEPTS

- Differentiating instruction through student-centered tools in New Zealand
- Using a Flow Map for simultaneously enriching Habits of Mind, multiple intelligences, and learning styles
- Facilitating emotional and cognitive development using Thinking Maps®

There are a number of ways in which we enrich the experiences our students have in our classrooms in any given year and over time in our schools. As we grow as teachers and administrators through these changes, we also enrich our learning community. In the short term, new techniques and theories implemented in schools may leverage new learning, but ultimately a long-term question may remain below the surface and undermine change: In what ways do these practices and theoretical models integrate with the existing approaches we have in place so that the individual efforts are unified? A school may react to yearly changes and become additive but not integrative. Sustaining a larger vision while creating a coherent educational experience for students requires constant orchestration of the overlapping teaching strategies, student tools, and various theories introduced into the school.

If the leadership of the school community does not address this question, then new processes may not be used together by teachers and students. The educational program risks becoming perceived by all concerned as merely a jumble of discordant instruments sounding off, rather than a richly synchronized, high-quality performance. As the headmaster of St. George's School, a K–8 private school in New Zealand, for 18 years, I had the opportunity to bring many practices and theories together and help facilitate conversations with our faculty, school board, and parents to make sense of this integration. I was equally concerned about both the practical and the theoretical integration of models. Over the years of my service, I have become particularly intrigued by how Thinking Maps have helped integrate the theories and practices of Goleman's views on emotional intelligence, Gardner's multiple intelligences, the Dunns' learning styles model, and Costa's Habits of Mind in our school.

INTEGRATING TOOLS FOR DIFFERENTIATION

The greatest advantage we as educators can give the wide, diverse range of students we teach is to enable them as learners. The drive toward the twin goals of common content and differentiated processes for individuals is one of the key educational challenges of the 21st century. For many school communities this dilemma can become a point of conflict, driving well-meaning people apart rather than functioning as a point of departure or an opportunity for growth.

In order to maximize learning for all students, individual differences must be sought out and explicitly developed in each of us as teachers and learners. To accomplish this, there is a need not only for the teacher to know how each individual learns but for the student to know that as well. Such information must be raised to the consciousness level. For example, while Thinking Maps are valuable in their own right as flexible tools for differentiating and unifying learning in a classroom, these tools become more useful for learners when they are connected to the other current learning theories and practices. As we found at our school, there are many connections to be made between the use of Thinking Maps in classrooms and emotional intelligence, multiple intelligences, learning styles, and Habits of Mind. When used together, they develop a synergy that truly benefits both the teacher and the student.

For a very long time now, seeking these connections has been the lifeblood of our school. This is because our school faculty has been particularly influenced by thinkers such as Alvin Toffler, Charles Handy, and Peter Senge. St. George's School has come to perceive itself as a learning organization preparing our students, our teachers, and even our parents for lifelong learning where the only constant is change and perhaps paradox. We want to go beyond teaching the curriculum and attaining high standards, important as they must be, to teaching behaviors that allow our teachers and our students to be confident problem solvers in areas where they do not know the answers; in areas where they have to ask their own questions; and in areas where, as Toffler has offered, they are required to learn, unlearn, and relearn.

THEORIES INTO PRACTICE

Over a dozen years our faculty has gone through extensive training in the theory and practices mentioned above. None of the training and other forms of professional development were isolated; instead they were brought into an ongoing conversation about the connections between approaches. Teachers' professional portfolios were an essential place for educators to muse, research, document, and reflect on how new processes integrated with existing structures. A large part of my investigation of how all of these processes worked together was to move in and out of classrooms on a regular basis.

During a span of time when I was observing a middle-grade class, the students were studying World War II and the Holocaust. I began focusing on two boys as a way of looking at how the learning styles approach worked.

One student, Harry, would be described in the Dunn and Dunn (1992) learning style profile as a near-extreme global learner. He always has his shirt out and constantly chatters, and thus it is no surprise that the sociological line in his profile states that he likes working with peers. As well, he is in constant motion and appears to avoid work. His teacher grasped the important point that it is not work as such that he avoids but analytic work, the factual stuff in encyclopedias and textbooks. Another student, Douglas, is the opposite. As an analytic learner, he prefers factual nonfiction, less emotive articles, and encyclopedic information. He wrote up the fact file on Auschwitz and drew the geographical map of Europe with great attention to detail. Harry would have none of this. He started by drawing a barbed wire border—anything to avoid or at least delay getting on with the work. He did read excerpts from *Anne Frank: The Diary of a Young Girl*, nonfiction reading, but not in the cold-hard-fact form. It was the emotional content that motivated him. He wrote a very good emotive poem. Harry constantly discussed research with Douglas that Douglas had found, but the teacher worried at times that neither was really learning because Harry seemed to be interrupting Douglas all the time.

However, both Harry and Douglas were learning, and they were using a common tool—a Flow Map—that served to focus their widely ranging styles (see Figure 4.1). One of them was engaged at the global, emotive level and the other at the analytical, factual level, but the information appeared together on their map. The map became a reference point and place that brought their two styles together. When it came time for the formal presentation to the class, Harry was quite verbose and could recall fully the information that was required in the study and shown explicitly in the map. This success story is a starting point for investigating, albeit in short form, the linkages made below between the Thinking Maps and very complex theories of emotions, intelligences, habits, and styles. A wider understanding may come about as we consider how teachers and students are becoming conscious and conversant about how these models work together to support deeper learning.

Figure 4.1   The Holocaust Research Flow Map

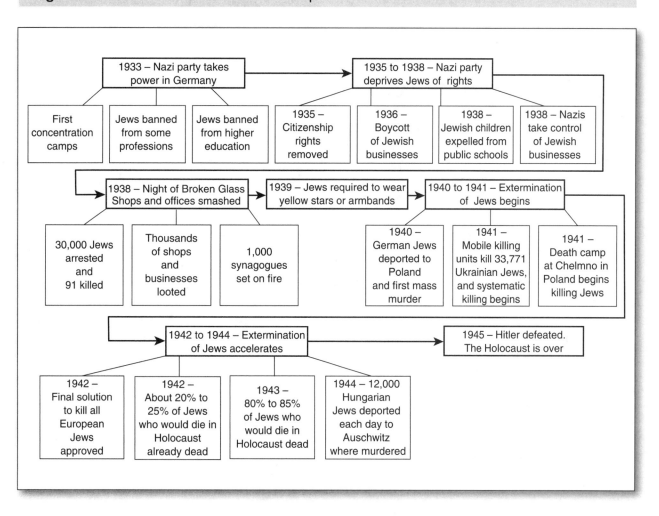

LINKING TO EMOTIONAL INTELLIGENCE

Confidence is necessary for both teachers and students in order for learning to occur, and it can be seen as a by-product of emotional intelligence (Goleman, 1995). Self-awareness and self-management, the first two components of emotional intelligence, are expressed by our abilities to manage ourselves effectively. The teacher of the two boys demonstrated this by having the self-confidence to try something with a risk attached. She did not know the ultimate outcome of allowing two opposites, as Harry and Douglas were, to work together. Many teachers would group kids together who seem to work in similar ways, not dissimilar ways. However, it was what Costa and Kallick (2000) call a responsible risk. Confident in her knowledge of the way the boys learned, the teacher was able to seize opportunities and turn the apparent weakness in the divergent learning style preferences of the boys into a strength. She made the connections by combining her understanding of the boys' learning styles and her internal thought processes with the use of Thinking Maps as the animating center for the boys' work.

Managing relationships effectively is a second component of emotional intelligence. The teacher's knowledge about how individuals learn gave her empathy for the learning styles of both boys, divergent as they were. She made the required organizational changes within the classroom to facilitate these styles, but she also had the social skill to do this effectively. Her empathy was not passive commiseration but active participation. As for the boys, they, too, demonstrated self-awareness. They knew their learning styles as learning strengths, because that was how the learning style profiles were openly referred to in the school. Consequently, the students had developed a strong and positive sense of self-worth. This aided their ability to self-manage and to adapt and seize a new and quite different working relationship—using a common visual tool—and use it in a way that made it work for each of them.

LINKING TO MULTIPLE INTELLIGENCES

There is a range of multiple intelligences, but the focus of this discussion is on intrapersonal and interpersonal forms, linking with Goleman's work. Intrapersonal intelligence is associated with the internal self. Howard Gardner (1993) defines it as "involving the capacity to understand oneself, to have an effective working model of oneself—including one's own desires, fears, and capacities—and to use such information effectively in regulating one's own life." A key word here is *capacities,* both for teachers and for students. It is a teacher's available repertoire, or the knowledge of the available tools and models, that will enable students to work more effectively. Interpersonal intelligence is more concerned with relationships, a key intelligence for teachers as they create a collaborative learning environment. Gardner's definition states that interpersonal intelligence is "to understand the intentions, motivations, and desires of other people and, consequently, to work effectively with others."

The teacher needs to understand how each individual student learns and to use that knowledge to enable the students to effectively use their individual learning strengths in groups. In so doing, the students, too, need to become aware of their personal intelligences by metacognitive reflection and teacher and peer feedback. The use of Thinking Maps as an open space for co-construction provided a mediating frame for the two boys to act out their styles toward a product that united their styles. The map was a safe place for collaboration. It was evolving and structured, mirrored their thinking, and had no one right answer. The boys were drawing out detailed information in a holistic form and together could evolve the ideas between them on paper.

LINKING LEARNING STYLES

Learning styles (Dunn & Dunn, 1992) are the way in which individuals begin concentrating on and then processing, internalizing, and, finally, retaining new and difficult information that they are taught. Integral to this is the realization that learning is individual—that students learn in many different ways, and teaching and learning are most efficient when these differences are taken into account. Just as theories of intelligence are complex, so, too, is the Dunn and Dunn learning styles model, having 21 different categories. However, there is a smaller subset of the whole, where learners are divided into global or analytic learners. It is this subset that Douglas and Harry were clearly exhibiting and their teacher was supporting, as displayed in summary using the Double Bubble Map in Figure 4.2.

Figure 4.2 Analytic and Global Learner Comparison Double Bubble Map

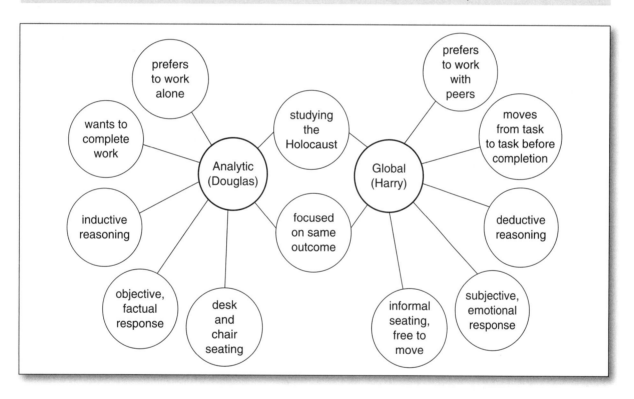

Harry, the analytic learner, was the conventional model pupil. He preferred being seated formally; he worked carefully and methodically through factual detail, completing each piece before moving on. Eventually, the details that he had compiled would become the whole—the complete picture. His work was also characterized by persistence, in the sense that he liked to complete what he was doing before moving on. Douglas, the global learner, was the conventional problem pupil. He needed a more informal seating arrangement, such as soft furniture or being allowed to sprawl on the floor rather than sit at a desk. He needed to be free to move. He focused on the emotional side of things by seeking the big issues, dashing about in this search rather than methodically working from the bottom up. Thus he could be said to lack persistence in that he did not complete what he was doing before turning his attention to something else, searching for the next big picture. Not even his barbed wire border around the Flow Map, an artistic touch, was completed before he was off doing another task. However, in the end, in his own time, he got it completed with Harry.

It was because of the teacher's awareness of and action on these understandings—personal intelligence in action—that these two diverse learning styles were able to be reconciled so successfully.

LINKING HABITS OF MIND

A wide range of Habits of Mind (Costa & Kallick, 2000) were also activated through this activity, especially when considering this situation from the teacher's perspective. It was the teacher who created this learning pair and took the risk of bringing these boys together with the Flow Map in hand.

One key Habit of Mind, metacognition, was formally undertaken by the teacher in her professional development portfolio. She brought to a conscious level the personal, practical knowledge that she developed and articulated as it flowed from her classroom interactions. She was thinking flexibly, listening to her students with understanding and empathy, taking responsible risks, asking questions, and above all remaining open to continuous learning. The students were doing likewise. The teacher noted in her portfolio that through this activity the students were beginning "to understand why they worked the way they did." This was clearly facilitating both their intrapersonal and their interpersonal intelligences. The understandings of how they learn increased their ability to understand the motivation and abilities of the other students and respond to them in such a way that they achieved a positive outcome. They were learning to self-manage and to manage their relationships—attributes that produce positive results far beyond the classroom walls. As the teacher noted in her portfolio, "It not only helped them individually, but it also helped them to understand, tolerate, and work with one another."

There is a strong match here between the theories of Goleman and Gardner and the Dunns' learning style models. As the students' capacities increased through their understanding of the learning styles of their partners, this internal, intrapersonal growth was transferred to interpersonal relationships so that they grew as well. This is ongoing, continual improvement of Habits of Mind through intrinsic rewards of learning. Jonathan Cohen (1999) describes it this way: "Awareness of ourselves and others provides the foundation for social and emotional competencies: a sense of self worth; the ability to solve problems and make responsible and helpful decisions, to communicate and collaborate with others, to become self motivating."

THINKING MAPS: A UNIFYING SET OF TOOLS

Given the short description above of the intersection of emotional and interpersonal intelligences, global and analytic learning styles, and Habits of Mind, we may begin to see how Thinking Maps provide a unique, unifying language across these four approaches, each of which is theoretically rich. The Thinking Maps provide the how-to tools that may be both linear and nonlinear, as well as detailed and holistic. Importantly, they are problem-solving tools used for executive processes (see Chapter 3, "Leveling the Playing Field for All Students"), not just information processors, and in the situation investigated above the teacher retreated to the background after creating the learning environment. Harry and Douglas did their work and problem solving, in this case with only the one Flow Map as the immediate, mediating agent. By their very nature, Thinking Maps are not content or task bound. They are adaptable and can be easily customized to suit individual learning styles and interdisciplinary problems.

There is considerable appeal in these tools for the global learner because the purpose of the map and the thinking process required are always emphasized. This immediately gives the big picture that global learners need. It becomes a large canvas of one or several thinking processes or multitasks such as comparing and contrasting, describing attributes, categorizing, and so on. Thus, the global mind is able to avoid rushing about looking for an organizing purpose as it settles in on it quickly and can then proceed to work deductively down into the detail.

The same map is flexible enough to provide the detailed structure that an analytical mind needs to build inductively, detail by detail, in order to arrive at the main idea. For example, the Flow Map for sequencing a complex event such as a war can be started with an overarching rectangular phase with smaller boxes expanding as stages, leading to ever more refined details shown as substages within each major stage. In the same way, the Tree Map for categorizing can be built with details from the ground up by the analytic learner, while the global learner is creating the same map from the top down.

However, there are extra spin-offs from this flexible, evolving, visual structuring of content and processes. The Habit of Mind Costa calls persistence is one of the major areas separating analytical and global learners in the Dunn and Dunn learning style model. At one end of the persistence continuum are those learners high on responsibility, who do not want to stop until they have completed their task. These learners are last to leave the classroom as they copy the homework fully and accurately. They are the students whose parents complain that there is too much homework because they spent two hours completing the half hour's work the teacher thought had been assigned. They are driven to be perfect. Part of that perfection is making sure that the task is completed exactly, with all the details in place. Each of the Thinking Maps has an adaptive structure and consistency so that students who are high on persistence can complete steps before moving on, or they can easily chunk the maps in order to provide for closure when there are time constraints. When several maps are being used in sequence, each map can be completed as a single unit in an overall project. In this way, closure is there at the end of each map, which satisfies those who see completion as an attribute of responsibility and removes the frustration of not completing an assignment.

For global learners, who are often low on persistence, moving from task to task is facilitated. Interestingly, the low-persistence student can keep on working for an extended period just as the high-persistence student can. The difference is that the low-persistence student often needs multiple tasks to work on, thus creating an interplay between focal points, but focusing nonetheless. Thinking Maps provide an alternative way of progressing through assignments. Continuity of task is not essential, so leaving off the work at any stage and then coming back later works. Where a sequence of maps is being used, the global learner can move through the sequence bit by bit, developing single ideas as they arise and moving back and forth between maps. In this way, the multitasking that provides optimum learning for the global learner is also made possible.

REFLECTIONS: EMERGENT THINKERS AND LIFELONG LEARNERS

The integrated Habits of Mind, emotional intelligences, and learning styles discussed above are obviously evolving well before a child steps into our school and becomes a student. It has become our responsibility, however, as an organization, to integrate these theories so that from the beginning and over time our students come to appreciate their capacities and learn how to use them to work effectively with others in the classroom.

The importance of Thinking Maps as a vehicle by which students are able to discover this is evident. However, the benefits do not stop there. By making these connections, positive attitudes toward learning are nurtured within boys like Harry who are often pigeonholed as difficult pupils. The maps become a way to get to the holism of their thinking. As a result, these students gain persistence, self-management, and self-efficacy as foundations for differentiated, lifelong learning. The added benefit is that we as educators learn more about ourselves and our students.

REFERENCES

Cohen, J. (Ed.). (1999). *Educating minds and hearts.* Alexandria, VA: Association for Supervision and Curriculum Development.

Costa, A., & Kallick, B. (2000). *Activating and engaging Habits of Mind.* Alexandria, VA: Association for Supervision and Curriculum Development.

Dunn, R., & Dunn, K. (1992). *Teaching elementary students through their individual learning styles.* Needham Heights, MA: Allyn & Bacon.

Gardner, H. (1993). *Multiple intelligences: The theory in practice.* New York: Basic Books.

Goleman, D. (1995). *Emotional intelligence: Why it matters more than IQ.* New York: Bantam.

5

Closing the "Gap" by Connecting Culture, Language, and Cognition

Yvette Jackson, Ed.D.

KEY CONCEPTS

- Pedagogy of Confidence in urban schools to develop cognitive mediation across cultures and language
- Revealing "codes of power" through using Thinking Maps® by students in underachieving schools
- Literacy results from urban school systems across the country

FINDING LEARNING SOLUTIONS FOR CHILDREN IN URBAN SCHOOLS

I had read about Reuven Feuerstein's (1980) work while I was doing graduate work in New York City in the early 1980s. He describes how he worked with kids who were displaced Jews during the early years of the development of the State of Israel, and how he helped them by bringing a deeper assessment of their learning. Knowing that these kids who had been considered low functioning really had more potential than an IQ test was showing profoundly resonated with me.

When I read about those kids, I said, "You know something? It's the same syndrome that my kids from urban settings are going through," meaning they have a lot more potential than is being assessed or addressed. They don't have mediators at home full-time because they are latchkey kids. Some of the kids are in foster care, and others are from poor homes where parents aren't home a lot. These students, like so many students in urban schools, are school-depend students: They depend on school to provide the mediation and enrichment needed to elicit and nurture their potential. I looked at Feuerstein's work, and that's when I said to myself, "I can capture the same idea if I know more about mediation." So often, students go through something called "remediation," but that is the basic remediation or redelivery of the content information and language skills. What we are talking about is the mediation of their thinking. The pedagogy that transmits this mediation anchored in the fearless expectation that urban students are capable of high intellectual performance is the Pedagogy of Confidence.

If you know about learning and how learning happens, you can improve the instructional technique, and if you really believe that kids have potential, you can set high expectations and have them meet those expectations with the tools that you give them.

WORKING WITH THE NATIONAL URBAN ALLIANCE FOR EFFECTIVE EDUCATION

I am now one of the leaders of the National Urban Alliance for Effective Education, and our mission is to substantiate in the public schools of urban America the irrefutable belief in the capacity of all children to reach high levels of learning and thinking demanded by our ever-changing global community. Our focus is on altering educators' perceptions and expectations of underperforming urban students, and this comes right out of my early interest in mediating learning. We recognize that when you believe in the intellectual potential of all students, you change the way you perceive the gap, and you strive to close that gap between underperforming students' potential and what they are achieving. When this gap is closed, the gap between different groups of students closes as well.

Many teachers of students labeled as underperforming have been led to believe that the students are deficient and that their underachievement is the result of limited potential. Yet when we talk about people having undeveloped muscles or physiques, we say they're "out of shape." We don't say they're deficient. In our work, we focus on the idea that the brain is like muscle; it requires specific exercises, guided personal training, and relevant and meaningful instruction to build competence and prevent dysfunction. It requires mediation. We address these misperceptions through professional development in the Pedagogy of Confidence based on research in brain-based instruction, cognitive development, and the impact of culture and language on cognition, critical thinking, and higher-order comprehension skills. We believe that when teachers are provided with the tools or strategies to strengthen intellectual development, learning, and literacy skills (or what Lisa Delpit, 1995, calls "codes of power"), urban students are able to demonstrate their potential through performance that changes the expectations of the teachers.

BRIDGING THE GAP BETWEEN TEACHERS AND STUDENTS IN URBAN SETTINGS

When teachers say there's a gap between themselves and their students, they are referring to a cultural gap regarding their frame of reference as well as their language. Many will say, "I can't communicate what I need to with these kids. I can't connect, so the students are resisting learning; they push back and don't want to learn."

The fact is that students do want to learn very badly and their teachers want to teach them. What teachers sometimes interpret as students not wanting to learn is really more what Jabari Mahari (1998) describes as the "out of sync rhythms between the students and their culturally different teachers." So a student may say, "You're not communicating, so I'm pushing back. It's not that I don't want to learn; I'm acting this way because we're not connecting." This misunderstanding of the student's intentions inhibits many well-meaning teachers from trying instructional strategies that motivate and support the learning of their culturally different students. Instead, they continuously use methods that not only minimize learning but very often result in students resisting. It's a vicious cycle resulting in the underachievement that we see around this country.

There are three interconnected factors that are key to bridging the gap between teachers and their underachieving urban students. One is addressing the fear that teachers have in not being able to address the needs of their underachieving students so they can meet the standards. The second factor directly relates to the first component of how to address the learning needs. To address learning needs we need to shift the focus from what has to be taught (content) to how learning happens (cognition, metacognition, process) and what affects it. The third factor is to provide teachers and students with a language that enables them to communicate with each other, building the mutual respect and relationships that are so vital to students of color.

I address the first and second factors by trying to simplify the research about learning through a symbolic representation that would illustrate the critical targets to address in learning instruction:

$$L: (U + M) (C1 + C2)$$

Learning: (Understanding + Motivation) (Competence + Confidence)

We know that in order for people to gain academic knowledge they have to understand the concepts of that knowledge. Another equally significant catalyst of learning is motivation. Both understanding and motivation are affected by what Eric Jensen (1998) describes as brain realization of relevance and meaningfulness. But the critical question we have to address in order to stimulate motivation is "What makes something relevant to an individual?" Well, it is a cultural frame of reference that makes something relevant and meaningful, thereby stimulating motivation. So we can't ignore that culture affects how one understands something, the perspective one takes on something, and the experiences one brings to reading affect how one infers. It's also one's cultural orientation that plays a large part in one's thinking. Feuerstein (1980) and Vygotsky (1962) point out that the other significant factors in stimulating motivation are competence and confidence. Jensen addresses the importance of confidence in relation to the positive impact challenge has on students when they feel a sense of competence and confidence to meet the challenge. Delpit (1995) refers to the importance of building confidence through competence as "codes of power" or higher-order thinking and literacy skills.

These understandings about learning and what affects it bring us to the third factor to address when bridging the cultural gap between teachers and students, and that is language. Just as culture shapes relevance, it's important to realize how language is affected by culture and how they both affect cognition, learning, and communication. Culture molds language, and language is a way of thinking. Addressing this interrelationship is critical in bridging the gap, and this is where Thinking Maps play a role of major importance.

I believe that Thinking Maps are essential tools in bridging the cultural gap between teachers and students because they address all three related factors. First of all, each of the eight Thinking Maps facilitates the development of one of the cognitive skills that are critical to learning and are also identified in all the state standards as skills students must have. They need to be able to define and generalize concepts or themes; describe, identify, categorize, and organize details; compare and contrast; sequence; identify cause and effect; analyze parts of a whole; and understand analogies. Second, Thinking Maps provide a language about thinking that allows teachers and students to communicate with precision, bridging the cultural gap. Equally important is that they provide students with the tools for building competence in learning and communicating and learning with confidence. The maps are like tools of power for unlocking the "codes of power" Lisa Delpit (1995) discusses.

THE PEDAGOGY OF CONFIDENCE

Pedagogy is an art that is developed and refined when teachers are confident in their ability to successfully affect students. Teachers become confident when they know what to do and believe that they have the skills and abilities to do what they know they have to do. When teachers are confident, they communicate to students confidence in students' ability to learn. A confident teacher is aware of the impact of culture on language and learning and uses this understanding to guide the selection of effective learning strategies that enable students to become competent and confident learners. The interplay of these elements and the forces at work in this complex system involving teachers, strategies, culture, and research are represented through the Multi-Flow Map (see Figure 5.1). Thinking Maps provide the tools and language for a teacher to confidently address the critical needs of underachieving students.

CRITICAL LEARNING NEEDS OF STUDENTS IN UNDERACHIEVING SCHOOLS

In every district in which we work, students who are underachieving have critical needs in verbal knowledge, inference, and academic language usage. These needs are compounded by what I call "learning blockers," things that obstruct the natural learning process, specifically, cognitive, linguistic, and textual blockers.

First of all, there is the cognitive blocker that occurs if students are not guided to identify the understanding, or concept, that should be the focus of the learning. Without this focus, students are unable to differentiate between relevant and irrelevant information, so critical details can't be identified, prioritized, analyzed, hypothesized, evaluated, or compared to personal experiences.

There are also language blockers that are manifested because the language of textbooks is so distinctly different from the language students use at home. Even though students are expected to read these texts with comprehension, very little discussion takes place in the classroom that engages students in using the vocabulary used in textbooks. The result is that the language necessary for comprehending texts is not developed. In high school, this lack of facility or understanding of the language of texts in different subject areas is extremely debilitating. The other language blocker is a lack of knowledge and understanding of patterns of language, from the most obvious one of decoding skills to syntax and understanding parts of speech and grammatical rules.

Last, there are textual blockers. There are two types of textual blocker: semantic and structural. Semantic blockers are words such as pronouns or idioms that are often not identified by teachers as problematic and don't necessarily require a deep understanding of language codes or patterns, yet they can severely inhibit comprehension of text. Structural blockers are the patterns that authors use to communicate information. These include descriptive, cause and effect, problem/solution, compare/contrast, and enumerative (main idea with supporting details). Each structure requires a different set of cognitive skills to analyze and construct meaning from the text.

The Thinking Maps become essential tools to address these learning blockers because they help students and teachers do what Reuven Feuerstein (1980) describes as "mediating learning" through these blockers. If teachers explicitly instruct students in the use of Thinking Maps, they are addressing language and cognitive blockers. All eight maps elicit the use of cognitive terminology and then provide vehicles for capturing the language so that students can go back and refer to that cognitive language, building their verbal repertoire of cognitive skills. If students can name the thinking they are doing, they will notice and seek that language in questions, assignments, and texts, thus owning the language the tool reflects.

While developing a level of fluency with this concrete visual language that represents cognition, Thinking Maps become the mediating tools for students' and teachers' learning and thinking. Thinking Maps mediate learning at many points, as represented by Figure 5.2.

Figure 5.1 NUA Organization Strategy Integration Multi-Flow Map

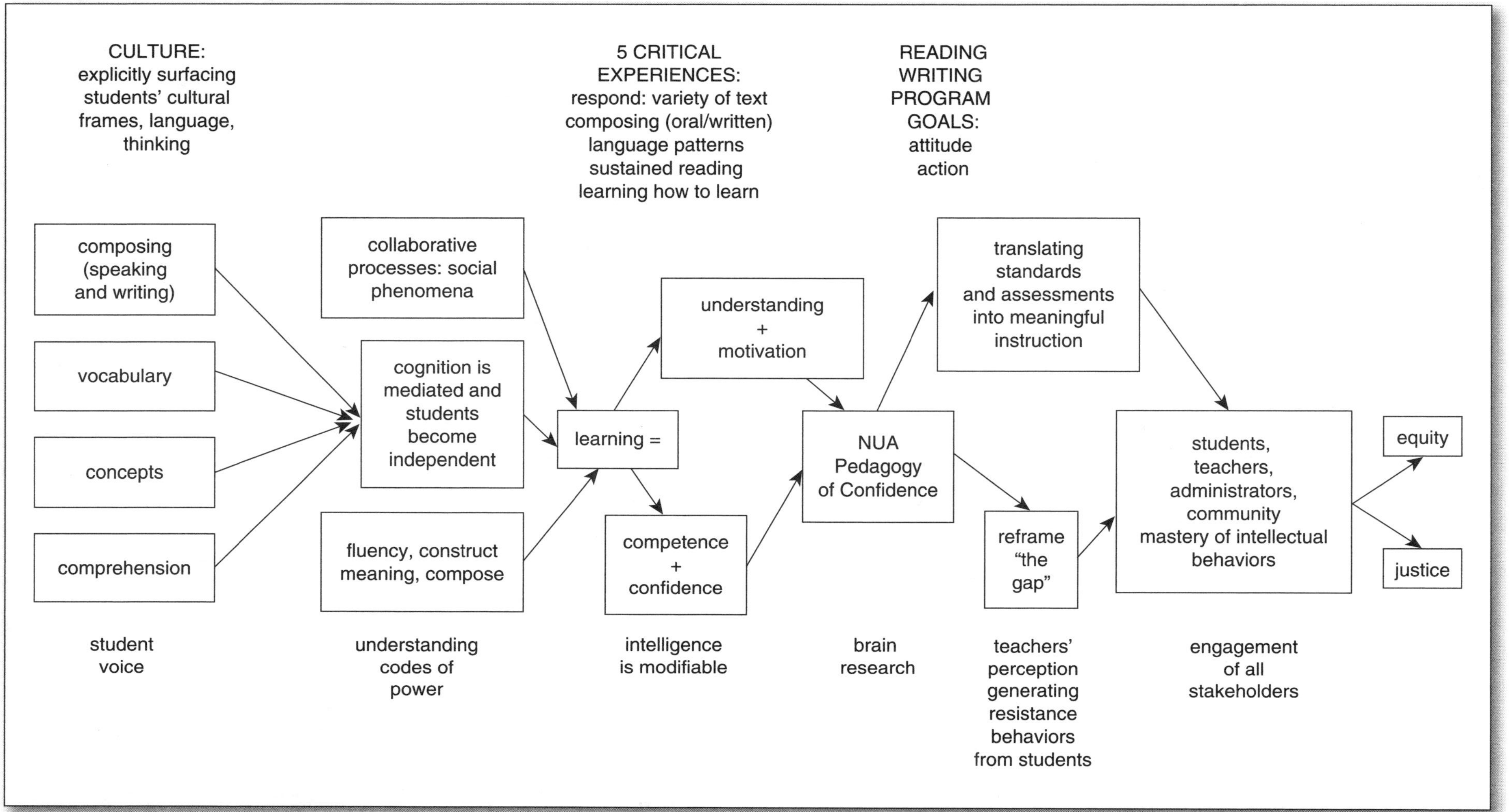

CULTURE:
explicitly surfacing
students' cultural
frames, language,
thinking

5 CRITICAL
EXPERIENCES:
respond: variety of text
composing (oral/written)
language patterns
sustained reading
learning how to learn

READING
WRITING
PROGRAM
GOALS:
attitude
action

composing
(speaking
and writing)

vocabulary

concepts

comprehension

student
voice

collaborative
processes: social
phenomena

cognition is
mediated and
students
become
independent

fluency, construct
meaning, compose

understanding
codes of
power

learning =

understanding
+
motivation

competence
+
confidence

intelligence
is modifiable

translating
standards
and assessments
into meaningful
instruction

NUA
Pedagogy
of Confidence

brain
research

reframe
"the gap"

teachers'
perception
generating
resistance
behaviors
from students

students,
teachers,
administrators,
community
mastery of intellectual
behaviors

engagement
of all
stakeholders

equity

justice

55

Figure 5.2 Points of Mediation Tree Map

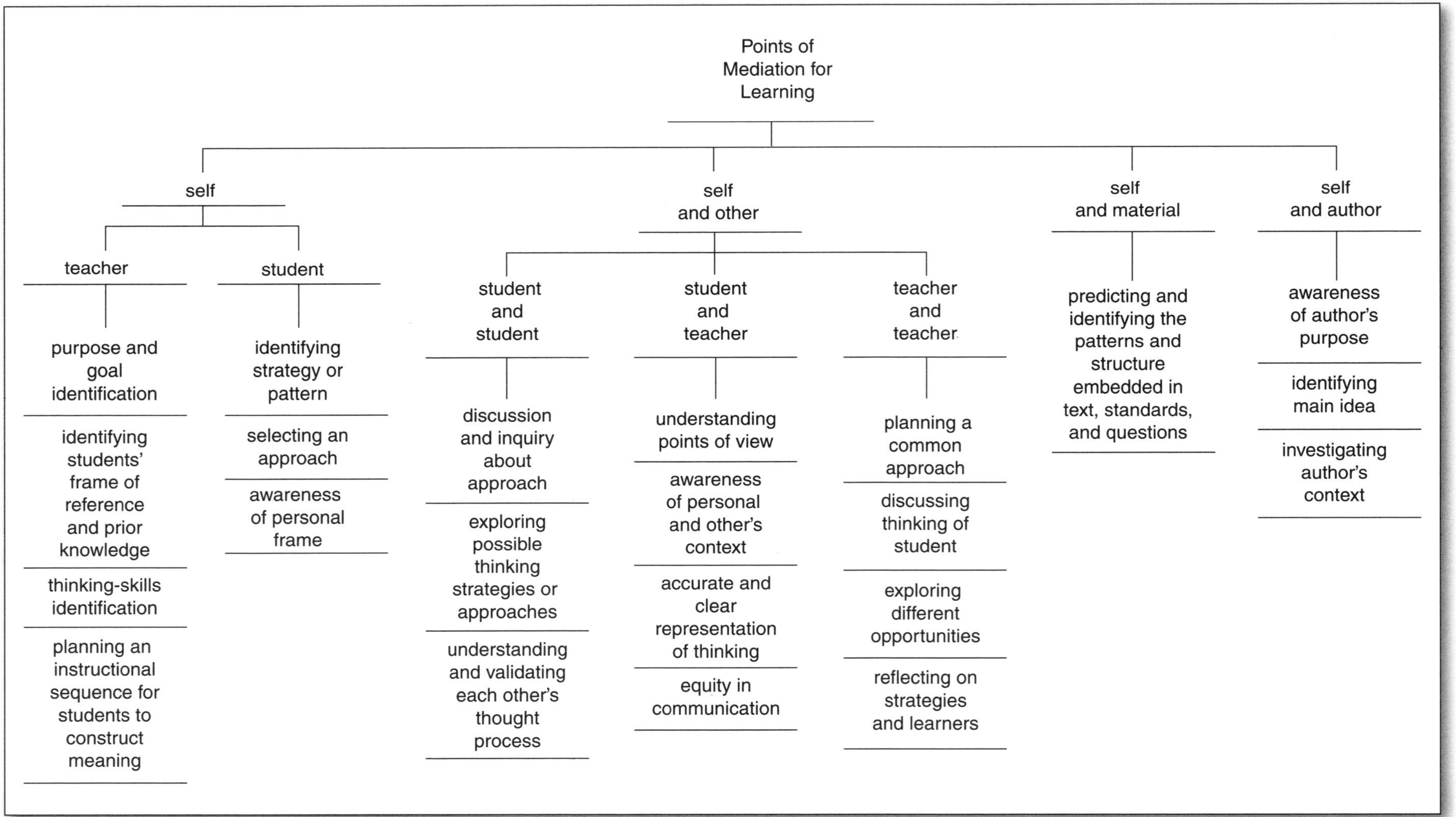

Points of Mediation for Learning

- self
  - teacher
    - purpose and goal identification
    - identifying students' frame of reference and prior knowledge
    - thinking-skills identification
    - planning an instructional sequence for students to construct meaning
  - student
    - identifying strategy or pattern
    - selecting an approach
    - awareness of personal frame
- self and other
  - student and student
    - discussion and inquiry about approach
    - exploring possible thinking strategies or approaches
    - understanding and validating each other's thought process
  - student and teacher
    - understanding points of view
    - awareness of personal and other's context
    - accurate and clear representation of thinking
    - equity in communication
  - teacher and teacher
    - planning a common approach
    - discussing thinking of student
    - exploring different opportunities
    - reflecting on strategies and learners
- self and material
  - predicting and identifying the patterns and structure embedded in text, standards, and questions
- self and author
  - awareness of author's purpose
  - identifying main idea
  - investigating author's context

56

Thinking Maps mediate students' and teachers' individual metacognition as they reflect on their own thinking about thinking. For the teacher, the Thinking Maps encourage the identification of the purpose and goals of the lesson before instruction in order to determine what kind of thinking is involved. Teachers' reflective conversations help them establish the prerequisites that students need to be able to construct meaning. Similarly, before students begin a task, they can ask themselves, by using the cognitive language embedded in the Thinking Maps, "How can I approach this task?" or "What do I notice about this assignment?" In both situations Thinking Maps foster metacognition, the first step in mediating one's own learning.

Besides supporting internal dialogue, Thinking Maps mediate thinking between individuals in the classroom. With the Thinking Maps, a teacher mediates learning by addressing specific learning needs in a way that engages students and activates those cognitive skills involved in the process of constructing meaning. The Circle and Frame Map, used for defining in context, is excellent for guiding students in analyzing and defining the focus of understanding or concept learning critical to guiding underachieving students in constructing meaning. The Thinking Maps encourage discussion between the teacher and the students about the kind of thinking required from the text by analyzing which Thinking Map is best for reflecting that kind of thinking. These explicit conversations about language, process, and cognition develop the focus on thinking, which can be transferred across disciplines. With shared visual representations, teacher and student can understand and communicate in the same language, shifting the power in the classroom.

In addition to understanding and communicating with oneself or with someone else, Thinking Maps mediate learning between student and teacher with text or content. Thinking Maps create a clearer pattern for a teacher to teach with and for students to analyze text and to demonstrate understanding of the text in the pattern required. Thinking Maps guide students in identifying and analyzing the understandings, skills, and text structures or patterns needed to construct meaning from a reading or unit of study in any discipline. Thinking Maps help teachers identify and analyze the kind of thinking that's going to be required to read a particular text as demanded by the text structure used by the author. The process fosters the great link between reading and writing. So Thinking Maps help students analyze text structure and really internalize the pattern, and then use that pattern to write their thoughts and demonstrate their thinking. This process of transferring between reading and writing is a complementary response to Ernest Boyer's (1983) definition of reading and writing. He said, "Reading is unlocking frozen thoughts and writing is freezing thoughts." Thinking Maps help students unlock the frozen patterns of thoughts and instead take their thoughts and freeze them in a pattern of thinking.

TEACHING INFERENTIAL THINKING

In regard to inferential thinking, the Thinking Maps are the most useful tools I have found. Teaching inference can be extremely difficult because inference is contingent upon connecting one's prior experience—and culture—with that of the author. Consider that individuals who are asked to author texts have years of expertise in their discipline or area of focus on which to base the ideas they want to convey and the meaning they want to imply. These books are given to students who often don't have any experience that connects to that of the author, and yet the expectation is that students should be able to infer, or read between the lines, to connect their experience with that of the author to speculate about ideas that are not literally presented. That's what you do when you're inferring. You've got to go from your personal reference to what the author is saying, which is why it's easier to infer with narrative or fiction than expository text.

Fiction is written about themes that everyone has experiences with or can relate to (such as love, fear, longing), but in discipline-based textbooks that are nonfiction or expository, concepts are more technical, more remote, and frequently harder for underachieving, school-dependent students to relate to. Guiding students without exposure to experiences that reflect what the author is writing about requires tools to engage the teacher and students in the kind of conceptual discussion that creates bridges for the students so that they can make a connection between the author's experience and their own. Perhaps Thinking Maps can mediate learning at yet another level—between the author of the text and the learner. A tool that engages students in this type of discussion is the Frame of Reference that can be drawn around any of the maps. An example of this would be using a frame around a Bubble Map to develop characterization. In the Bubble Map shown in Figure 5.3, you identify adjectives that describe a character; the frame elicits exploration or inferences of why the adjectives were selected to describe the character. Why is the character the way he or she is? If "angry" is identified as one of the descriptions, in the frame a student would infer why the character was angry. If the character is described as discontented, the frame would elicit why he or she is discontented. What happened in the characters' lives to cause them to be this way? The Frame of Reference enables students to infer ideas, speculations, or theories about who this character really is. It's not just about description; it's the inference behind the description that is the core of characterization.

Figure 5.3 Supporting Inferential Thinking With Bubble and Frame Map

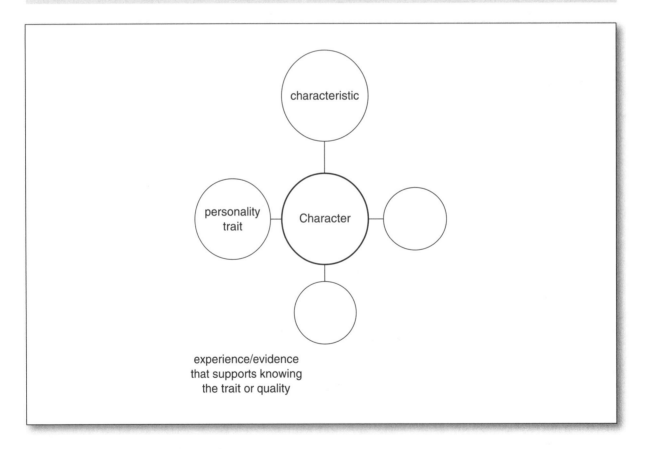

DEVELOPING MEMORY AS PART OF THE MEDIATION OF A STUDENT'S LEARNING

Unfortunately, memory has been associated with rote learning, and that's not what we're talking about here. Eric Jensen (1998), Mel Levine (1993), and others have written extensively on memory and its impact on learning. The shame is that teachers too often ignore the use of powerful memory devices such as mnemonics to strengthen student learning, because they believe that any memory focus is associated with rote learning. The key here is that rote learning is not about patterning but memory is. Students' achievement has a lot to do with their memory of things. The Thinking Maps strengthen learning by becoming external memory patterns for students when they use them to freeze their thinking. The maps provide a place where students can refer to all the interrelated ideas and from these ideas make the extractions. If students tried to hold the quantity of ideas their brains explore, they would be expending a lot of their mental energy focusing on just trying to remember all the details instead of generalizing and elaborating on these ideas. Thinking Maps elucidate patterns and function as external memory, so the maps can fortify and expand students' learning that relies on memory. In a sense, first students refer to the pattern of information, and then they can infer from that pattern. This is the shift from frozen information to the construction of knowledge.

REVERSING UNDERACHIEVEMENT IN LITERACY AMONG URBAN LEARNERS

We work to reverse underachievement, predominantly underachievement in reading and writing, the major deficit being identified in inferential thinking, vocabulary, and language usage. We focus our professional development around the acceleration of intellectual performance, specifically in literacy. We know that literacy is the catalyst to empowering students, so we go beyond the standard definition of literacy and embrace the definition described by Elliot Eisner (1994) as the ability of an individual to construct, create, and communicate meaning across disciplines in many forms of representation (such as written text, drawing, mathematical symbols, and dance). We resonate with this definition because it expands pedagogical focus to include the cognitive functions that are the prerequisites to accelerating learning and achievement throughout life.

We believe that literacy for urban learners is best developed when the teacher mediates the learning process by providing lessons that foster social interaction for language development and guide the application of cognitive skills that assist students in constructing and communicating meaning. The Thinking Maps are a core component of the cognitive strategies we provide because they are tools that have a direct impact on how students construct, communicate, and create meaning. In each district in which we work, we have witnessed how teachers immediately employ Thinking Maps as one of the most-used tools of their pedagogical repertoire. The result has been what administrators and parents associate with the most impressive and valued impact our literacy initiatives have on learning—significant growth in the achievement of students who have previously been labeled "low achievers." In Indianapolis, schools experienced a 12- to 20-point jump in scores, which is significant. While across the state of Indiana scores had fallen since 1998 by 1.2%, the "vanguard schools" in Indianapolis participating in the literacy initiative experienced an average increase of 10.4%, with seven of the elementary schools showing double-digit gains. In Seattle, a study showed that African American students who failed the reading section of the Washington Assessment of Student Learning (WASL) in 1999 and then spent at least two years with teachers who participated in the initiative passed the 2002 test at twice the rate of those students who spent a year or less with participating teachers. In just three years of implementation by the City School District of Albany and the National Urban Alliance, students in Grades 3–8 who met or exceeded proficiency standards on the New York State exams increased by 14% in English language arts (ELA) and 21% in mathematics. In 2009, the entire district's elementary and middle schools exceeded New York State Education Department ELA benchmarks for students in Grades 3–8. Overall, 61% of the district's students in Grades 3–8 achieved proficiency this year, attaining Level 3 or Level 4. That's a 24% gain over 2008, when 49% of the district's students achieved the top two levels in ELA. Aside from the quantitative data, we are seeing improved student performance with tasks requiring higher-order thinking such as reasoning, problem solving, and theme-based classroom projects.

This evidence has been significant in demonstrating the learning potential of under-achieving students, which has in turn altered the expectations of thousands of educators, but to me there is additional evidence that has great implications regarding the impact of the Thinking Maps. Insights about the benefits of district-wide institutionalization of the use of the Thinking Maps as critical instructional tools have been felt from the classroom to the boardroom.

After our third year in the Indianapolis project, the board of education summoned the assistant superintendent to explain why it should continue to fund the literacy initiative. We decided that the most convincing way to respond would be for teachers from kindergarten through high school to share with the board the effects of the strategies and practices they had been implementing in their classrooms. Every one of the teachers talked about the impact the Thinking Maps had on the achievement of their students: A kindergarten teacher presented samples of her students' studies in science through each of the eight Thinking Maps; middle school literacy teachers shared examples of student expository and narrative writings; a chemistry teacher demonstrated how he applied the maps in chemistry. Beyond the strong impression these presentations made on the board, the real epiphany was experienced by the high school teacher who exclaimed, "Wait! The kindergarten teachers are using the same maps we are. If every teacher is working on this kind of thinking with his or her students, think how strong they'll be by the time they get to high school." A similarly impressive revelation was the focus of a story told by a teacher about two brothers doing homework. A kindergartner said to his middle school brother, "Oh, you're doing a Bubble Map. That's for describing." The older brother asked how he knew that. The younger brother informed him that he learned about that at school, surprising the older brother completely. The very same presentation took place last spring by teachers and administrators in the Albany Public Schools for their school board, with identically passionate responses.

Thinking processes are universal, and Thinking Maps help students transfer these cognitive skills across content areas and grade levels. Children are born understanding cause and effect. They know how to think sequentially. In urban settings where there may be historic underachievement, providing tools that enable teachers to build on the capacity of the students to think critically through instruction that provides them with the means to fortify their understanding, competence, and confidence results in students who are motivated to excel and do excel. It becomes part of the common culture of the classroom, of the school, and, as we have seen, of whole systems.

REFERENCES

Boyer, E. (1983). *High school: A report on secondary education in America.* New York: Harper and Row.

Delpit, L. (1995). *Other people's children: Cultural conflict in the classroom.* New York: New Press.

Eisner, E. (1994). *Cognition and curriculum.* New York: Teacher's College Press.

Feuerstein, R. (1980). *Instrumental enrichment.* Baltimore, MD: University Park Press.

Jensen, E. (1998). *Teaching with the brain in mind.* Alexandria, VA: Association for Supervision and Curriculum Development.

Levine, M. (1993). *All kinds of minds.* Cambridge, MA: Educators Publishing Service.

Mahari, J. (1998). *Shooting for excellence.* New York: Teacher's College Press.

Vygotsky, L. (1962). *Thought and language.* Cambridge, MA: MIT Press.

Section 2

Integrating Content and Process

6

Maps for the Road to Reading Comprehension

Bridging Reading Text Structures to Writing Prompts

Thomasina DePinto Piercy, Ph.D., and David Hyerle, Ed.D.

KEY CONCEPTS

- Linking reading text structure research to cognitive patterns
- Results from first graders' fluency with Thinking Maps®
- Multiple Thinking Maps applied to phonics, vocabulary, and reading comprehension

"While I am reading, my mind adds to my Thinking Maps all by itself, and suddenly I know more than I knew!"

—student in Christina Smith's first-grade class,
Mt. Airy Elementary School, Maryland

At Mt. Airy Elementary School, in a classroom of first-grade students, on a morning in mid-May, we watched as a third-year teacher read the guiding question for the day: "How will you organize your thinking about this book?" While this may seem to be an unfocused question, the teacher knew the students could meaningfully respond. The book, *How Leo Learned to Be King*, rested on the chalkboard tray with its colorful picture of a crowned lion on the cover, set there after it had been read aloud the day before. This is an inclusive classroom of students in a modest suburban neighborhood school, a school that had experienced a 15% decline in writing scores over the previous two years and mediocre reading scores as the population swelled beyond the original building and into portables.

This year, student performance moved significantly upward. This was reflected on state tests, while scores across Maryland generally fell. Mt. Airy Elementary School has become the highest-performing school in its county since it started using Thinking Maps in reading and writing instruction. Data support the observations we see in classrooms: Thinking Maps significantly impact instruction and improve student performance.

While this is important news, a closer look shows that students have changed how they are understanding texts: They are surfacing dynamic patterns of content from the linear landscape, the wall of text. The range of structures bound within line-by-line text becomes unveiled in the form of mental maps as shown in Figures 6.1a–g. They are changing the form, trans*form*ing text. Step into a classroom and observe a teacher and you will see how this works.

Figure 6.1a   Leo Circle Map

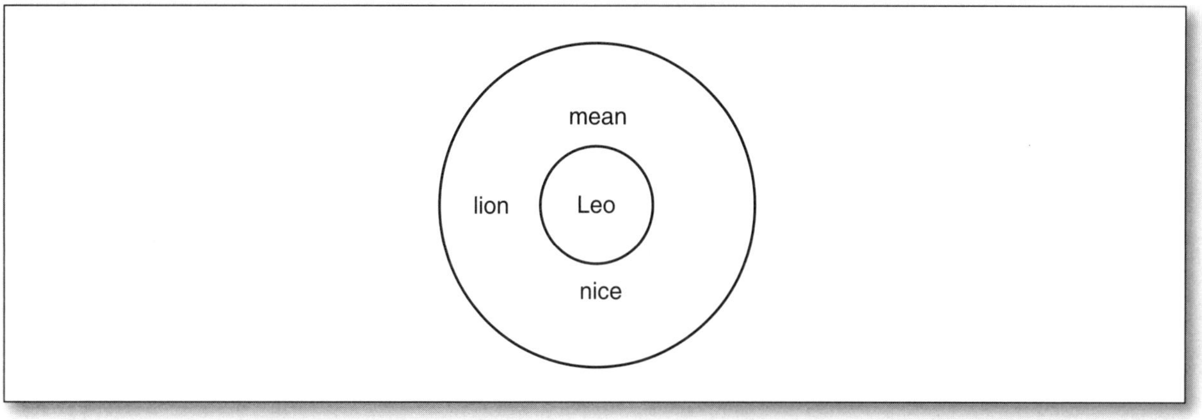

Figure 6.1b   Mouse Bubble Map

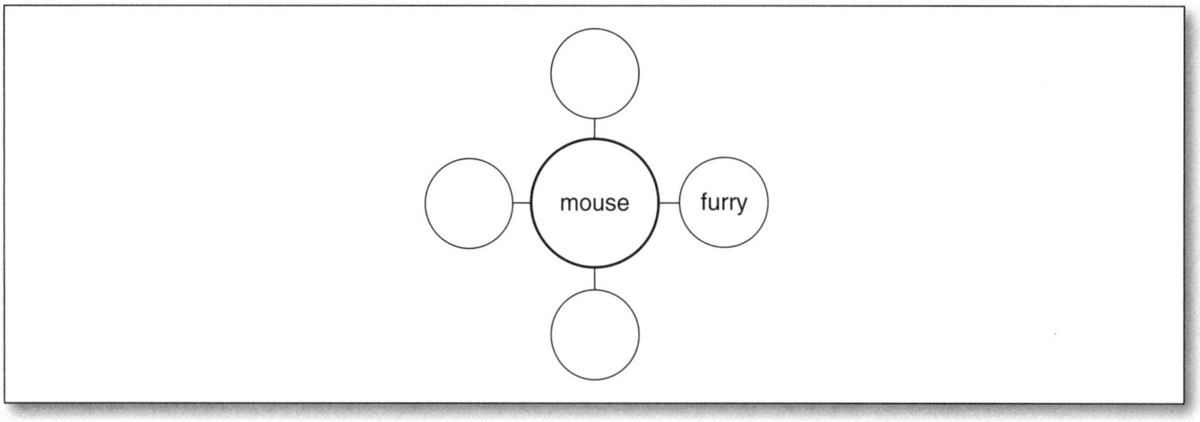

Figure 6.1c Comparing Two Books Using the Double Bubble Map

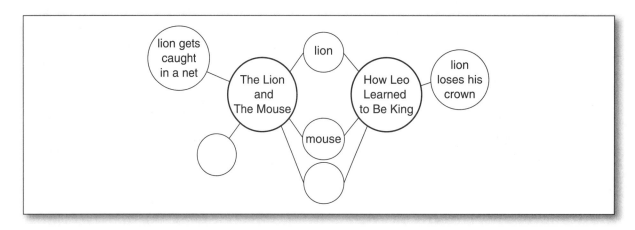

Figure 6.1d Leo Character Analysis Tree Map

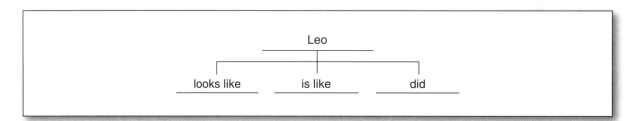

Figure 6.1e Leo Character Development Flow Map

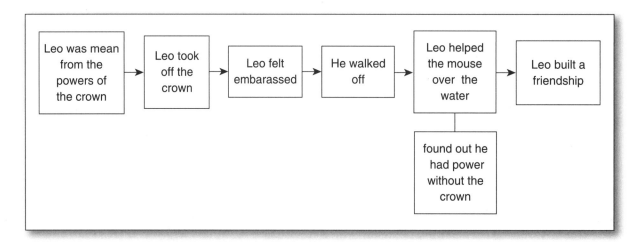

Figure 6.1f Cause of Leo's Being Mean Multi-Flow Map

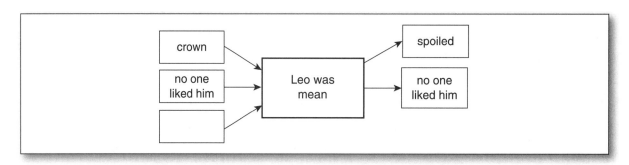

Figure 6.1g Bridging Qualities of Characters Across Text

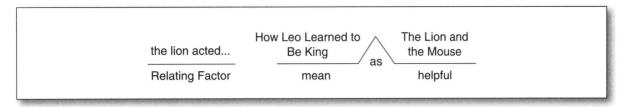

While observing Ms. Christina Smith's classroom, I sat down behind the students: As principal and instructional leader, I began clacking away notes on my laptop. Students gathered on the floor near their teacher, just below the blank, open space on the chalkboard that held the guiding question for discussion. The book *How Leo Learned to Be King* had been read aloud the day before, but the students and all of the teachers and administrators across our school had learned about Thinking Maps the year before. These excerpts and the related maps may heighten your understanding of Thinking Maps and still underrepresent the richness of the classroom conversation. Here is how first graders organized their thinking about this book:

Erin: You could use the Circle Map . . . put the topic in the middle and all ideas that you get in your mind from that topic, you write down in the circle . . . Leo . . . details about Leo . . . he was mean and he was nice.

Megan: A Bubble Map about a mouse. You say a word about what the mouse is . . . like furry . . . describing words.

Billy: We could do a Double Bubble. We could compare *How Leo Learned to Be King* and *The Lion and the Mouse* . . . they [both books] both have a lion and a mouse.

Mark: A Tree Map. I am thinking of . . . about Leo . . . what he looks like . . . and, um, I think, and what he is like . . . and what he did.

Thomas: You could organize it with a Bridge Map. In *The Lion and the Mouse,* the lion was mean to the mouse, but in *How Leo Learned to Be King,* the lion was nice to the mouse by helping him get over the river.

Alexis: You could use a Flow Map. First, he was mean. Then, when they took off the crown he, like, got a little embarrassed. He walked away, he got surprised, because he met a mouse. And at the end he helped the mouse and *they became friends.*

Regan: Multi-Flow . . . what caused him to be mean. The crown made . . . the crown could have caused him to be mean.

Erin: No one liked him. They took away . . . they didn't want him to be their king.

Shawn: We've got a lot of maps, don't we?

Teacher: That makes me think . . .

Shawn: . . . that we are like second graders!

The discussion between Ms. Smith and her students is within reach of any school, is replicable, and may refine and even reframe reading and writing instruction or offer a new direction for cognitive science research. This teacher had brought students to such a high level of fluency with Thinking Maps that they could begin to identify text patterns on their own. They were able to use fundamental thinking-skills vocabulary (words such as *describing, compare, causes,* and so on) and respective cognitive maps (Bubble, Double Bubble, Multi-Flow) and had the metacognitive awareness to be able to explicitly transfer these processes and tools to reading comprehension through identifying text structures. They were then able to return to their seats with blank sheets of paper and, with varying results, choose a Thinking Map and expand their thinking. They later went on to write about the story using the maps they had chosen to organize their ideas.

This sample of classroom activity is a practical and symbolic representation of a new form of literacy and a transformation of how we perceive the interrelationships between thinking patterns and the fundamentals of reading comprehension.

THINKING AND MAPS

"Thinking Maps are the paper of my mind."

—third-grade student, Mt. Airy Elementary School, Maryland

If text on paper is what we produce for linear communication, Thinking Maps are the paper for the mental mapping that goes on in our brain and through our minds. The U.S. Department of Education–sponsored publication, *Put Reading First* (Armbruster, 2002), targets semantic maps and graphic organizers as the keys for unlocking both text structures and reading comprehension and as bridges to writing prompts. The strength of graphic organizers is the visually scaffolded structure of each form. The weakness is that there is a static nature to many of these templates and only an episodic use of the tools by students. There is also a glass ceiling on thinking—students go from grade to grade and classroom to classroom across schools, often filling in prestructured blanks on a worksheet without much reflection or higher levels of thinking. Thinking Maps bring together the creative uses of webbing and brainstorming semantic maps with the organizing uses of prestructured graphic organizers.

As shown above, Thinking Maps provide the dynamic thinking patterns and thus the cognitive link to common text structures. The tools also link these text structures to organization patterns often found in writing prompts, and this is shown in summary form in Figure 6.2. For example, the ability to comprehend a text based on problem-solution mode depends on the student understanding the fundamentals of cause-effect reasoning. Cause-effect reasoning is an essential thinking skill for being able to produce a coherent and well-organized piece of writing in response to a prompt based on prediction (see Chapter 7, "Empowering Students From Thinking to Writing").

READING AND WRITING: FROM PHONEMIC AWARENESS TO METACOGNITIVE PROCESSES

"Thinking Maps just happen! They work automatically while I am reading!"

—fifth-grade student, Mt. Airy Elementary School, Maryland

If you accept the premise that we mostly teach and assess using written, spoken, and numeric languages, it is easy to see how we are still caught in the dichotomous debate between phonics and whole language. This debate is nestled within the most heavily researched and publicly financed area in education, namely, improving literacy. Teachers, researchers, major publishers, and test developers have attempted to synthesize the two sides, yet the practice in the field remains discordant and failed. Our cyclical failures to break through this dichotomy reveal that the problem lies not merely in balancing phonics and whole language or taking a radical swing to one side or the other.

Figure 6.2 Reading, Thinking, Writing Connection

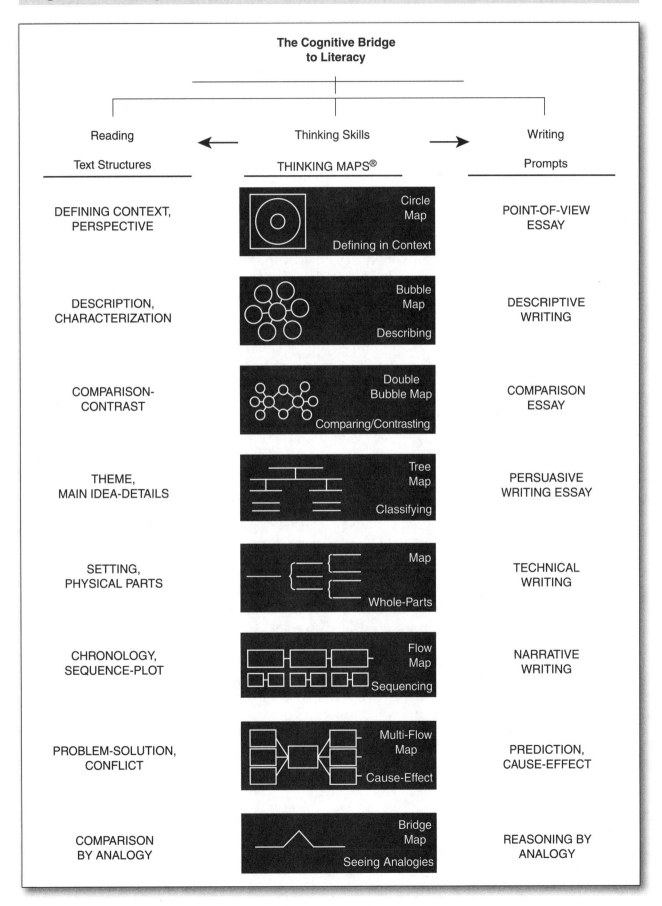

How else does one explain the deficits our nation is experiencing in reading as indicated by National Assessment of Educational Progress (NAEP) scores from 1971 to 2000? NAEP has reported that our at-risk population has improved only slightly despite receiving enormous resources. For our students who are not at risk—those who have the fundamentals of decoding, fluency, and pertinent vocabulary—reading comprehension scores are not much better than they were 25 years ago. It is time to accept the minimal impact on reading comprehension that the present paradigms of research and translations into instruction have made since the 1980s. Why has there been limited change in standardized and performance-assessment scores of reading comprehension despite the enormous effort over nearly two decades to overhaul reading comprehension instructional techniques?

Our work with Thinking Maps points to a third way. One missing link is the cognitive underpinnings, interconnections, and interdependencies between the processes of phonemic awareness, vocabulary learning, and meaning making. Sasha Borenstein (as quoted in Hyerle, 2000), director of the Kelter Center, which serves students from the Los Angeles region, states that

> the recent research in the area of literacy done by the National Institute of Child Health and Human Development has documented the need for explicit, systematic instruction in "breaking the code," phonics and word study, as well as in "making meaning" strategies for comprehension. The research supports an active, thoughtful instructional approach rather than a return to repetitive, passive work.

Reviewing the three areas of the *Put Reading First* (Armbruster, 2002) report distributed widely by the U.S. Department of Education reveals how Thinking Maps provide a cognitive bridge to phonemic awareness, vocabulary instruction, and text comprehension.

Phonemic Awareness

Sasha Borenstein has found that Thinking Maps are also a set of tools for helping students to see words, break them down, and put them back together. Through her work with students who are at risk and falling behind in the Los Angeles area (for a related story from Los Angeles, see Chapter 11, "A First Language for Thinking in a Multilingual School"), she and her staff have found that Thinking Maps work as microcognitive tools for seeing how to work with words:

> Thinking Maps are flexible, active tools for exploring literacy. The maps are student-centered, pushing learners to discern patterns and interactions in materials and concepts. Thinking Maps are used in discerning the concepts which organize the expectancies and rules of phonics. Performing the sounds of the past tense, /t/, /d/, and /id/, can lead to the understanding that the sound of this morpheme is based upon the last sound in the root word to which it is affixed. The Brace Map is used by students to identify these **part-whole** relationships. Finding the **similarities and differences** between syllable types using the Double Bubble Maps leads to the understanding that each syllable is defined by its vowel. Creating a Flow Map for **sequencing** the spelling of /ch/, ch or tch, /j/, ge or dge, and /k/, k or ck, at the end of a word can lead to the concept that the spelling depends upon what type of vowel is in that word. (Hyerle, 2000)

The summary page for phonemic awareness research in *Put Reading First* recommends guiding students to categorize phonemes, see part-whole patterns in words, and put them back together through blending. These are key strategies for developing this one area of early reading development while facilitating language and cognitive skills development.

Vocabulary Instruction

A second area of *Put Reading First* focuses on learning vocabulary. Vocabulary learning is a networking process involving not only direct vocabulary learning through word-learning strategies and repetition but also the indirect acquisition of vocabulary in different contexts. This is because the brain is constantly networking bits of information, and the maps facilitate patterning of related words, which become a context for definitions (see Chapter 2, "Why and How Thinking Maps Work: A Language of Brain and Mind").

Returning to the above reading of *How Leo Learned to Be King*, Thinking Maps create multiple pathways for students and teachers to gather vocabulary from the story into several patterns. These are explicit visual patterns that show a word *in context*. When a student independently voiced that the Circle Map could be used, she stated that you put the topic (Leo) in the center and the details around it. The Circle Map is defined by the visual representation of a circle within a circle and by the thinking skill of defining in context. Students learn to use this tool to look for and gather in the outer circle of the map context words and build vocabulary and meaning around a key topic in the center. Contextualization *requires* that students attempt to give definition to a word not just by what precedes it, but often by reading ahead so that the full context may be brought to bear on the word. All eight Thinking Maps are vocabulary builders, and in practical and metaphorical terms, they are the scaffolds for the building process.

Text Comprehension

Correlating with NAEP data is the national report explaining that future implications for reading comprehension include evidence-based assessments. Affirming this concern, Donald Graves (1997) asserts that educators and the public are in a frenzy over how to boost reading comprehension scores.

We must teach students how to synthesize and show their thinking. What we have needed is the physiology of reading comprehension, the actual working parts as a reader interacts with text. But what would the working parts look like? Graves writes that when a reader engages with print, in the past we have had no idea what types of thinking are in process. Over 20 years ago, Lauren Resnick (1983) noted that if we cannot produce a more substantial explanation of the internal events that produce improved comprehension, it will be difficult to develop an instructional training approach. She later suggested that research has located a psychological (metacognitive) space, in which educationally powerful effects seem to occur, but it has not yet adequately explained what happens in that space to produce the effects. A synthesis of these reading researchers (DePinto Piercy, 1998) confirms the need to change our instructional focus. We must move from the panoramic lens of a wide variety of strategic instructional techniques to include a zoom lens for specific instruction focused directly on what students do during the process of reading.

In the document *Put Reading First* (Armbruster, 2002), proficient readers are described as active and purposeful, and strategies are suggested for guiding students to self-monitoring and metacognition. Central to this section of the report is the focus on graphic organizers and maps that support students in identifying text structures within fictional and nonfictional texts. The report states that these visual tools

- help students focus on text structure as they read,
- provide students with tools they can use to examine and visually represent relationships in a text, and
- help students write well-organized summaries of a text.

Dr. Bonnie Armbruster, one of the lead authors of *Put Reading First,* was an early leader in the research on text structures. For example, her work showed that using a problem-solution graphic before reading gave students an advanced organizer of this key structure, and their comprehension improved on those specific texts. Of course, texts are not identified as problem-solution or chronology texts for students, and quality responses to open-ended writing prompts are not completed by staying inside the lines of a graphic template (see Chapter 7). Thinking Maps extend this work by having students become fluent in a cognitive and metacognitive tool set for adapting their thinking to varying contexts.

READERS AT RISK: A MAP FOR THE ROADS TO READING COMPREHENSION

When we are out driving in an unfamiliar region, we need a map. The reading comprehension landscape is much more complex, as students' eyes hit the page running. Reading instruction traditionally walks students right up to the road of comprehension and says, "Now you're on your own." After being motivated and developing prior knowledge, teachers then expect students to cross the road of comprehension alone, greeted on the other side with comprehension questions. Students, especially children at risk, so often make a run for it, thinking that the faster they get down the page, the better. Then teachers provide fix-up or remedial strategies when students can't respond to the questions. Lev Vygotsky's (1962) zone of proximal development is the critical region beyond a learner's immediate, autonomous performance, where instructional guidance is crucial. Yet it is exactly in this zone of comprehension where there are limited instructional strategies available.

Rather than dropping students off at the edge of the road, Thinking Maps help them *see* their way through to the end. By guiding them across an unfamiliar text with Thinking Maps, we are providing direct instruction for using reading strategies independently. Providing direct Thinking Map instruction for use *during* reading allows students to cross the reading comprehension road safely. Ultimately, Thinking Map instruction for reading and writing provides students with instruction beyond what- and how-to-use strategies. Thinking Maps require students to understand why and when to use them. Strategic reading behaviors—and writing processes—require that it is the learner who selects an action for a specific purpose. It is the intentional self-selection and self-regulation of a particular strategy to achieve a specific goal that is the critical component of strategic reading behavior (see Chapter 3, "Leveling the Playing Field for All Students").

LITERACY IN A NEW LANGUAGE

"My Thinking Maps have power. I have all these ideas and nowhere to put them. Thinking Maps let me get them out!"

—first-grade student, Mt. Airy Elementary School, Maryland

The outcomes described above have been attained because of ongoing professional development commitment within the unit of change that makes a difference for individual students over time: the whole school. The faculty members of Mt. Airy Elementary School were and still are committed to ongoing training. Teachers left the initial training in Thinking Maps with the goal of explicitly training their students to use these tools independently, in cooperative groups, and for the whole class, thus supporting them in internalizing the tools for direct transfer to content learning and process outcomes. The central outcome of the initial training and ongoing follow-up design is represented not only in the high-quality first-grade classroom conversation at Mt. Airy Elementary School, but in the quantitative results on the school's state assessments. Following the first year's implementation of Thinking Maps, writing scores realized a 15% increase on the state-mandated assessment, the Maryland School Performance Assessment Program. Later, Mt. Airy Elementary rose from being a school in the middle of testing to becoming the highest-performing school of the 21 elementary schools in Carroll County.

In addition, the No Child Left Behind legislation requires that each state test content knowledge and how well students perform. Maryland meets this requirement by using the new 2003 Maryland School Assessments. The cornerstone for Maryland's accountability system is the measure of Adequate Yearly Progress (AYP). Again this year, Mt. Airy Elementary is the highest-performing school in the county. Mt. Airy's scores are higher than the Maryland state average and higher than the county average, remarkably achieving AYP in all eight subgroups, including special education. The results across our student population show that literacy and cognitive development work together as teachers help students cross the road to reading comprehension with Thinking Maps as a new language for literacy.

To move beyond the inadequacies of past research and practice and to shift literacy to a new form require a shift in tools and a mind shift by leaders. Literacy alone is not power in the age of information and technology, multicultural and multilingual communication, and global economies (see Chapter 15, "The Singapore Experience"). A new critical literacy is required, based on research showing that phonemic awareness and metacognitive strategies must develop together with vocabulary development and comprehension strategies across first *and* second languages. Many students, and unfortunately most students at risk, are given an overwhelming, repetitious panoply of strategies that merely heighten their awareness of words without deepening their comprehension abilities. From our experiences and results, we have found, however, that students are not left behind on the road to reading comprehension when given tools for actively reflecting on how they are thinking and the patterns emerging from text.

REFERENCES

Armbruster, B. (Ed.). (2002). *Put reading first.* Washington, DC: U.S. Department of Education.

DePinto Piercy, T. (1998). *The effects of multi-strategy instruction upon reading comprehension.* Unpublished doctoral dissertation, University of Maryland–College Park.

Graves, D. (1997). *Forward: Mosaic of thought.* Portsmouth, NH: Heinemann.

Hyerle, D. (2000). *A field guide to using visual tools.* Alexandria, VA: Association for Supervision and Curriculum Development.

Resnick, L. B. (1983). Toward a cognitive theory of instruction. In S. Paris, G. Olson, & H. Stevenson (Eds.), *Learning and motivation in the classroom.* Hillsdale, NJ: Erlbaum.

Vygotsky, L. (1962). *Thought and language.* Cambridge, MA: MIT Press.

7

Empowering Students From Thinking to Writing

Jane Buckner, Ed.S.

KEY CONCEPTS

- Writing as thinking from a developmental viewpoint
- The Tree and Flow Maps as organizing structures for developing written expression
- Results from Thinking Maps® schools using a common language for thinking and writing

According to the business community and those in higher education, it is time for a writing revolution in American schools. In September 2002, the College Board—composed of more than 4,300 schools and colleges—established the National Commission on Writing in America's Schools and Colleges. The decision to create the commission was motivated in part by a decision by the board to make a writing assessment an additional component of the new SAT beginning in 2005. However, a greater impetus for the study was a growing concern within the education and business communities regarding the quality of student writing.

In April 2003, the commission issued a report, *The Neglected "R,"* that revealed disturbing findings regarding the writing proficiency of students in the United States. Among those findings was the fact that most fourth graders spend less than three hours per week writing. This is 15% of the amount of time they spend watching television each week. In grades 4, 8, and 12, only 50% of students assessed met basic requirements for writing, while only 20% were considered to be proficient. In addition, 66% of high school seniors do not write a three-page paper as often as once a month for their English teachers. Further findings revealed that 50% of college freshmen are not able to produce papers that are relatively free of language errors. It is estimated that these writing weaknesses of incoming college students cost campuses up to $1 billion annually for remediation. Unfortunately, this writing deficiency is spilling over into the business world as business leaders complain about the writing skills of new employees. This grim picture was the motivation for numerous recommendations presented in *The Neglected "R."*

The commission called for a major effort to improve teacher training in writing to include all discipline areas, as well as a greater allocation of time devoted to student writing instruction both during the school day and in the form of daily homework assignments. The commission acknowledged that our problems regarding writing proficiency did not occur overnight and that to fix the problem "the amount of time and money devoted to student writing must be dramatically increased in school districts throughout the country, and state and local curriculum guidelines must require writing in every curriculum at all grade levels." In addition, the commission report suggested that writing has been shortchanged in the school reform movement launched 20 years ago and, since writing has not received the attention it deserves, the acquisition of proficient writing skills now must be put squarely in the center of the school agenda beginning in elementary school.

Eight years later, the business community is still focused on the ability of its future employees to communicate well, both orally and in writing. According to an article in *USA Today* (Marklein, 2010), 89% of those surveyed regarding what they want most from future employees said "effective communication, both orally and in writing." In other words, just *having* a college degree is not the most important concern; rather, the degree must have *value*. The results of these two surveys reflect the need for quality instruction in written communication that spans from the early grades through college.

As elementary and high schools prepare to develop greater writing proficiency among their students, they must find a high-quality writing approach and a professional development plan that systematically supports the writing process from idea generation to the final product, as well as writing development from the early grades through high school. Currently, schools across the nation have improved whole-school writing performance through comprehensive training in a developmental K–12 writing framework: *Write . . . from the Beginning* (Buckner, 2000) and *Write . . . for the Future* (Buckner & Johnson, 2002). Both frameworks use Thinking Maps as the foundational tools to teach the thinking patterns and processes involved in composing in the narrative, expository, and other domains of writing, thus uniting writing *explicitly* with thinking.

DEVELOPING COMPOSITION

Child development experts contend that writing proficiency begins with oral communication well before the elementary grades. From the moment of birth, children use their newly developed lungs to communicate with those around them. Caregivers soon learn to distinguish among the different cries of an infant and to associate those cries with the specific needs of their young charges. As children grow into toddlers, language begins to develop, and the early babbles and coos become decipherable verbiage through which the child learns to communicate. At approximately the same time that language is developing, fine motor control is developing, thereby enabling these youngsters to make their first written marks on the world, often in the form of crayon scribbles in inappropriate places.

By the age of three, a child's scribbles become more decipherable, yet primitive, drawings that represent something or someone in the child's world. For a developmental period, drawing actually becomes the child's form of written communication. Once the child is exposed to picture books, environmental print, and the opportunity to observe adults engaging in writing, an awareness of the distinguishing attributes of written communication develops, and the child comes to the understanding that a message is communicated through the written word as well as through pictures. At this point, the child seeks to imitate what he has observed.

The earliest attempts to imitate writing often appear to be squiggles and nonsense to the untrained eye. However, the value of these scribbles and squiggles has been documented as an indicator of early developmental stages in writing. Marie Clay (1975), among others, has studied extensively these early writings of children and has described certain principles children must master to make marks that resemble writing. Clay maintains that seven basic principles must be learned by children before they can be said to write, and that many of these principles may be seen emerging in the scribbles of children before anyone notices that they are trying to produce real writing. With repeated writing practice, children will produce marks, according to Clay, that resemble more and more the writing they see in print around them. At first the child's writing will appear as a form of "mock" writing. Over a period of time, and with opportunities for practice, the writing becomes decipherable. For this reason, children in preschool and kindergarten should be encouraged to engage in writing throughout the school day. In some instances the teacher will provide a model for writing, while in other instances the teacher will facilitate spontaneous and self-selected writing engagement.

Once students have begun to communicate with confidence through the written word and can produce several sentences using inventive spelling, they are ready for formal instruction in writing in much the same way that they become ready for formal instruction in reading. Just as a teacher's manual serves as a valuable resource to provide a guide for the how-to of reading instruction, Thinking Maps can be and have been used by teachers to facilitate, enhance, and expedite the acquisition of writing proficiency for students from the primary grades through high school. Reading and writing share common text structures, and for this reason each is taught most effectively through a step-by-step cumulative process, vertically aligned from one grade level to the next.

WRITING AS THINKING

In an effort to alleviate the writing fears of their students, teachers have been known to tell their charges that writing is just "talk written down." This statement is a gross oversimplification of a complex process—writing is actually "thinking written down." Perhaps one reason for inefficiencies in student writing is connected to this misunderstanding. To write well, one must first think well about what is to be communicated. The foundation of formal writing instruction begins with the essential understanding of the purpose for writing, as well as the various organizational patterns that can be used to accomplish this purpose. These patterns correspond to the types of thinking that are involved for a reader to be able to comprehend the writer's message. Each organizational pattern needed for writing can be visually represented by one of the eight Thinking Maps, depending on the specific purpose for writing. For example, the purpose of narrative writing is to entertain through relating a story or memorable experience in sequential order; therefore, a Flow Map would be used to organize the writing. Teachers who consistently model the use of Thinking Maps for organizing writing have witnessed increased writing proficiency in their students and in their schools.

Within the past several years, more and more states have begun to implement an assessment to ensure writing proficiency in their students. In Florida, for example, all fourth-grade students are assessed annually on either narrative writing or expository writing "to explain why." A passing score is a 3.0 on a 6-point holistic scale. In 1999, the percentage of fourth-grade students passing the Florida Comprehensive Assessment Test (FCAT) at Brookshire Elementary School in Orange County was approximately 84%. The goal of the teachers and administration at this site was to move their overall school grade of C to an A by targeting improvement in their writing scores. Kindergarten through fifth-grade teachers participated in training at the beginning of the school year in the use of Thinking Maps in all curriculum areas. Follow-up sessions focused exclusively on using Thinking Maps for organizing and modeling writing. Teachers were taught the specific attributes of both narrative and expository writing, as well as the thought processes and Thinking Maps to use with each.

Following the training, a spiraled curriculum plan for teaching writing using consistent visual tools was implemented school-wide. Grade-level training sessions for writing were held to ensure that teachers knew how to model the use of the Thinking Maps for organizing writing with their students and how to demonstrate taking the information "off of the map" and onto the page. All teachers had the opportunity to observe demonstration lessons using Thinking Maps for student writing. The administration monitored and supported the teachers' efforts, providing individual assistance as needed. Within one year, the number of students passing the writing assessment had risen to approximately 97%. At the end of the second year, every student taking the FCAT writing assessment scored at least a passing 3.0, and the school achieved a state grade of A.

Principal Ken McGuire and his staff at Bluebonnet Elementary School, part of the Keller Independent School District in Fort Worth, Texas, led their students to outstanding writing achievement on the Texas Assessment of Knowledge and Skills (TAKS) in 2008. Following two full years of implementing *Write . . . from the Beginning* (Buckner, 2000), the number of students scoring a 4 (the highest possible score) rose from 3 to 75. The same year, 81% of fourth-grade students received "commended" status on the TAKS writing test. This was one of the highest levels of commended performance in the state of Texas, which had a 30% state average for commended performance that year.

At Euclid Elementary in Ontario, California, Principal Rhonda Cleeland and Literary Coach Monica Ibarra Ayala led their school in a school-wide implementation of Thinking Maps and *Write . . . from the Beginning* (Buckner, 2000). Within two years, the school's Academic Performance Index on the California Standards Test had risen from 624 to 735. In addition, 90 out of 100 fourth-grade students passed the state writing assessment. Of the 90 students, 50 *exceeded* the state expectations. According to Ayala, "The difference was having the right tools and a common language."

This same escalation of writing scores can occur all the way through secondary school as students are taught to plan and organize their writing using Thinking Maps. In 1995, Melba Johnson, a high school English teacher in Brunswick County, North Carolina, attended Thinking Maps training and immediately used the maps in her classroom to teach her students how to organize for writing. Within one semester, the scores of her students taking the 10th-grade state English II Writing Examination on literary analysis rose 5 points. One year later, Johnson attended training on the use of Thinking Maps specifically for the teaching of writing, and for the last five semesters of her teaching career, 100% of her students have passed the high school English II Writing Examination. The only difference in her instruction was teaching her students how to use Thinking Maps to plan and organize for writing based on the specific purpose and thought processes involved in the assignment. In addition, Johnson experienced the same success with her 11th- and 12th-grade advanced placement students by using this same process.

STRUCTURES FOR ORGANIZATION

While single classrooms can experience success, the most effective use of Thinking Maps for teaching writing involves whole-school commitment and vertical alignment of writing instruction. The "nonplagiarized," authentic research report that is difficult for many upper elementary and secondary students can be made easier if, beginning in first grade, students learn how to use a Tree Map to organize information by categories prior to writing. For example, a first-grade student has written a report about his favorite vegetable. Prior to writing, the student organized his information on a Tree Map (see Figure 7.1) according to the categories of information about which he would be writing. Note the correlation between the categories on the Tree Map and the organization of the writing.

Figure 7.1   Student Report-Writing Tree Map

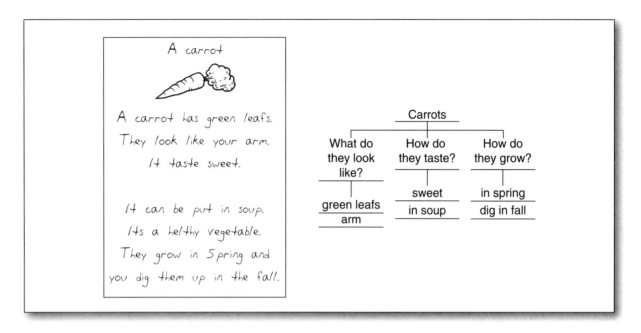

By organizing in this manner, the writer ensures better comprehension by his reader since the writing is set up like a familiar reading text structure. Another familiar text structure found in literature is the presentation of a series of events in sequential order to establish a story line. Another first-grade student used a Flow Map to organize her writing to tell a story about what her grandmother did when she came home (see Figure 7.2). The sequence of the Flow Map will become the sequence of the writing. Writing to explain why requires the writer to take a stance or make a choice that is supported with reasons. This type of writing has yet another organizational pattern that can be represented with a partial Multi-Flow Map. Figure 7.3 is a sample of writing by a first-grade student to explain why a certain food is her favorite snack.

Figure 7.2   Student Narrative-Writing Flow Map

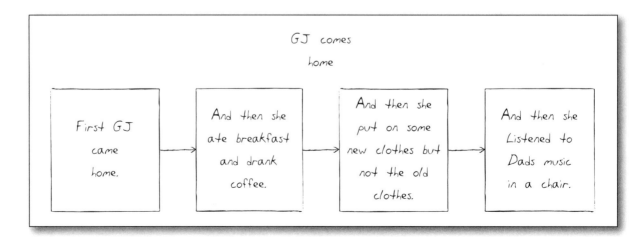

Figure 7.3   Writing-to-Explain-Why Multi-Flow Map

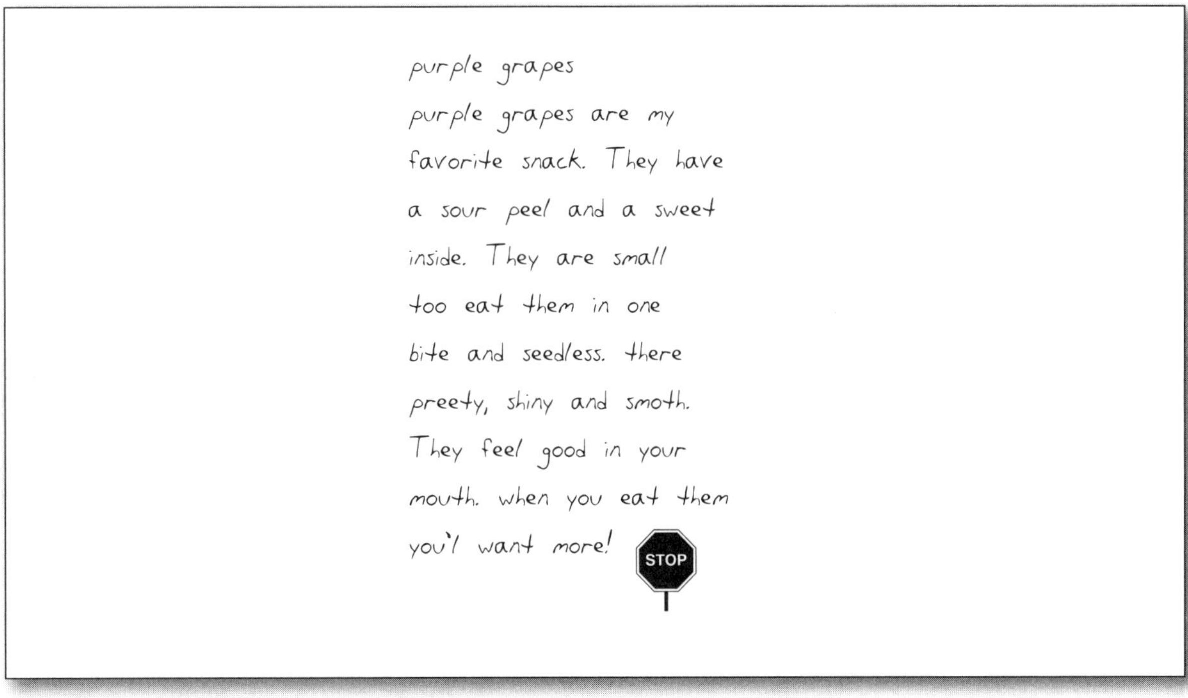

purple grapes

purple grapes are my

favorite snack. They have

a sour peel and a sweet

inside. They are small

too eat them in one

bite and seedless. there

preety, shiny and smoth.

They feel good in your

mouth. when you eat them

you'l want more! STOP

The teacher had modeled how to use a Circle Map and a partial Multi-Flow Map to develop reasons (the initial thinking part of writing) and then to organize for writing. The student began by brainstorming all of her favorite snacks in a Circle Map. Once this was done, the student was instructed to make a choice regarding the food about which she would write and to compose a sentence about her favorite snack and write it in the center box of the partial Multi-Flow Map. Next, the student engaged in thinking about "what caused me to select this snack as my favorite" or "what are the reasons why this snack is my favorite" and then recorded her thoughts in the small boxes on the left-hand side of the map. The teacher had explained that when others read her writing, they will be thinking about her choice and her reasons for that choice. The readers should "see" her thinking as they read.

An example of narrative writing by a second-grade student who used Thinking Maps to help him plan and organize for writing shows that this student has combined two Thinking Maps to help with his plan (see Figure 7.4). He used a combination of the Flow Map for sequencing events and the Tree Map for recording details related to those events. The flexibility of the maps allows students to combine maps as needed when engaging in a task that requires more than one thought process. Had the student used only the Flow Map, his writing could have become nothing more than a sequence of events that reads like a list. The elaboration or details related to each event were planned on lines borrowed from the Tree Map and located just under each of the stages or events. Note also that the Flow Map is nonlinear in appearance, allowing the student to plan a beginning and an ending to his story.

As students mature, the Thinking Maps used for writing become more sophisticated in appearance; however, the correlation between the maps, the thinking, and the writing is still apparent. Figure 7.5 is a re-creation of a visual representation of eight-year-old Cagney's thinking about her favorite summer vacation and the reasons why it is her favorite. She began with a partial Multi-Flow Map to develop her reasons; she then used a combination of a Flow Map

Figure 7.4 Combining Sequence and Details in Narrative Writing

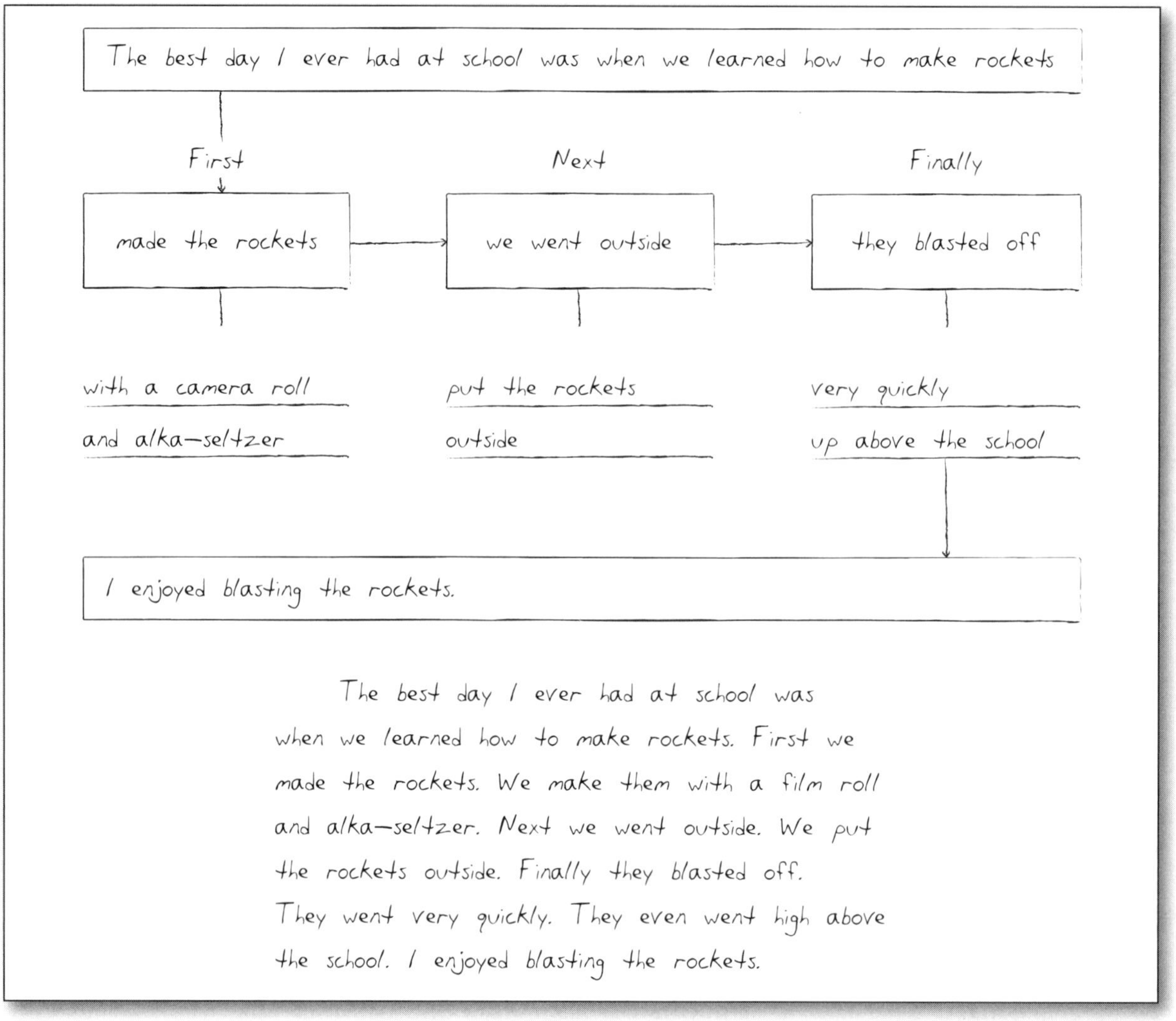

The best day I ever had at school was when we learned how to make rockets

First

made the rockets

with a camera roll
and alka-seltzer

Next

we went outside

put the rockets
outside

Finally

they blasted off

very quickly
up above the school

I enjoyed blasting the rockets.

The best day I ever had at school was when we learned how to make rockets. First we made the rockets. We make them with a film roll and alka-seltzer. Next we went outside. We put the rockets outside. Finally they blasted off. They went very quickly. They even went high above the school. I enjoyed blasting the rockets.

and a Tree Map to organize the parts of her writing, to decide the most appropriate sequence for presenting her reasons, and to plan the elaboration of her selected reasons. By the time Cagney wrote her essay, the hard part of the thinking had already been done. It is important to notice in this example how multiple patterns of thinking—based on common, well-defined, and flexible graphic structures—are adapted by the student to progress to more complex thinking and more elegant writing.

Thinking Maps for writing can be valuable to the global learner as well (see Chapter 4, "Tools for Integrating Theories and Differentiating Practice"). In every classroom, there are those students who do not grasp the concept of putting together a piece of writing from the parts to the whole as it is often modeled by teachers. With these students, teachers can use a process referred to as "reverse mapping," in which the teacher assists the student in analyzing his essay from the whole to its parts. The teacher provides a blank template of the Thinking Map that is used for organizing the particular type of writing, and the student cuts apart a copy of his essay and places the parts on the template. The student can immediately see the "holes" that represent the parts of the essay that are underdeveloped. At this point the student

Figure 7.5 Using a Multi-Flow Map, a Flow Map, and a Tree Map to Plan Expository Writing

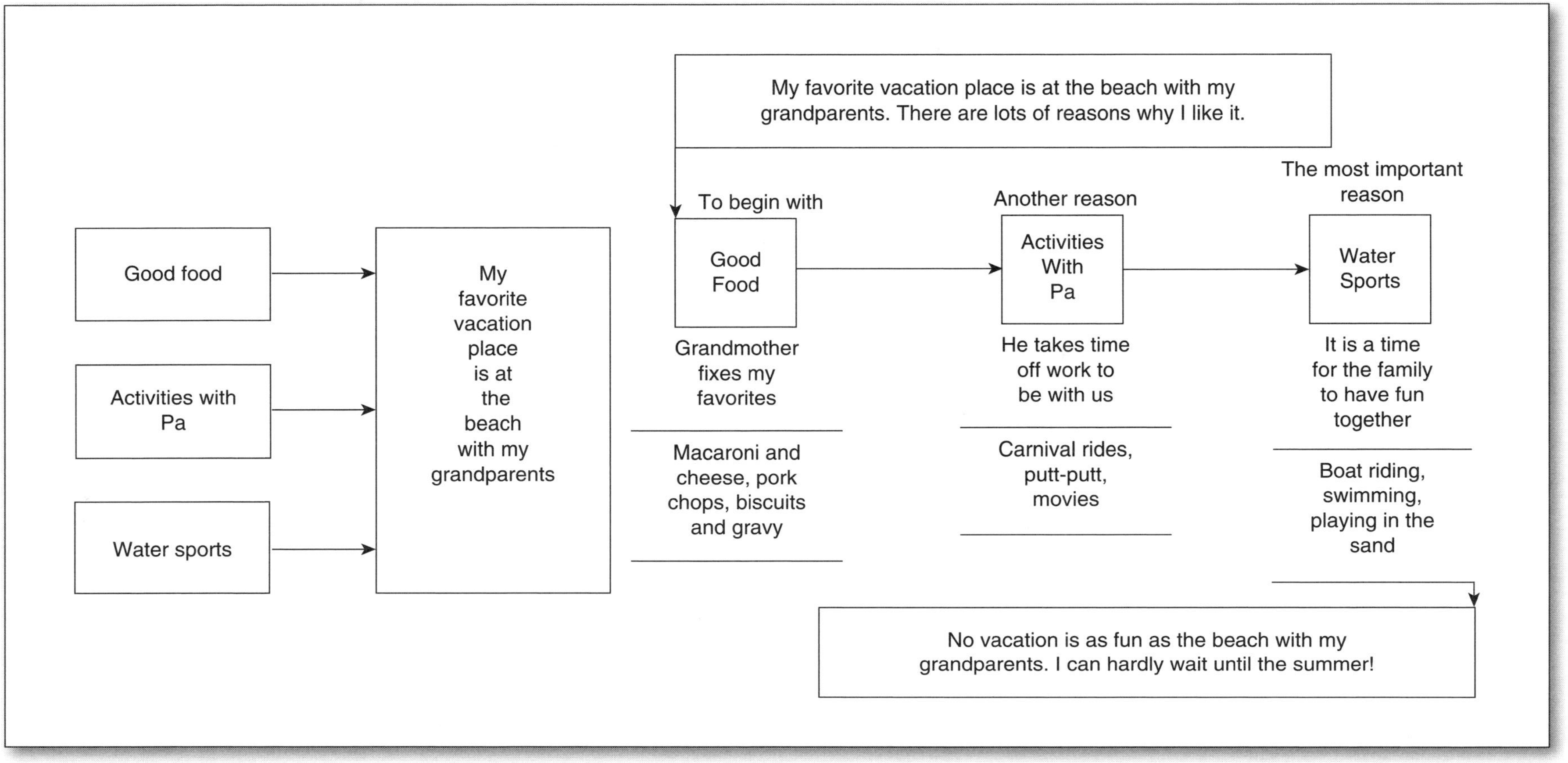

My favorite vacation place is at the beach with my grandparents. There are lots of reasons why I like it.

To begin with

Good Food

Grandmother fixes my favorites

Macaroni and cheese, pork chops, biscuits and gravy

Another reason

Activities With Pa

He takes time off work to be with us

Carnival rides, putt-putt, movies

The most important reason

Water Sports

It is a time for the family to have fun together

Boat riding, swimming, playing in the sand

No vacation is as fun as the beach with my grandparents. I can hardly wait until the summer!

Good food

Activities with Pa

Water sports

My favorite vacation place is at the beach with my grandparents can create the needed information and fill the "holes." The flexibility of the Thinking Maps empowers teachers to adjust instruction to the individual needs of students.

Eight-year-old Alecia was a student who needed individualized assistance in her understanding of the components of narrative writing. She was attentive in class and conscientious about completing her assignments correctly. However, as she tried to use the Thinking Maps modeled by her teacher for organizing writing, she often produced an underdeveloped story. Using the reverse mapping procedure, the teacher was able to instruct Alecia in how to develop her story more fully. Alecia's work has been reverse mapped with teacher assistance (see Figure 7.6).

Figure 7.6 Reverse Mapping for Revision and Elaboration

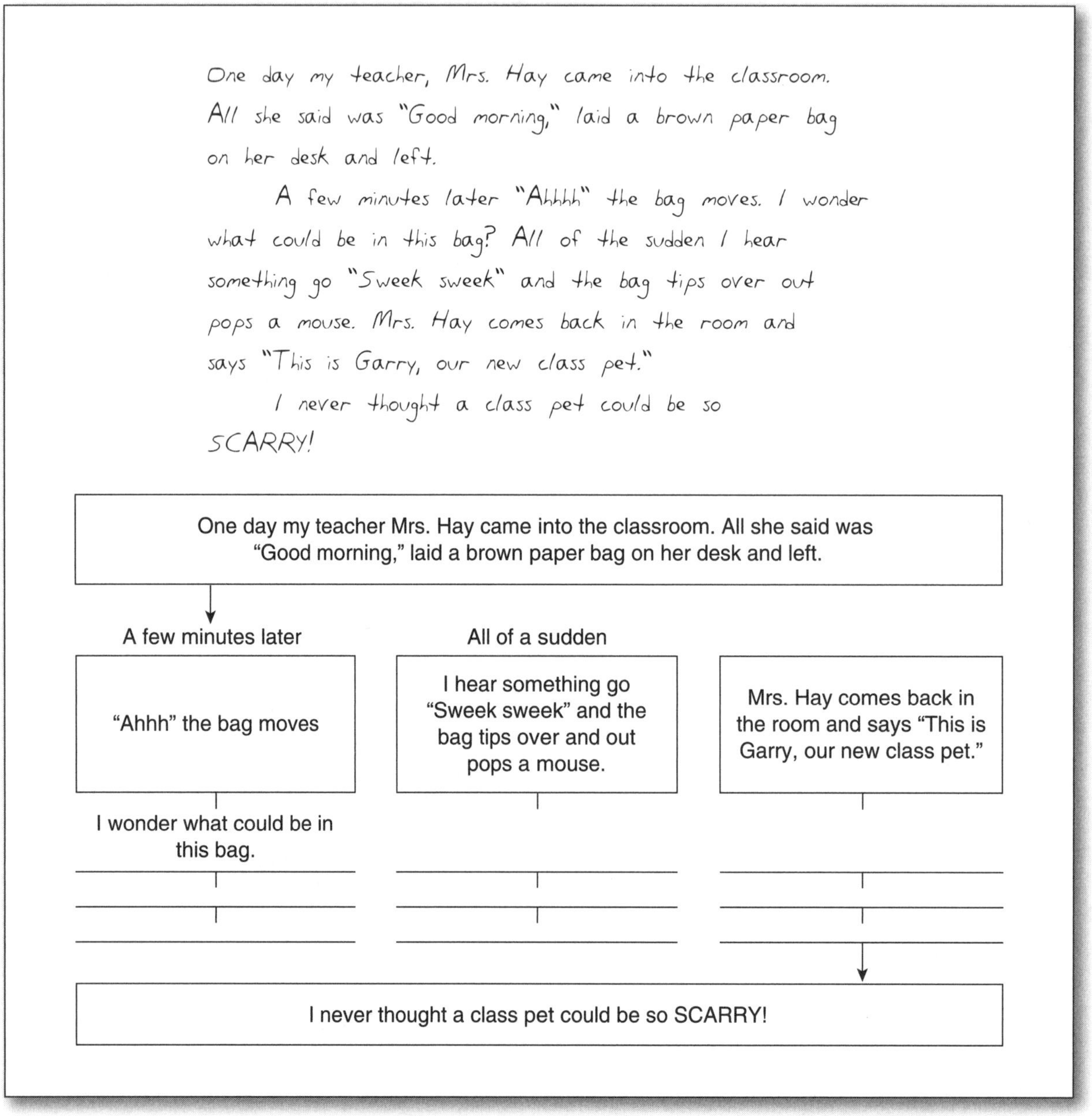

One day my teacher, Mrs. Hay came into the classroom. All she said was "Good morning," laid a brown paper bag on her desk and left.

A few minutes later "Ahhhh" the bag moves. I wonder what could be in this bag? All of the sudden I hear something go "Sweek sweek" and the bag tips over out pops a mouse. Mrs. Hay comes back in the room and says "This is Garry, our new class pet."

I never thought a class pet could be so SCARRY!

One day my teacher Mrs. Hay came into the classroom. All she said was "Good morning," laid a brown paper bag on her desk and left.

A few minutes later — "Ahhh" the bag moves

I wonder what could be in this bag.

All of a sudden — I hear something go "Sweek sweek" and the bag tips over and out pops a mouse.

Mrs. Hay comes back in the room and says "This is Garry, our new class pet."

I never thought a class pet could be so SCARRY!

PRECISION OF THOUGHT AND LANGUAGE

Learning the organizational structure for different domains of writing is a first step for students. However, there must be a focus on the quality of the content of that writing as well. Word choice as well as clear, precise language gives life, color, and voice to a piece of writing. One of the 16 Habits of Mind for developing thinking is defined as *precision of language* (Costa & Kallick, 2000). Many of the Thinking Maps have proven to be effective in helping students to achieve this goal. For example, when a student is contemplating how to describe a noun such as *cactus* in his writing, he must consider two things: the words he *could* use and the words he *should* use. As Mark Twain said, "The difference between the right word and almost the right word is the difference between lightning and a lightning bug."

Understandably, upon first sight teachers often construe the Bubble Map as just another brainstorming web, but as defined within the Thinking Maps model, this tool is based on the cognitive process of identifying and describing the attributes of things, not the cognitive process of defining all of one's associated ideas (which is easily accomplished using the Circle Map). This precision of definition of the cognitive skill of identifying attributes using the Bubble Map guides students to more precise word usage and vocabulary development that then can be used effectively to help the students with this task. In this example, the word *cactus* is placed in the center of the Bubble Map, and the student records adjectives and adjective phrases in the smaller bubbles surrounding it. The immediate goal for the student is to think of as many adjectives as possible that could be used to describe the word *cactus.* The next step is for the student to evaluate the adjectives selected and to determine the most appropriate, unique, and precise one to use. The quality of writing will improve when the student uses tools and strategies that help him to ponder and wrestle with language in the same way that a sculptor, a singer, or an athlete wrestles to develop a particular skill.

QUALITY ASSESSMENT TOOLS

As governors and legislators incorporate writing into their state school standards, a new commitment to measuring writing quality is sure to follow. Multiple-choice tests used in the past are likely to disappear, as a new commitment to measuring writing quality will result in requiring students to produce a piece of prose that someone reads and evaluates for quality. Also on the education horizon lies a swing away from current assessments that dictate the type, or domain, of writing a student must use to respond to a prompt, thereby requiring that the student have a repertoire of writing domains from which to select.

Not too long ago the state of Texas implemented just such a writing assessment that allows students the choice of how to respond to a given prompt. When given either an "on demand" or an "extended time" writing task, success for these students lies in the knowledge of various visual tools for organizing the information they wish to present. Through extended exposure and practice, the student will acquire a range of organizational tools for writing and will be able to select appropriately the organizing tool that best accomplishes the purpose of the writing task. In addition, with practice in the thought processes related to the quality of the content of writing, an overall improvement in writing proficiency will occur.

While Thinking Maps have been used as effective tools for improving writing, the greatest proficiency occurs when the students also understand how to assess quality in their own writing. Most state assessments are scored using a focused, holistic scoring guide. The holistic score that is given assesses a "general impression" and is useful as a snapshot of writing achievement. However, holistic scoring provides little information that can be used to plan and develop successive instruction geared to improving writing proficiency. According to a publication of the International Reading Association, analytic scoring, unlike holistic general impression scoring, looks at multiple elements or characteristics associated with effective writing and provides the most information from which to draw conclusions about writers and writings. As an assessment system, analytic scoring offers information that can best assist instruction because each element in the writing is evaluated separately, with each characteristic marked on a scale that indicates how well it has been presented.

Students who are trained in analytic scoring rubrics and understand the meaning of "quality content" have a better chance to be successful on writing assessments. The tools of Thinking Maps to organize their writing and a means to self-evaluate the quality of their content are the very least that teachers should provide during writing instruction.

SHARING THE LANGUAGE OF WRITING

For years there have been those in education who have believed that writing is a special language owned by English teachers. We know, however, that this can no longer be the case. Writing must now become the responsibility of all grade levels and all curriculum areas. If we view writing as intimately linked to teaching thinking and recognizing organizational patterns in text structure, then teachers of all subjects teach writing. The Thinking Maps provide teachers and students with a visual language for transferring both writing and thinking skills into every content area. Precise language, transition words, and reasons of elaboration are part of expository writing in textbooks that students need to comprehend while reading. If students transfer these reading skills from one subject to another, writing can improve as they replicate what they have seen in text. While this is not an easy task, it is one that can be accomplished with appropriate teacher training and commitment. Teachers must be empowered with knowledge about writing before they can be the most effective models for their students. If we expect students to write effectively, then our job as educators is to model how to build a bridge between what is within the heart and mind of the student and the written word. This bridge can and should be in the form of visual tools that help students construct the information they wish to relate.

Writing is not an easy task; it is a skill that takes time to develop in both teachers and their students. It involves becoming aware of patterns of thinking and knowing how to build a strong organizational structure. It engages students' creative and analytical minds as they audition words for themselves and for their readers. The goal of writing should be always to "go for better" and not settle for *red* when *crimson* is the word you need. Most important, writing is an act of courage, a willingness to share oneself with others. It is that skill that allows us to leave a part of ourselves in the world when we are gone; it is that symphony of sounds that allows us to understand the hearts and minds of those who have gone before us; it is that essential skill that we must give to those students who are entrusted to us.

REFERENCES

Buckner, J. (2000). *Write . . . from the beginning.* Raleigh, NC: Innovative Sciences.

Buckner, J., & Johnson, M. (2002). *Write . . . for the future.* Raleigh, NC: Innovative Sciences.

Clay, M. (1975). *What did I write? Beginning writing behavior.* Portsmouth, NH: Heinemann.

Costa, A., & Kallick, B. (2000). *Encouraging and engaging Habits of Mind.* Alexandria, VA: Association for Supervision and Curriculum Development.

Marklein, M. B. (2010, January 20). Group wants emphasis on quality in college learning. *USA Today.* Retrieved October 31, 2010, from http://www.usatoday.com/LIFE/usaedition/2010–01–21-collegelearning21_ST_NU.htm

National Commission on Writing in America's Schools and Colleges. (2003, April). *The neglected "R": The need for a writing revolution.* Princeton, NJ: College Entrance Examination Board.

8

The Challenge of High-Stakes Testing in Middle School Mathematics

Janie B. MacIntyre, M.Ed.

KEY CONCEPTS

- Students moving from concrete to abstract mathematical concepts using Thinking Maps®
- Multiple-year results from research on Thinking Maps applied to procedural knowledge by students with special needs
- Fostering clear and meaningful communication between students and teachers in mathematics classrooms

FACING MYSELF AND MY STUDENTS

In the early 1990s, North Carolina initiated major educational reforms that continue to become more rigorous. Student proficiency must be demonstrated on annual statewide math and reading end-of-grade tests for elementary and middle schools. Secondary school assessment is conducted through end-of-course tests in core areas. Student performance and proficiency are directly linked to promotion, unit credit, and graduation. With the knowledge that students with special needs would have to meet the same standards as their regular education counterparts to be eligible to receive a high school diploma, a pivotal personal and professional realization occurred. Morally, and with full awareness that my students were counting on me and others like me, it became essential to find and develop strategies that would allow them to adapt to and compensate for learning difficulties, differences, and deficits to have an opportunity to earn what would represent the pinnacle of formal education for many of my students: a high school diploma.

Prior to the reforms, the underachieving students in my seventh-, eighth-, and ninth-grade mathematics classes at George R. Edwards Middle School in Rocky Mount—both those coded as having a learning disability and those achieving in the lower quartile—performed basic computation for whole numbers and decimals, learned to tell time to the nearest 5 minutes, made change for purchases of under $20, and, perhaps, studied fractions. Today, my students have made cognitive leaps and are successfully mastering concepts of solid and plane geometry, exponents and scientific notation, two-step equations, and graphing linear and nonlinear systems of equations, to mention only a few. Students are truly light-years ahead of where they were and are able to access and master those concepts, as our research has shown, because of Thinking Maps.

From the onset of Thinking Maps implementation within the instructional process, I have been astounded by the ease with which students with learning disabilities and those in the regular education program have been able to not only grasp new concepts but also demonstrate comprehension and application with accuracy. For over a decade, teachers at my school have observed that Thinking Maps provide the vehicle by which students with special needs are able to adapt to and effectively compensate for learning difficulties and perceptual deficits with tremendous efficiency and success. This inherently concise, consistent, and flexible visual language transcends age and ability and aids students by providing accurate, concrete connections between what is already known and new skills to be acquired. For example, by using a Circle and Frame Map with my students (see Figure 8.1), I was able to connect the concrete ideas of coordinate planes within a real-world context for their reference.

Figure 8.1 Coordinate Plane Circle and Frame Map

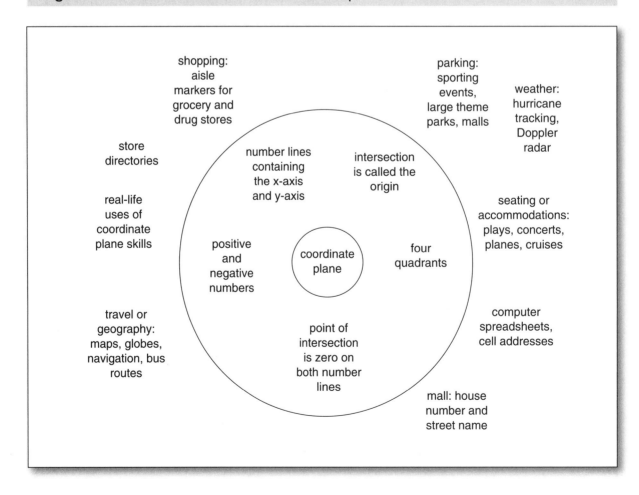

While I intuitively knew the value of Thinking Maps from over a decade of results gained from examples as shown in the figure, I also knew that in today's data-driven field of education, increases in student performance need to be stated in observable, measurable, and replicable terms to be valid. I used my opportunity as a Christa McAuliffe Fellow in 1999–2000 to conduct a control group study to determine the impact of Thinking Maps on math achievement. I found that after an entire year of Thinking Maps implementation, end-of-grade test results for both exceptional and traditional students indicated four years' worth of developmental gains in one year's time.

BEYOND INTUITION

During the first two years of integrating Thinking Maps, a variety of experiences convinced me that Thinking Maps positively influence student performance. Many times in sharing student accomplishments I was told, "Yes, but Janie, you are a wonderful teacher." In response I would state, "I know I'm a good teacher, but this is not my magic—this is because of Thinking Maps!" I used Thinking Maps throughout all stages of the instructional process: from determining prior knowledge of a given topic through directed and independent instruction to assessment and self-evaluation of curricular growth. If we were working on a particular skill, I could use the same tool to differentiate instruction depending on the developmental level of the students involved. In Figures 8.2a and 8.2b, two students were working through a process of how to make a graph using a Flow Map for sequencing. Notice the different levels of sophistication each student applied.

Figure 8.2a How to Create a Graph Level I Flow Map

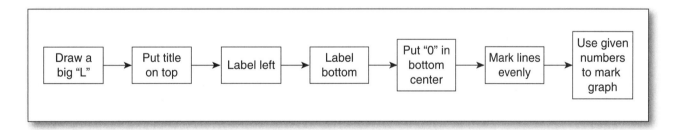

Figure 8.2b How to Create a Graph Level 2 Flow Map

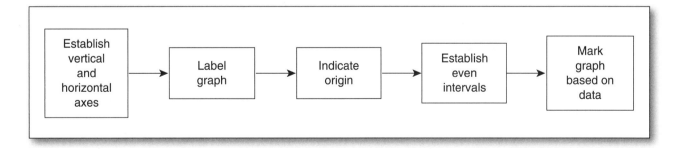

In Figure 8.3, the Bridge Map, used for analogies, was applied to transfer familiar language to the mathematical language needed for this concept. This is just one example in which Thinking Maps scaffold the learning of mathematical language and processes.

Figure 8.3 Bridge Map for Building Math Language

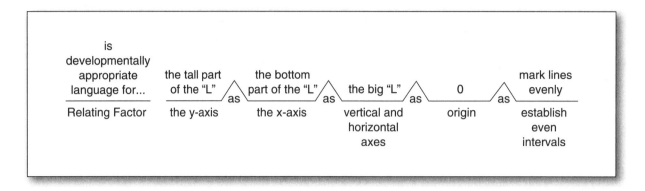

Not only did the maps foster students' increased personal awareness of their individual cognitive and metacognitive style, but they allowed me to glimpse students' metacognition, thus enabling me to assess areas of inherent student strength and weakness.

As a result of this type of instruction in my math classes, 6 out of 11 students with special needs scored "proficient" or "exceeds expectations" in math. Eighth graders were learning 46% beyond what they were expected to learn in one year's time, with one student demonstrating a remarkable 21-point gain in developmental growth. In an even more needy population, in an intensive math remediation class for ninth graders who had previously failed the eighth-grade exit exam, 84% passed the retest. It was apparent that when Thinking Maps applications were incorporated consistently and frequently within the math instructional process, these exceptional students were able to demonstrate, on average, two years' worth of growth in one year.

RESULTS: GAINS IN DEVELOPMENTAL GROWTH

In 1999–2000, I was selected to serve as the North Carolina Christa McAuliffe Fellow. I structured independent research to measure the impact and statistical significance of Thinking Maps instruction on North Carolina eighth-grade end-of-grade developmental growth of lower-achieving students in math. The research targeted the 291 lower-achieving, rising eighth graders in the Nash-Rocky Mount Public Schools. The schools in Rocky Mount, located in eastern North Carolina, serve both an inner city and a rural population of middle- to lower-class families. Over time the area has changed from an agricultural economy of mainly tobacco farms to a more diverse economy including bank, restaurant, mechanical engineering, and biotechnology headquarters and facilities. The student body also reflects this diversity, with students who are about 50% African American and 50% White, including a small migrant and ESL (English as a second language) population.

Approximately 30 system-wide eighth-grade math teachers attended Thinking Maps professional development throughout the year, including monthly follow-up sessions that provided model and videotaped demonstration lessons, classroom observations, and coaching opportunities, as well as assistance in the collection of anecdotal evidence and documentation logs indicating the frequency and types of Thinking Maps being used. Participants were provided with over 200 Thinking Maps applications in math that were aligned to all curricular goals and objectives and the state-adopted text.

Due to the pre- and posttest design model used by the state to determine a student's developmental growth, test scores from the sixth and seventh grades determined developmental growth prior to Thinking Maps applications. Seventh- and eighth-grade scores determined developmental growth subsequent to the implementation of research strategies. Therefore,

North Carolina end-of-grade math tests for three consecutive years were mandatory to be included in the project's comparisons. A variety of factors may prevent the administration of a test to individual students, including illness, exemption, transfers into a system, or moving. Of the 291 students identified in the research, 133 possessed a score for all three consecutive years. Based on individual performance, the increases in the developmental growth of these students after the implementation of Thinking Maps strategies are significant.

The average developmental growth of the exceptional children as eighth graders at all three school sites for the 1997–1998 and 1998–1999 school years, prior to the implementation of the McAuliffe Fellowship project in 1999–2000, is shown in Table 8.1. I included data from the students in my classes (*MacIntyre*) who had used the Thinking Maps during both the 1997–1998 and 1998–1999 school years. The students in my classes exceeded exemplary growth in both years, and, in one case, their growth was almost as much as 7 times that of seventh graders at another site. Shown in Table 8.2 are the scores that indicate the 1999 pretest and 2000 posttest developmental growth scores for eighth graders who participated in the Thinking Maps implementation during the McAuliffe Fellowship project in 1999–2000.

Table 8.1   Test Results for Seventh-Grade Developmental Growth

School Sites	Exceptional Children Developmental Growth in Math	
	1997–1998	1998–1999
Expected	5	3.8
Exemplary	5.5	4.3
Edwards	6.25	3.7
Nash Central	4.33	1.6
Southern Nash	3.88	2.7
MacIntyre	7.33	7.6

Table 8.2   Test Results for Eighth-Grade Developmental Growth

School Sites	McAuliffe Fellowship Developmental Growth 1999–2000	
	Pretest	Posttest
Expected	3.8	3.7
Exemplary	4.3	4.2
Edwards	4.93	8.02
Nash Central	1.28	6.94
Southern Nash	1.33	9.71

At the time of the 1999 pretest, expected developmental growth for these students was 3.8 points, while exemplary developmental growth was 4.3 points. As the figure indicates, the actual pretest developmental growth for the students involved in the research was measured at 1.28 points for Nash Central Middle School and 1.33 points for Southern Nash Middle School. Therefore, at the time of the pretest, only students at Edwards Middle School, who had to some extent used Thinking Maps, met the expected growth. In fact, they exceeded it.

Figure 8.4   Thinking Maps Applications to Diminish Learning Difficulties Tree Map

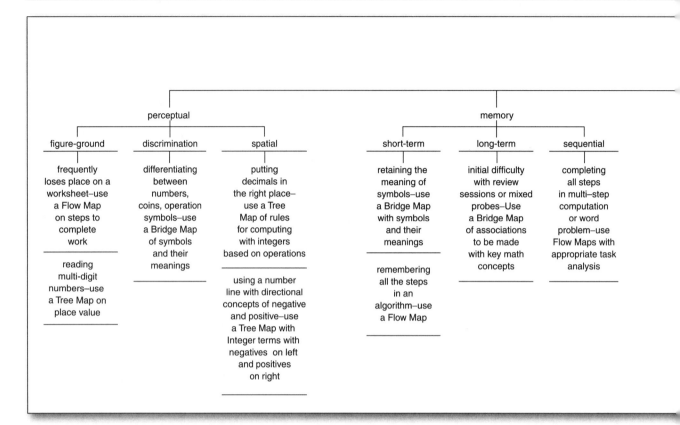

In the 2000 posttest, given after Thinking Maps implementation, the results show a fivefold increase in the average developmental growth scores of the research participants at Nash Central Middle School and a sevenfold increase in the average developmental growth scores at Southern Nash Middle School. As expected, the more profound change in individual developmental growth occurred overall at our sister schools that had not previously used Thinking Maps at all. The less dramatic increase in scores at Edwards could have been due to my six-week absence from my classroom to conduct the Thinking Maps training as part of my fellowship. Of the 133 students formerly labeled as low-achieving, 71 demonstrated proficiency on the first trial.

What we have learned about Thinking Maps during this era of high-stakes testing and accountability continues to evolve, but this study confirmed two findings:

1. When Thinking Maps are utilized in daily math instruction, student learning and demonstration of mastery exceed exemplary developmental growth expectations on state tests.

2. Thinking Map strategies and applications in math are replicable.

THINKING MAPS: A BRIDGE TO SUCCESS

The statistics indicate considerable growth in mathematical achievement, so how and why does applying Thinking Maps in math instruction improve math ability as measured on these tests? Qualitative results in the form of student and teacher anecdotal reports and instructional logs indicate that Thinking Maps support mathematical thinking by enabling students and

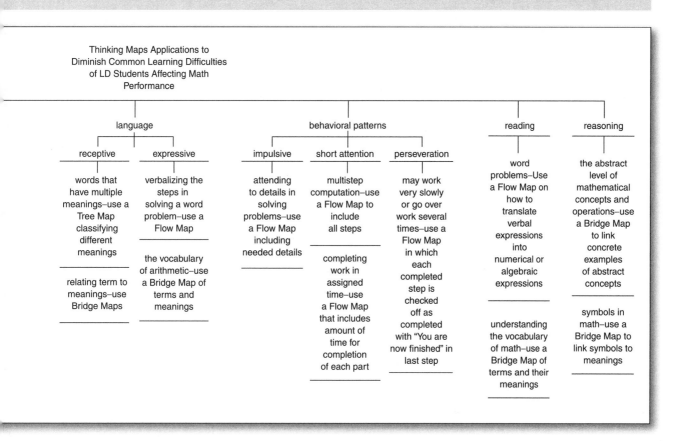

teachers to clearly and visually explain, understand, monitor, and assess mathematical processes and problems.

Students who typically find math enjoyable and readily grasp new concepts are those who have developed and use analytical skills. According to some researchers, "giving students advanced organizers does have the desired effect of increasing recall of critical information" (Deshler, Schumaker, Lenz, & Ellis, 1984). In addition, students with learning disabilities "experience deficits in cognitive processes including disorganization, acquisition, retrieval, integration or association, expression, sequencing, analyzing, and evaluating information," according to Wallace and McLoughlin (1988). With Thinking Maps, teachers are able to graphically demonstrate and model analytical thinking to students, furthering opportunities for them to develop, practice, enhance, and apply the analytical skills necessary to be able to truly understand and apply mathematical concepts.

In addition to analytical skills that may be immaturely developed, some students possess learning difficulties, differences, or disabilities that can directly impact math performance. In the following Tree Map, Cecil Mercer's (1983) work has been expanded to include sample Thinking Maps applications (see Figure 8.4). The application of Thinking Maps is directly targeted to diminish the impact of the acquisitional and behavioral problems experienced by students with learning disabilities in math. From this Tree Map, it is clear that language and procedure play a large role in contributing to mathematical understanding.

Students need support not only with the concepts of math but also with the symbols and multiple steps involved in the construction of the concept. In the following multiple map example (Figures 8.5a–c) introducing and explaining "the coordinate plane," teachers and students work together to understand the language, processes, points, and purposes of plotting and using coordinates.

Figure 8.5a Coordinate Plane Tree Map

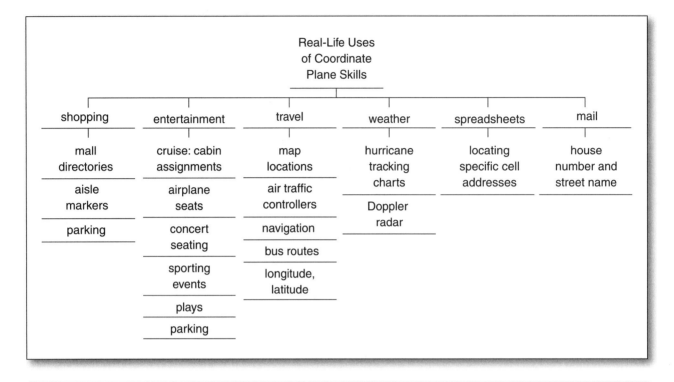

Figure 8.5b Determining Points on the Coordinate Plane Flow Map

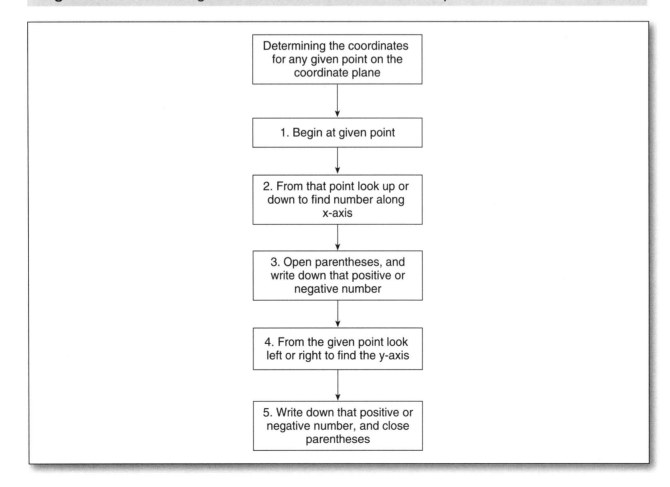

Figure 8.5c Finding Points on the Coordinate Plane Bridge Map

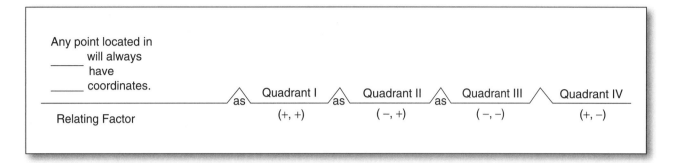

We also know from theories of brain-based research and theories of emotional intelligence (Goleman, 1995) that for learning to occur, new information must have either personal relevance and meaning or an emotional connection to the learner. Through the use of Thinking Maps, particularly the Frame of Reference, graphics can be constructed depicting the relevance of math goals to real-life applications in ways that are compatible with the triune brain's innate, natural preferences for pictures, determining patterns, establishing order, making connections, and completing processes. While students should realize that perhaps only in a math class would they be asked to determine the coordinates for a point on a coordinate plane, those skills are used often in real-life situations without being referred to specifically by name. Real-life applications can and should be made for every goal and content area to enhance student awareness of personal relevance and the need to acquire those skills.

We can see that Thinking Maps foster clear, deliberate, and meaningful communication between students and teachers. When students are involved in study where instruction is effective, goals are clear, and opportunities for success are frequent, enhanced levels of self-confidence will emerge and render students willing to take more frequent appropriate academic risks leading to upward spirals of student achievement.

In applying the theory that all knowledge is either declarative or procedural to the area of mathematics, declarative knowledge would include content vocabulary, theorems, laws, rules, and contributions of mathematicians—the factually based, continually true information, or the absolutes. Procedural knowledge would include everything else: How to bisect an angle or use the Pythagorean theorem to determine a missing measurement of a right triangle; how to graph a point on a coordinate plane; and how to determine the mean, median, mode, and range of a set of data are all examples involving procedural knowledge. Because of the inherent procedural nature of math, the list could go on and on. Using a Flow Map for a procedure, students can guide themselves or can be guided from where they presently function toward the acquisition and subsequent mastery of curricular goals with amazing rates of growth.

A student from Edwards Middle School explained how Thinking Maps scaffolded her learning by translating abstract thinking processes and mathematical processes into explicit and tangible visual representations: "Thinking Maps help me in math class by explaining something complex or abstract in a simple way. They allow you to see where you have made your mistake, and how *to show* your math in words that make sense. I wish someone had taught me math this way before. Now, I can understand exactly what we're doing in class." The student added, "The more we use Thinking Maps, the more I understand, and the easier the work becomes to do."

Teachers also celebrate the changes in students' organizational ability, self-efficacy, and attitude toward learning: "Students get excited and are becoming much better at organizing and maintaining their 'map' notes. . . . Students are consciously aware of wanting to have their math Thinking Maps with them. The students know the tools are helping and will refer to previous maps to verify their current work. It is very encouraging to me to assist students to develop strategies that enable them to become independent learners." Students and teachers indicated that Thinking Maps fostered students' ability to articulate how they were thinking or to reflect with a metacognitive stance to self-assess. Students who previously had trouble organizing now had a predictable road map that they could navigate.

Math teachers in general have a tendency to be highly organized and analytical. Because that can be such a natural part of our way of thinking and frame of reference, we sometimes fail to remember that others don't necessarily think that way, particularly adolescents who are still developing cognitively. The use of the Flow Map for procedural knowledge acquisition in math forces highly organized, analytical teachers to view concepts and skills from the student's perspective to determine what is truly needed to ensure student mastery while incorporating the language that is developmentally appropriate for that particular group of students.

The Flow Map used for sequencing is the same graphic design used in math, English, science, social studies, physical education, art, foreign language, or any other subject being taught. This repetitive and consistent link to cognition is extremely positive and beneficial in helping students, particularly students identified as having special needs, to become more efficient and organized in their thinking across all facets of educational pursuit. This success breeds increases in self-esteem and the willingness of students to take appropriate academic and responsive risks during the instructional process. Through the use and internalization of this consistent language, students are enabled to quite literally state a more figurative phrase: "I see what you mean."

BEYOND TEST SCORES

Developmental and cognitive gains like these have tremendous implications for instruction, assessment, services, and expectations of this population. By examining data scored in groups with decimal points and percentages, we might forget that those numbers represent individual students. The data validated my suspicions about Thinking Maps as tools for learning. Thinking Maps affirm students' ability to think, with a positive ripple effect on their sense of self-worth. The gravity of this situation struck me when I told one of my students his test results. Tension filled the air as he approached my desk. Anticipating failure, he lowered his head and said, "I didn't make it, did I?" "As a matter of fact," I replied, "you did." With tears in his eyes, this towering eighth-grade boy picked me up and spun me around. We immediately called to share the great news with his mother. It was during that interaction that I understood the true meaning of my results. Relief and praise washed over this student and his family. He exclaimed, "I am smart—I can do this!"

REFERENCES

Deshler, D. D., Schumaker, J. B., Lenz, B. K., & Ellis, E. E. (1984). Academic and cognitive intervention for learning disabled adolescents, Part II. *Journal of Learning Disabilities, 17,* 170–179.

Goleman, D. (1995). *Emotional intelligence: Why it matters more than IQ.* New York: Bantam.

Mercer, C. (1983). Common learning difficulties of LD students affecting math performance. In *Arithmetic teacher* (p. 345, Table 14.2). New York: Reston Publishing.

Wallace, G., & McLoughlin, J. A. (1988). *Learning disabilities: Concepts and characteristics.* New York: MacMillan.

9

Thinking Like a Scientist

Lou-Anne Conroy, M.A., and David Hyerle, Ed.D.

KEY CONCEPTS

- A pattern language for the science inquiry process
- The cognitive foundations of scientific thinking in elementary and secondary classrooms
- Explicit thinking in an inquiry classroom

Have you noticed over the past 10 years how often scientists in fields such as biology and the neurosciences—as well as the social sciences—use the term *mapping* for describing how they understand and solve problems within complex areas such as weather systems, ecosystems, the human genome system, and, of course, the human brain? *Mapping* has become the overarching metaphor for research, discovery, invention, creative and analytic thinking, and, in practical terms, a new way to visually represent knowledge in the 21st century. There is even a new field: *knowledge cartography.* Increasingly, scientists are becoming aware that we must *consciously* learn how to transform bits of information and data (as our brain does unconsciously) into mapped patterns of knowledge.

Across the sciences, we are mapping the human genome system, as well as all the systems of the brain and body. The brain is based on pattern seeking and mapping, and thus we even now use cartographic means to discover how we think; for example, we use fMRIs (functional magnetic resonance imaging) to *map* that organ of our body that is continuously and unconsciously remapping reality for us at every moment. This is because we now accept that our world is more fully understood when we investigate interdependent *patterns* in systems rather than isolated, linear data points for informing our scientific research. The use of mapping in the 21st century represents a paradigm shift in the way the "contents" of knowledge are generated and represented. The *form* in which we present knowledge is thus a critical dimension of scientific process, inquiry, and innovation.

Thinking Maps® are, simply, a *pattern language* that supports teachers and students in discovering and *representing* linear and nonlinear knowledge structures. These visual tools based on generative cognitive structures—when used in combination and embedded within each other—are congruent with the patterns at work within our brains. Below we will view a correlation of the underlying cognitive processes of Thinking Maps to scientific processes and then investigate classroom-based work that shows the dynamic use of the tools from elementary to high school.

SCIENTIFIC PROCESSES AND THINKING MAPS

How can we engage students in mapping information and transforming it into knowledge across the fields of science in K–12 classrooms and into college and the workplace? Let's start with the basics. The direct relationship between fundamental cognitive patterns based in the Thinking Maps and the foundational processes used across the sciences is clearly visible in Figure 9.1. The summary correlation between the maps and scientific processes offers teachers and students patterning tools that may be used across the sciences for understanding scientific concepts and, ultimately, for the scientific processes of conducting in-depth research and inquiry-based learning. As you review this correlation, notice that what we often consider to be simple, lower-order cognitive skills are actually the nuts and bolts of scientific processes.

Figure 9.1 Fundamental Scientific Processes and Thinking Maps

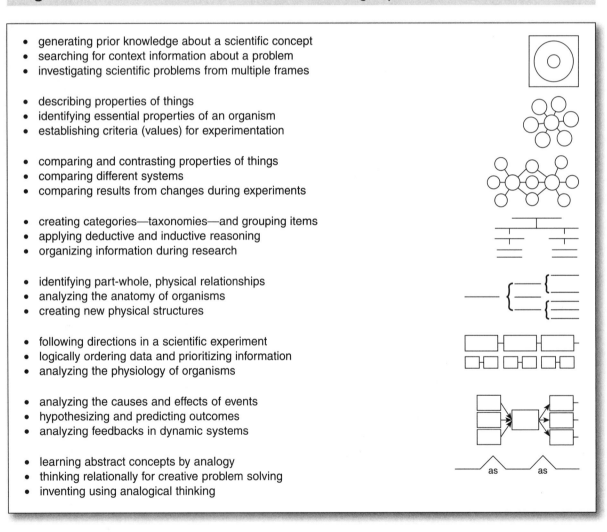

- generating prior knowledge about a scientific concept
- searching for context information about a problem
- investigating scientific problems from multiple frames

- describing properties of things
- identifying essential properties of an organism
- establishing criteria (values) for experimentation

- comparing and contrasting properties of things
- comparing different systems
- comparing results from changes during experiments

- creating categories—taxonomies—and grouping items
- applying deductive and inductive reasoning
- organizing information during research

- identifying part-whole, physical relationships
- analyzing the anatomy of organisms
- creating new physical structures

- following directions in a scientific experiment
- logically ordering data and prioritizing information
- analyzing the physiology of organisms

- analyzing the causes and effects of events
- hypothesizing and predicting outcomes
- analyzing feedbacks in dynamic systems

- learning abstract concepts by analogy
- thinking relationally for creative problem solving
- inventing using analogical thinking

The scientific method that is often found inside science textbooks has an overarching, often dull linear design from hypothesis building to testing. Yet within this method the scientific thinking, discovery, problem solving, and invention are *not* linear processes and involve seeking complex nonlinear patterns, interdependencies, and systems within information. Scientists think by

- defining a problem in context (Circle Map),
- describing properties of things (Bubble Map),

- comparing things and establishing criteria for evaluation (Double Bubble Map),
- creating taxonomies and hierarchical categories (Tree Map),
- analyzing the part-whole anatomy of objects (Brace Map),
- ordering information in sequences (Flow Map),
- analyzing the physiological feedback systems (Multi-Flow Map), and
- using analogies and metaphors to understand concepts (Bridge Map).

Above all, scientists are often constrained and/or enlightened by the existing body of research and theoretical paradigms within their domains. In the best cases, scientists seek to understand how their own belief systems and the existing body of research inform their biases and frame their perceptions and beliefs while also influencing their methods and interpretation of evidence. Within the language of Thinking Maps, a rectangular frame (Frame of Reference) may be drawn around the map(s) as a metacognitive mirror for establishing and reflecting on the personal and cultural influences on one's thinking.

How does this all play out in the classroom? We first look at a unit of study at the elementary level focused on students' collaborative learning about scientific discovery and how to create a rubric for further analysis of data. We then turn to a few examples from a high school student who mapped out *an entire biology textbook*. These foundational pieces lead us into an in-depth view of how Thinking Maps may be integrated into the processes of inquiry in science.

Mapping Scientific Processes, Patterns, and Inquiry

Bob Fardy was a science curriculum coordinator in Concord, Massachusetts, when he began to conduct a systematic evaluation of the effectiveness of Thinking Maps through practical classroom work. He worked with multiple second-grade classrooms. As he used the maps with students, he captured the collaborative processes they used and reported on the outcomes. In the report below, Bob discusses and then reflects on how he used multiple maps and the frame during an action research design to help second-grade students learn how to understand different types of rocks and how to develop a rubric for further scientific discoveries. He reveals how Thinking Maps may be integrated in classrooms through practice that is developmentally appropriate and reflective.

DEVELOPING A ROCK RUBRIC USING MULTIPLE THINKING MAPS
BY BOB FARDY

At the beginning of a "rocks and minerals" unit, I introduced second-grade students to three Thinking Maps: the Circle, Bubble, and Double Bubble maps. In our school district, classroom teachers often use the KWL strategy (Ogle, 1988–1989) when their students begin a new topic or unit of study. The strategy is an effective way for students, at the beginning of the unit or lesson, to identify what they already know (K) and what they want (W) to know about a topic, and to identify what they have learned (L) at the conclusion. As both teachers and students were familiar with this approach, I introduced the students to the Circle Map and asked them to share what they already knew about rocks. The Circle Map (see Figure 9.2) proved to be an effective brainstorming tool for the students. I recorded and displayed the students' responses within and around the concentric circles of the map. This tool helped me to carefully avoid any kind of linear listing, clustering, or linking of their responses that might imply

(Continued)

(Continued)

or infer some kind of hierarchical ordering of their ideas and/or making connections between and among their comments. In this way, the Circle Map served as a classroom mirror, reflecting the fluency and flexibility of students' thinking, ideas, and information at that moment in time. As the students continued to brainstorm what they knew about rocks, I began to see the Circle Map as more than a mirror that reflected the students' responses. The map was also serving as a window, providing a means to access and assess the students' thinking. I could identify their prior knowledge and surface some possible misconceptions and alternative conceptual frameworks. Indeed, the Circle Map was emerging as an effective tool for both assessment and brainstorming.

Figure 9.2 "What Do You Know About Rocks?" Circle Map

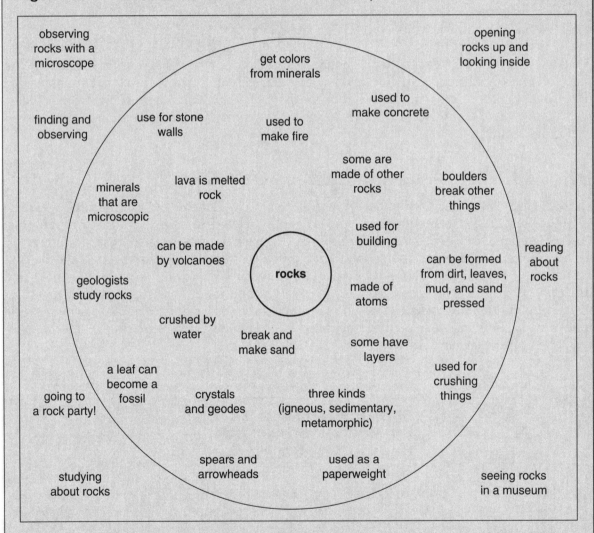

For me, the distinguishing feature of the eight Thinking Maps, as compared with more traditional visual tools, is the "Frame of Reference," which, as a metacognitive device, added another dimension to the lesson. As the students and I reviewed the Circle Map, we acknowledged that "we already knew many things about rocks." Transferring our attention to the Frame of Reference, I asked the students, "How did you learn what you already know?" In responding to this question, the students reflected on their own learning and at the same time informed me as to the diversity of learning experiences that had been their avenues for acquiring knowledge and constructing meaning. The students identified their "ways of knowing and learning" in the outside frame.

Having surfaced and assessed the students' prior knowledge, I distributed rock samples (granite) to each student and introduced the Bubble Map. With the aid of hand lenses, the students examined the samples of granite using multisensory observations and, using the Bubble Map, recorded their descriptions of the properties of granite. After a few minutes, the students shared their map (see Figure 9.3).

Figure 9.3   Describing Properties of Granite Bubble Map

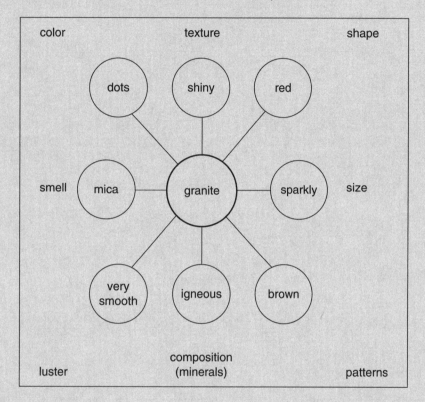

Most important, as they shared their maps, the second graders identified the discrete types of properties that they had been observing: color, texture, shape, patterns, luster, minerals in the rock (composition), size, and smell. We defined the generated list of rock properties as "Our Rock Rubric." The students subsequently referred to the rock rubric as they began to observe more rock samples (gneiss) and recorded their observations using a new Bubble Map and Frame of Reference.

Having shared their Bubble Maps about granite with their classmates and by using the rock rubric as a guide, the students made and recorded even more observations about the gneiss samples. As the students increased the number of observations, they began to expand their map, adding more "bubbles" of properties as needed. Now the students were beginning to take greater ownership of the visual tool, using and adapting it to meet their needs. For the students, the Bubble Map was not a static "fill-in-the-bubbles worksheet." Instead it became a dynamic, versatile, open-ended graphic with a certain "elasticity" that could be stretched in tandem with their thinking.

In the concluding moments of this lesson, I asked the students, "How are granite and gneiss alike and different?" Each student literally had both samples in hand in order to compare and contrast these two types of rocks, but to facilitate our discussion, the students also had two Bubble Maps that could be merged into a third Thinking Map, a Double Bubble Map (see Figure 9.4).

(Continued)

(Continued)

Figure 9.4   Comparing and Contrasting Gneiss and Granite Double Bubble Map

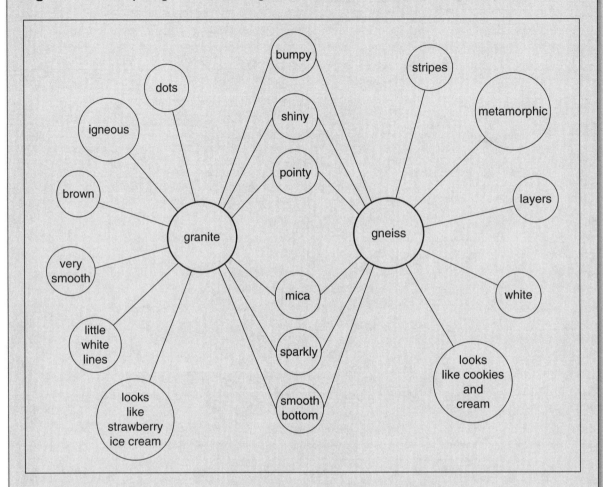

In the area of science, students are constantly comparing and contrasting objects, organisms, phenomena, events, and ideas within and about the natural world. It has been my experience that teachers often use Venn diagrams as "the" graphic organizer for comparing and contrasting. However, I have observed that certain graphic organizers—such as Venn diagrams—often can be problematic. Children, particularly young children, as concrete learners can at times become focused on the seemingly fixed format and nature of the graphic. For example, if the Venn diagram is drawn with a relatively narrow area of intersection, does that imply a limited commonality between the objects being compared? If I had asked the students to compare granite and gneiss by constructing and using a Venn diagram, how would they have determined to what extent to overlap the circles? The Double Bubble Map clearly was a more "user-friendly" tool for the students to manipulate as they compared granite with gneiss; it developed naturally from the separate Bubble Maps they had created and was more in keeping with a constructivist approach to learning. Following this first lesson with rocks and minerals, the students had opportunities to observe and describe the properties of 10 other types of rock including conglomerate, sandstone, pumice, obsidian, slate, shale, limestone, marble, basalt, and granite schist. These additional rock explorations set the stage for the second lesson (a week later), when the students sorted and classified the 12 kinds of rock according to their own classification systems. I then introduced the Tree Map that supported students with another key scientific process, categorization, or the creation of taxonomies.

As I reflect on my efforts at using these four visual tools, I find the insights gained and discoveries made about the relationship between visual tools and teaching, learning, and assessment to be both rewarding and challenging.

As this practical investigation shows, Bob and his students were able to fluidly move *with* their thinking to the conceptual outcomes of this discovery process through the use of multiple Thinking Maps. Even though Bob's lesson plan was linear, the kind of scientific thinking and discovery required was not; students needed to flexibly pattern information in different forms—as maps—to construct understandings. They could evolve ideas from brainstorming to the development of a rubric and finally to the creation of a taxonomy: a Tree Map. During this process, the students also used the Frame of Reference to reflect on the content and experiential background that influenced their perceptions.

MAPPING A BIOLOGY TEXTBOOK

Now let's shift from second graders who were novice users of Thinking Maps to an honors biology student and expert in the tools who mapped out an *entire* biology textbook, independently, over the course of a year. Some years ago, we received a document from a high school biology teacher outside of Chicago who, along with her colleagues, had systematically trained all of the students in the school to use Thinking Maps and Thinking Maps software (Hyerle & Gray Matter Software, 1997, 2007) at a very high level (see Chapter 10, "Thinking Technology"). The examples shown in Figures 9.5, 9.6, and 9.7 were excerpted from a much larger document containing over 40 Thinking Maps that had been generated using the software during the yearlong course. All eight maps were used at different times by the students and teacher as formative assessments as the year progressed. With most chapters, the students decided which maps best reflected the key information in the text and, with accuracy and great clarity, displayed, for example, types of muscle cells and their properties using a Tree Map, the cycle of cells using a Flow Map, and dozens of intricate interrelated parts of a muscle using a Brace Map.

Figure 9.5 Tree Map of Muscle Cell Types

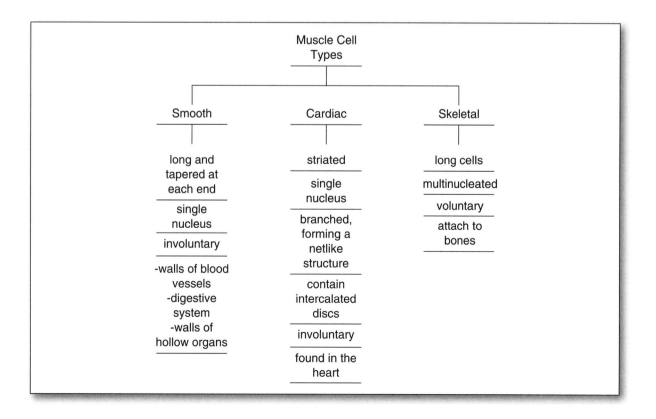

Figure 9.6 Cycle Phases Using a Flow Map

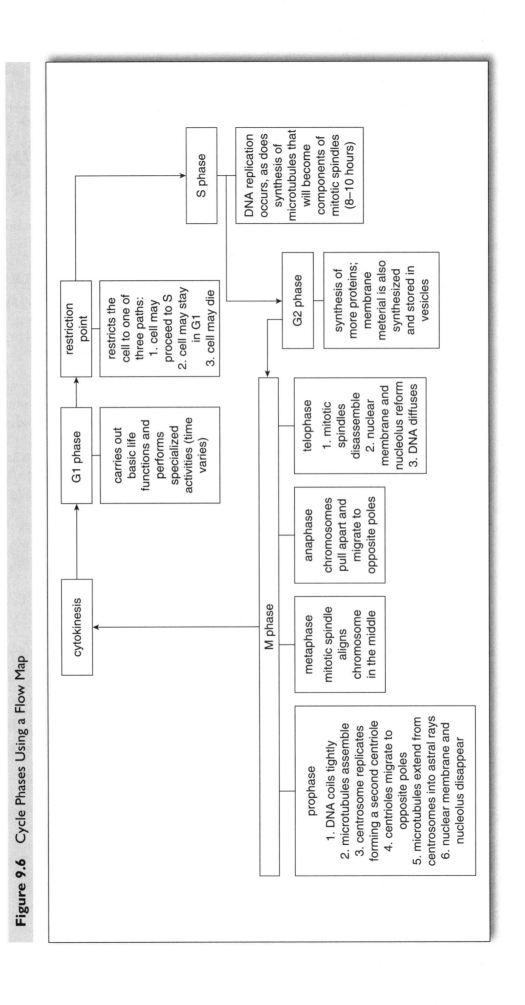

Figure 9.7 Brace Map of a Muscle

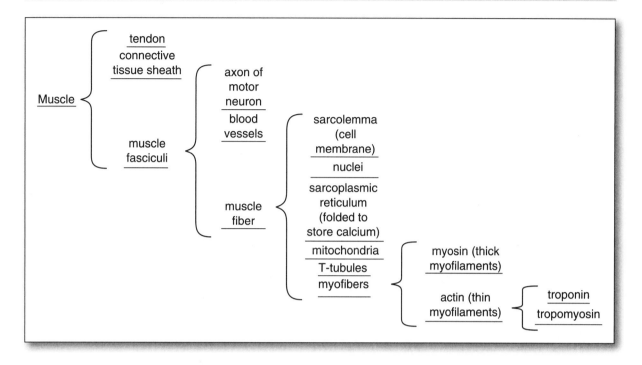

In addition to the examples shown, this student was also able to show that she could map out the feedback loops of different body systems using a Multi-Flow Map, comparisons of different processes using a Double Bubble Map, and properties of unique parts of the body using a Bubble Map. By midterm and at the end of the year, with her notes contained in maps reflecting the academic language and the conceptual content of the chapters, she was able to spread her documents out for review for exams. Her teacher was also able to *assess* how this student drew the information and scientific language in the chapters together conceptually as the year progressed.

STUDENTS THINKING LIKE SCIENTISTS: NOVICE TO EXPERT

From rocks to human biology, the two examples above from second grade and high school reveal that all of these students were working at higher orders of thinking relative to the developmental level of the scientific concepts being taught and assessed. These experiences also exemplify the key aspects of the five qualities of the Thinking Maps language that support students to move from novice to expert thinkers. As discussed in Chapter 1, Thinking Maps are graphically consistent, flexible, developmental, integrative, and reflective, and these five dimensions offer a way of analyzing students' evolution from novice to expert users of the maps.

Consider the accumulated work of the high school student who mapped her biology textbook as an example. The *graphic consistency* and *flexibility* of each tool enabled the student to start with different graphic primitives and expand each map while holding onto the basic forms. Because of the common graphic form for each map, the student's teacher and peers could easily "read" and assess the map for factual content, conceptual clarity, and interpretation. This student also showed the advanced developmental progression from learning the basic elements of each map to complex applications, in this case using Thinking

Maps software. We see this *developmental* aspect of the maps as first-grade students, college students, and school administrators alike are able to use each map in novel applications. Given a full view of the 40 pages of Thinking Maps developed by the high school student over the course of the year, we also witness both the *integrative* and *reflective* dimensions of the language. She was able to integrate multiple maps (e.g., a Tree Map on types of cells, a Brace Map of the anatomy of a muscle, and a Flow Map of the cycle of a cell) and developed a deeper understanding of how this information is interdependent. The 40-page document also shows that through the rich mapping of content knowledge, this student was able to work across multiple types of map representing different knowledge structures in the sciences as noted in Figure 9.1: properties (Bubble Maps), comparatives (Double Bubble Maps), taxonomies (Tree Maps), anatomy (Brace Maps), sequences (Flow Maps), and physiology (Flow and Multi-Flow Maps).

Ultimately, we want students to become self-assessing and develop the capacity for critical examination of research, including being able to detect their own biases for how they are interpreting knowledge presented to them. The high school student, along with her teacher, could use the maps for what Arthur Costa (personal communication) has called "displayed metacognition" and "bifocal" assessment (Chapter 3). This is an example of how students can actually *see* the development of content/conceptual knowledge by focusing on the development of thinking patterns. Most often in classrooms content knowledge held in the minds of students is assessed using various methods—including linear written essays, isolated problem-solving formats, projects, and multiple-choice items.

Yet this is not enough, because ultimately we envision students as citizens in the 21st century being able to grapple with real scientific issues and problems confronting our world—and not just in classroom science labs but through inquiry processes and "the scientific method." The work presented above—an elementary-level "rock rubric" and samples of high school biology text "mapped out" from beginning to end—offer examples of foundational work for "thinking like a scientist." Yet the essence of scientific thinking is *inquiry,* the capacity to independently and collaboratively engage in the nonlinear processes of following your thinking to new discoveries. In the section that follows, Lou-Anne Conroy goes deeper into this process with an analysis and reflections on the use of Thinking Maps.

THINKING MAPS FOR INQUIRY-BASED LEARNING IN SCIENCE

By Lou-Anne Conroy, M.A.

While an educator who participated in a science inquiry course I taught was at home reviewing a video of a high school chemistry class, her 10-year-old son remarked, "Who is teaching the class?" This child's comment went straight to the heart of teaching science through the inquiry process. Teachers become facilitators as they provide the scaffolding necessary to question, explore, and guide. As I viewed the same video and watched the students make observations about chemical reactions and then design investigations around their own questions, I found myself applying the eight Thinking Maps to the process I saw unfolding and began to wonder again how we can more deeply and directly facilitate students' thinking.

In the video, as students in this ninth-grade chemistry class designed and shared their experiments, it was clear that they were *implicitly* applying the cognitive processes upon which Thinking Maps are based: These processes included categorizing observations made about an initial chemical reaction, sequencing the steps to their investigations, comparing and contrasting experimental results, preparing to organize the physical materials and equipment needed for investigations, defining the chemistry they were exploring, and drawing analogies to other experiences in chemistry. I immediately could see that these fundamental thinking processes would come to the surface *explicitly* using visual patterning and thus engage students at a deeper level.

For most of my career as a public school teacher, I spent my summers immersed in scientific research at Woods Hole Oceanographic Institution, Woods Hole Marine Biological Lab, and Dartmouth College. I loved the opportunity to surround myself with people who were always figuring something out about the living and physical world, asking questions, debating results, pushing each other to explain and clarify, and creating an order out of what seemed like chaos. I vowed to create a classroom experience where such energy and passion could thrive. Each experience gave me the opportunity to develop inquiry-based units connected to my research. I developed units around paleoclimate research, cephalopod ecology, and river ecology. These experiences were my inspiration to continue infusing my science teaching with genuine research and to encourage all learners to dare to step out of their comfort zone in terms of learning and risk discovery.

With the perspective of 25 years of teaching science to a wide range of students from a variety of socioeconomic backgrounds and rural, suburban, and urban communities, I have found that my work with Thinking Maps has transformed the "tool kit" I carry. Thinking Maps allow students to map out their thinking in nonlinear ways and see the rich complexity and simplicity of the ecosystems they impact, live in, and depend on.

Every step of the inquiry process lends itself to Thinking Maps. As students pose questions, gather background knowledge to a problem, formulate hypotheses, design methods and their data collection format, troubleshoot, revise steps, and share results and new questions, Thinking Maps help both individuals and the community of learners to see the thinking. In a busy science room, students are always discussing, showing, explaining, and revising. Inquiry science invites sharing of one's thinking for peer review and for general camaraderie around discovery. Thinking Maps complement what Pat Clifford refers to as the "public space" in classrooms where students are assessed not only in the very individual space of tests, quizzes, and lab reports but also in the realm of collaboration and sharing of ideas (Clifford & Marinucci, 2008). As inquiry-based teaching and learning take learning from the front of the classroom to the heart of the classroom, Thinking Maps are the tool to facilitate this process.

As classroom teachers witness, most students are excited about science and the possibilities of exploring questions they have about the world around them. Too often science educators deaden the process of inquiry by using only one tool for both formative and summative assessment of the progress and success of a student's relationship to the varied fields within science. This common assessment tool is the lab report. It doesn't take too long for teachers to realize that if they are going to hook students on science, they must use a variety of tools to help them both communicate their thinking and learning and show their thinking in both linear and nonlinear ways. Thinking Maps are a natural visual language for inviting all learners into what should be experienced as an exciting world of scientific exploration. This language directly facilitates the kinds of nonlinear thinking learners need to do to truly *show* their scientific thinking. Instead of providing them with only one way to organize and communicate their ideas, questions, and findings, Thinking Maps allow students to see, in multiple ways, how they are thinking as they explore a topic. The maps help them communicate their ideas, design plans for the exploration of these ideas, and then share their ideas and results in a form from which they can then write a more formal scientific paper if necessary. Scientific investigations into the questions we ask about our world require a boldness and a daring to delve into the unknown and discover. As a science educator, my job is to facilitate this boldness in each one of my students regardless of how they learn or how they view themselves as "discoverers" when they first arrive in my classroom.

THINKING MAPS AND UNIT PLANNING

As a high school biology and environmental science educator, my work with Thinking Maps has transformed my approach to inquiry-based science. I have found it extremely helpful in the design of units, logistical planning for student field study, presentation/introduction of science concepts, and student investigation design. As an example, I will focus on a river ecology inquiry-based unit I developed.

I started by asking myself questions around the big ideas. I discovered that Thinking Maps are a natural tool for system-related science inquiry teaching. Scientists are faced with system-level problems never before addressed on such a global scale. Climate change, diminishing global freshwater supplies, and catastrophic depletion of the biodiversity of our ocean ecosystems are a few among many present and future problems that all citizens need to understand. To address these challenges, people will need to communicate beyond their disciplines as scientists join efforts with economists and businesspeople. With this in mind, Thinking Maps can be used in teaching science to equip students with the skills they need to envision and explore complex connections in their world.

The maps allow me to clearly follow the flow of my thinking. They are flexible enough to allow me to add ideas and move them around as my unit takes shape. Just like my lessons, they are dynamic in their ability to be seamlessly combined with other maps and to reflect the basic and complex ways I approach unit design. When planning my unit, a Flow Map like the one shown in Figure 9.8 allows me to see the flow of my ideas. I can link Tree Maps easily to the Flow Map events that then allow me to tease out and see the details of differentiated activities and assignments, identifying the formative and summative place- and project-based components and the state standards I am addressing in the activities. Since my units are a work in progress, where I change and add information as I think through the layers of my units, I find that the maps are flexible and allow for this dynamic approach to unit planning.

I can also post the unit Flow Map in my classroom so colleagues and students can see where I am heading or so administrators can observe my unit planning in a glimpse on any given day.

USING THINKING MAPS IN THE INQUIRY SPACE

Pat Clifford (Clifford & Marinucci, 2008) refers to designing science units to integrate "inquiry space." The following are examples of how specific Thinking Maps may be applied to the specific inquiry components in a river ecology unit I use with high school biology, environmental science, and aquatic ecology classes. For example, to introduce the concept of conflicting interests around a natural resource, the Circle Map and Frame of Reference in Figure 9.9 are assigned for students to become aware of different perspectives from which to think about the value of a river for different community members. Today's students' world demands understanding, engaging in empathy, and tolerating a variety of perspectives to grapple with the planet's challenges. It is important to include activities that address Frames of Reference in a formal way. Thinking Maps and the use of Frames of Reference are powerful learning tools that do just that. The Circle Map focus with individual students leads to a group activity through which students compare different Frames of Reference and identify similarities and differences using a Double Bubble Map. These maps are then the basis of group and class discussions around how best to preserve a local river ecosystem in light of the variety of uses and pressures on the river. In addition, students then look at the local Conservation Commission and state and federal wetlands regulations and discern whether or not they think the present regulations address the value of the river they have identified.

In Figure 9.10, the Bridge Map is used to help students learn about the functional ecology of a river's food chain. The function of an ecosystem refers to the complex relationships that exist between living systems. The Bridge Map represents an example applied to the ecology of

Figure 9.8 Planning River Ecology Unit

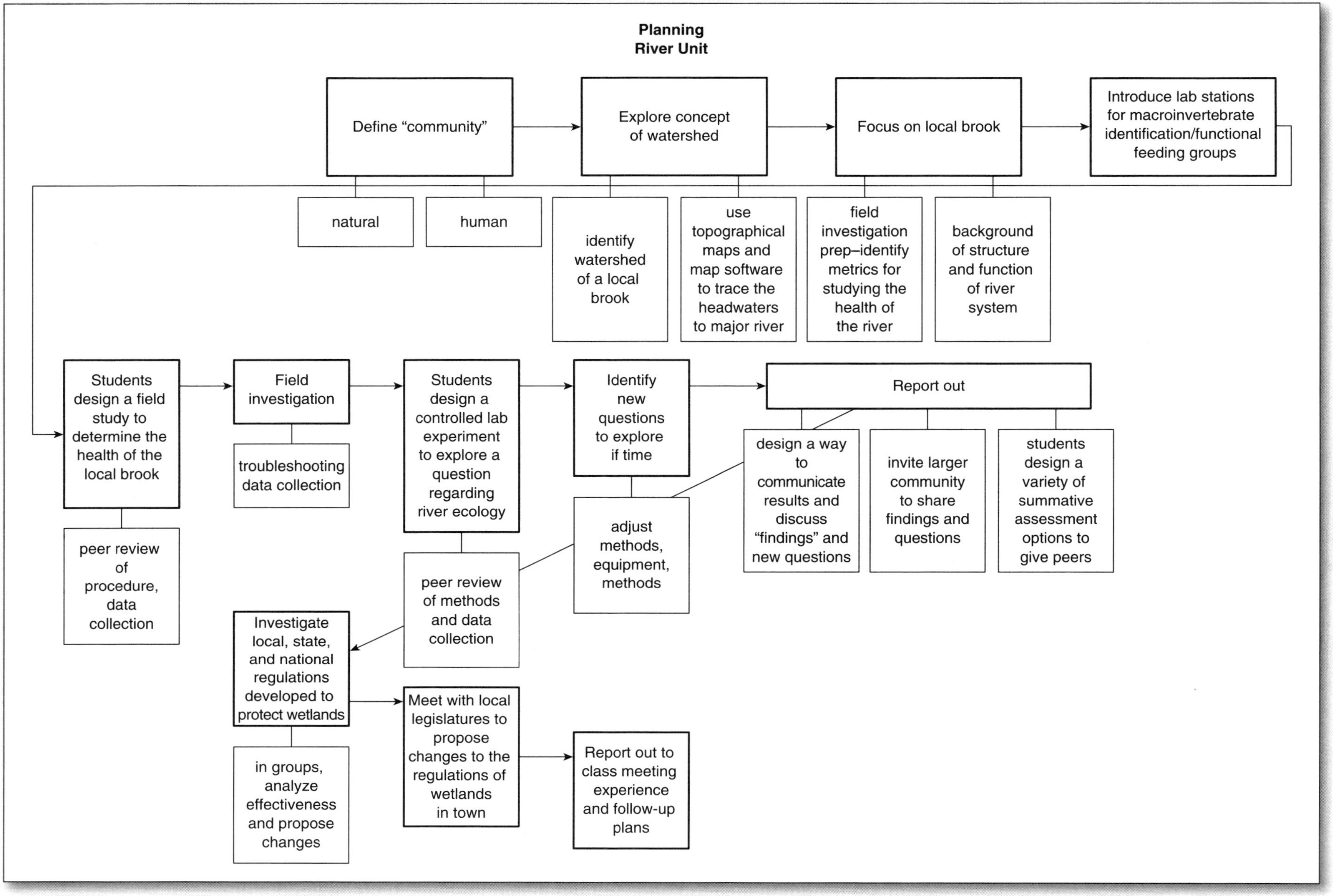

Planning River Unit

Define "community"
- natural
- human

Explore concept of watershed
- identify watershed of a local brook
- use topographical maps and map software to trace the headwaters to major river

Focus on local brook
- field investigation prep–identify metrics for studying the health of the river
- background of structure and function of river system

Introduce lab stations for macroinvertebrate identification/functional feeding groups

Students design a field study to determine the health of the local brook
- peer review of procedure, data collection

Field investigation
- troubleshooting data collection

Students design a controlled lab experiment to explore a question regarding river ecology
- peer review of methods and data collection

Identify new questions to explore if time
- adjust methods, equipment, methods

Investigate local, state, and national regulations developed to protect wetlands
- in groups, analyze effectiveness and propose changes

Meet with local legislatures to propose changes to the regulations of wetlands in town

Report out to class meeting experience and follow-up plans

Report out
- design a way to communicate results and discuss "findings" and new questions
- invite larger community to share findings and questions
- students design a variety of summative assessment options to give peers

105

the variety of macroinvertebrates and how they relate to other important feeding groups within the river ecosystem. By identifying possible food sources for the relating factor, students then make important connections to the human impact of clear-cutting around headwaters, logging along first- and second-order streams, nutrient loading of wetlands associated with rivers, and using in logging operations such ubiquitous herbicides as what is commonly known as Roundup. If I ask students to help me map the relationships of food sources to an organism, I can then pose questions regarding how and why they think the variety of human impacts would affect the system. New questions are then sparked and lead to interest and curiosity used in the design of their own field and lab investigations. Figure 9.11 is a Bridge Map used in a similar way to continue the discussion of food chains in a variety of wetland ecosystems that are interconnected from headwaters to the mouth of a river as it flows into the sea. In the case of Figure 9.11, the students *see* the effect of climate change on Atlantic salmon that reside part of the year near Long Island Sound as they migrate from breeding grounds in the upper reaches of the Connecticut River and its tributaries to the feeding grounds of the Atlantic.

I am convinced that sharing the natural world with students is a motivating hook to stirring a sense of awe and interest in the "wild" members of their communities. I can only hope that a sense of responsibility for the stewardship of these wild places is also cultivated. Within the river ecology unit, I bring my students out into the rivers as soon as possible; in fact, my whole yearlong curriculum is determined by the seasons. After scaffolding a variety of activities by bringing specimens from rivers and wetlands into the classroom in the form

Figure 9.9 "How Do Members of a Community Value a River?" Circle Map

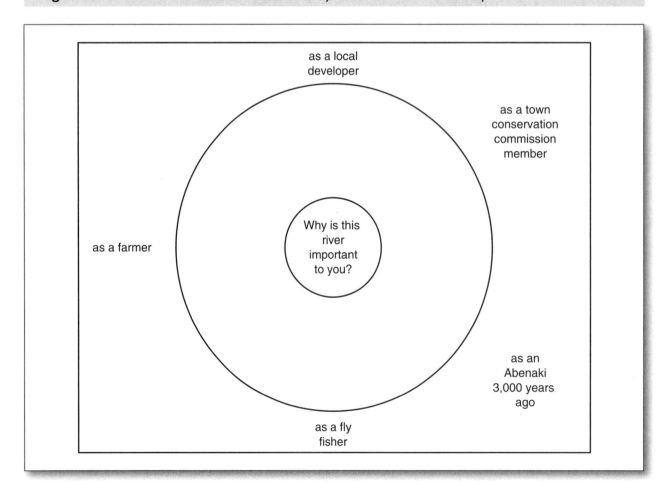

Figure 9.10   River Functional Feeding Groups Bridge Map

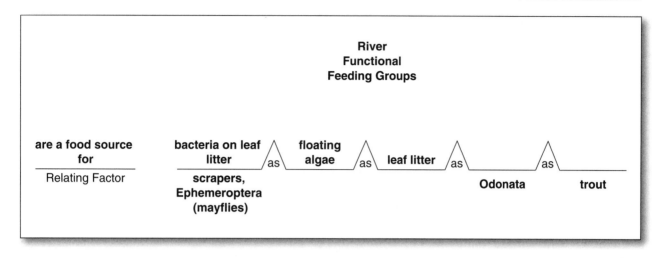

Figure 9.11   Aquatic Ecosystems' Food Chains Bridge Map

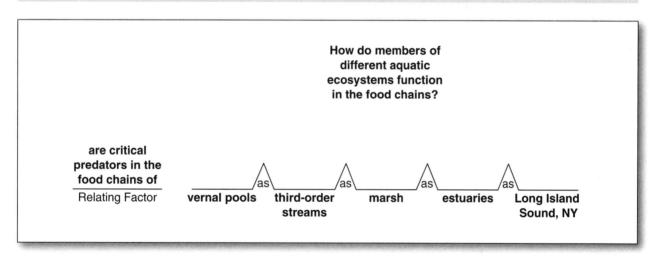

of bubbling aquaria and kiddie pools filled with pond water and water striders, diving beetles, and tadpoles, the students and I work toward planning a field investigation that considers human impact. Over the years, these activities have included the impact on the surrounding ecosystems from golf course maintenance, municipal sewage treatment, clearcutting, and agriculture.

Of course, a large part of fieldwork is the hands-on tools that students love to use for investigation, assessment, and collection of specimens. Figure 9.12 is a Brace Map that organizes all the field equipment necessary to investigate the health of a river using macroinvertebrates as an indicator. This map can be used as developed, or, better yet, student groups can create their own maps and then show them to peers for criticism and ideas for additional equipment. Again, the maps are easy to revise as students share in the seeing of the whole and parts of the practical needs of implementing an ecosystem field investigation.

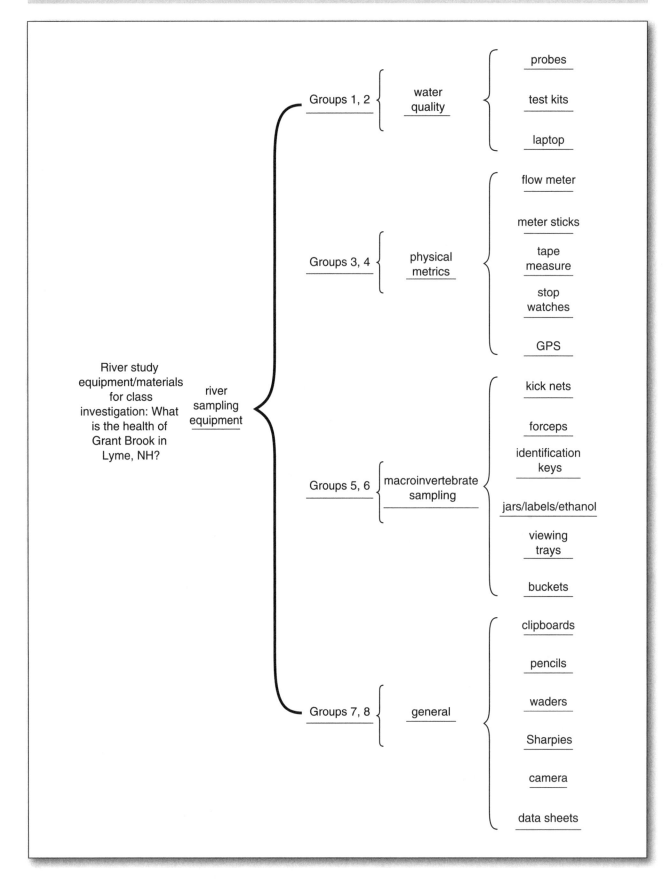

RIPPLE EFFECTS USING THE MULTI-FLOW MAP

Inquiry-based learning integrates "space" for genuine student-directed investigation into the curriculum. As students begin the investigation process, they first research the big ideas around their investigation. In my classes, after students have the opportunity to experience a field investigation in the river, they are given the chance to explore a specific question related to human impact on wetlands. One of the first phases of the investigation design process is background research. Students need to explore and then show that they have the background knowledge needed to design a meaningful investigation, one that reflects real-life situations in the natural world. Figure 9.13 is a Multi-Flow Map that a student used to see the cause-and-effect relationships between nitrogen loading in a local wetland and the degradation of the river habitat. Nitrogen loading and its impact on wetlands is the topic this student wanted to explore. As a member of this student's "peer review" group, in the company of classmates, I needed to be able to see the cause-and-effect relationships and make suggestions regarding investigable questions that would be feasible given the limitations of the classroom lab facilities and time availability. The student investigator would then use any feedback and suggestions to refine the question, design the methods of investigation and data collection formats, and share the troubleshooting and results.

Once students have background knowledge regarding a topic to investigate, a Flow Map helps them plan in sequence the major steps in the investigation (see Figure 9.14). A Flow Map is conducive to sharing "the plan" in a visual way that all students can easily understand; students elicit feedback, add to the map posted on the wall or computer, and revise based on peer feedback. The flexibility of the maps to reflect changes and the addition of details to each major step make it a valuable tool in the planning of an investigation. Given the permission and the opportunity to genuinely "put their heads together," students are great at asking probing questions and bringing to light unexpected perspectives and insights that can drive experimentation.

Figure 9.13   Background Knowledge for My Lab Investigation Multi-Flow Map

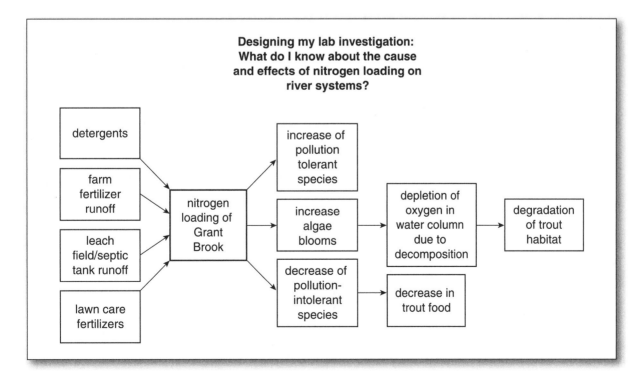

Figure 9.14 Designing My Lab Investigation Flow Map

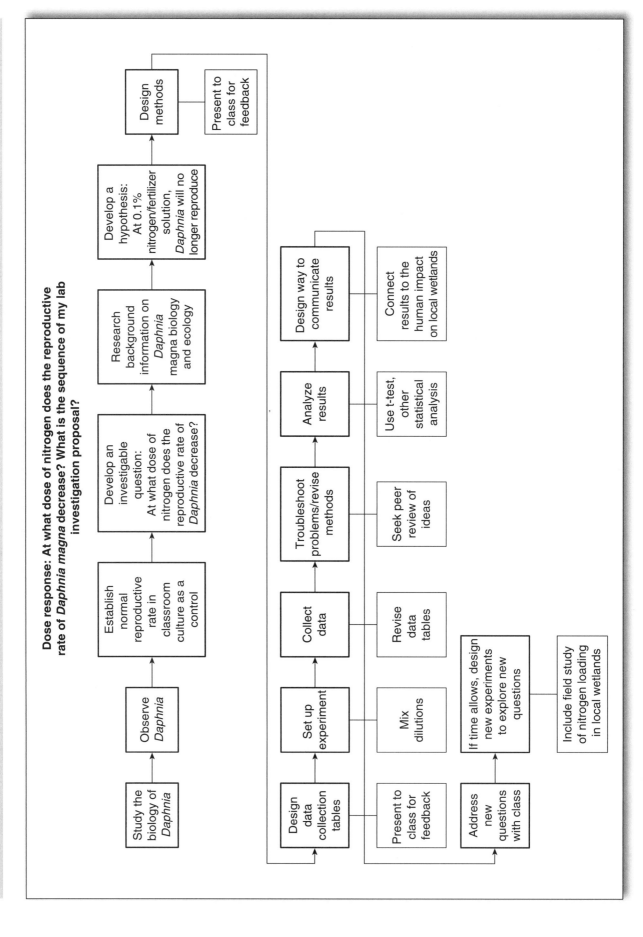

Dose response: At what dose of nitrogen does the reproductive rate of *Daphnia magna* decrease? What is the sequence of my lab investigation proposal?

THE SCIENTIFIC METHOD AS DYNAMIC THINKING AND INQUIRY

An all-too-common introduction of students to science involves "the scientific method" found in the beginning chapters of most science textbooks. This method is often described in lengthy paragraph format. Students see the process of scientific thinking as a list of steps to memorize for a chapter quiz. In reality, scientists approach problems and questions in nonlinear ways as they test out ideas on colleagues in the form of diagrams. Brainstorming sessions and background research into a problem are often more like complex networks and maps that have diverging and converging routes that link and inspire new directions of thought and approaches to addressing a question or solving a problem.

The 21st-century world and the problems educators face will require creative and innovative problem-solving approaches and collaboration at whole-system levels and across disciplines. Importantly, systems are based on complex patterns of information and patterns of different kinds as demonstrated in this chapter. Thinking Maps offer teachers and students an additional way of looking closely and over time at the development of thinking processes, and an opportunity to see what it actually looks like to think like a scientist.

With this in mind, Thinking Maps can be used in teaching science to prepare students for envisioning and exploring the complex connections in the world in which they live and in turn for contributing innovative solutions to a planet that will need them more than ever.

REFERENCES

Clifford, P., & Marinucci, S. J. (2008). Testing the water: Three elements of classroom inquiry. *Harvard Educational Review, 78*, 675–688.

Hyerle, D., & Gray Matter Software. (1997). *Thinking Maps* (Version 1.0) [Computer software]. Raleigh, NC: Innovative Sciences.

Hyerle, D., & Gray Matter Software. (2007). *Thinking Maps* (Version 2.0, Innovative Learning Group) [Computer software]. Raleigh, NC: Innovative Sciences.

Ogle, D. (1988, December–1989, January). Implementing strategic teaching. *Educational Leadership,* (46), 47–48.

10

Thinking Technology

Daniel Cherry, M.Ed.

KEY CONCEPTS

- Uniting networking capacities in the brain, the mind, and machines
- Making the explicit connection between higher-order thinking and technology applications
- Using a common language of thinking patterns through software for mapping the standards

THE BRAIN, THE MIND, AND MACHINES

It seems odd to think that soon we will be celebrating the 25th anniversary of the personal computer in public schools. I remember loading programs from the cassette drive on TRS-80s and Commodore PET (Personal Electronic Transactor) machines. I was even impressed that I could write a five-line program in BASIC (Beginner's All-purpose Symbolic Instruction Code) and have my name show up all over the screen. From the time I was an elementary school teacher beginning to use technology, to when I took a position as a district-wide technology coordinator, to my present work as director of New Hampshire School Administrators Leading with Technology (NHSALT, one of 50 state leadership programs funded by the Bill & Melinda Gates Foundation), I have been part of and observed with a critical eye the slow and, more recently, rapid progression of technology use in our classrooms.

The computer, in one of its earliest and simplest definitions, is an input, process, and output device. Many early computers were described as "thinking machines" that would ultimately mimic the sensory input, mental processing, and productive output of the human mind. Artificial intelligence programs were being created to challenge chess champions before the intelligence quotient was challenged and before a theory of multiple intelligences was offered. At this time the brain was also described as a black box that could be simply broken down into two separate hemispheres, but the new functional magnetic resonance imaging (fMRI) brain scanning tools show that *holistic* is a more accurate description of the complex circuitry of the human brain.

When a person works with computers, neurons accept visual input through the optic nerve, and the brain processes all of the shapes, colors, and bits of information at lightning speed. An interaction occurs between the user (a strange slang term often linked to people struggling with addiction) and the machine: a transfer or an exchange of data. Amazement and wonder take over. The wiring and firing of neural pathways in the brain are readied as the user tries to relate to and make conscious sense of the data presented. What does this mean? Thousands of calculations that would take weeks to accomplish by hand, the ability to accept variables and build projections, and answers, answers, and more answers. Think of the possibilities, think of the impact on education, think of . . .

WAIT! WHAT IMPACT ON EDUCATION?

Now here's a question worth considering. Schools have spent billions of dollars on wires, boxes, routers, hubs, displays, calculators, probes, and printers. Despite this effort and expense, at a time of high-stakes testing, accountability, and financial benefits from research-based best practices, few can respond with deep data when the words "show me the research" are uttered.

There is no way to tie computers to improved student outcomes without taking a great leap of faith. Just to say "kids love computers" gets us only halfway. So where can we begin to examine the connections and the impact of technology on higher-order thinking skills?

Jamie McKenzie (n.d.), a longtime leader and critical reviewer of educational technology, emphasizes that students need to be "info-tectives," savvy with a set of problem-solving tools and adept at moving information around and seeing information in different forms and from different points of view.

One of the keys to instruction and learning is the visual domain. Bridging technology to graphic representations is not something new. In fact, the two fields intimately overlap. Beyond a few bells and whistles and maybe downloaded music playing backup, most of the output from the computer is visual. This means that technology, graphic representations, and the human brain with its dominant visual nature are uniquely bound by visual representations, a meshing of circuitry.

Inspiration and OmniGraffle, now commonly used for webbing and creating visual organizers for content-specific tasks and processes, are highly flexible, open-ended graphical software programs, with infinite template starters. However, the critique of graphic overload as students and teachers are inundated with graphic organizers (Hyerle, 2009) is mirrored in the graphical creations on these software programs: There are so many graphics that the cognitive load on students (not to mention teachers) ultimately outweighs the benefit. There is little theoretical coherence to most graphic organizers as they show up in many basal texts and books of graphic organizers, and the same is true for graphical software programs through which an infinite number of graphics can be spun out on the screen.

Many of these graphics serve only one aspect of Bloom's (1956) taxonomy: They simply capture the factual knowledge within preformed organizational structures that have no real connection to fundamental thinking processes. Often these graphics structure the thinking for students rather than offering students flexible tools that can support them in consciously performing at higher levels of thinking. Chris Moersch (2002) refers to this as "chroming" a lesson: just adding something for the sake of using technology, but not bringing the lesson to any new levels of thinking.

TECHNOLOGY FOR THINKING

As education continues to identify best practices, and cognitive scientists discover more about how people learn and the workings of the brain, educators must focus efforts on delivering quality educational opportunities with tools that are common and transferable to learners in a variety of environments. Thinking Maps® software (Hyerle & Gray Matter Software, 2007), having evolved out of the language of Thinking Maps, is one pathway toward this outcome.

When I started working with teachers and technology through the use of Thinking Maps and the accompanying software, I was amazed that, given the same set of tools, first graders and eighth graders were sharing ideas about writing styles of authors. When the work was displayed in a hallway, third-grade students, not familiar with the sixth-grade content, could name the cognitive process that was being used to communicate information through a common Thinking Map. Students were given tools that organized and allowed them to communicate their thinking, and were motivated by the ability to create graphic representations of their thinking on the computer. We were creating a culture of thinking in our schools that integrated technology into the center of the community, improved pedagogy, and promoted thinking.

As a technology coordinator, I saw new effective communication across content areas and grade levels as parents, teachers, and students used a common visual language to teach and share complex thoughts and ideas. We offered Thinking Maps software training to parents. Some parents attended formal instruction in the evening at school, and many parents experienced informal sessions, with their children providing examples and teaching them how to use the software in the labs at school. Not only were students sharing maps with parents, but parents were sending maps to teachers! Administrators included maps in newsletters to describe processes for student placement. They also used maps to explain the results of programs on high-stakes tests. At an open house, parents and children explored the various uses of the maps on computers. We even had parents bring in examples of maps that they had created for use in their workplace. This seemed to be an integration point, a crossroads for best practices focusing on higher-order thinking, a delivery system using the personal computer, and a common visual language built on the cognitive processes embedded in Thinking Maps. This also produced a systemic change across one of the schools, Hanover Street School, that resulted in improved scores for students on the New Hampshire statewide test.

ELEMENTS OF THINKING MAPS SOFTWARE

Thinking Maps, a visual language, offers common symbols or elements and a flexible structure and is easily communicated and transferable in the learning community. For teachers, Thinking Maps software creates in the computer environment relevant activities to what is being used in the classroom. By the nature of the visual language, a Thinking Map asks students to define in context, sequence, compare or contrast, describe, identify whole-to-part relationships, determine cause and effect, create or identify analogies, or classify information. Planning units or developing lesson plans takes on a deeper focus when the cognitively based maps are used as a tool to inform instruction. The software is designed for both teachers and students through a three-window approach: a window for lesson planning for the teacher, a window for the dynamic generation of Thinking Maps by students, and a final window for students to transfer their maps into writing (see Figure 10.1). In the software environment, teachers can use the tools in the same way as students, or they can create plans and assessments or capture and collect evidence of success that can be shared with other educators.

A simple tool that can be used in very complex ways, Thinking Maps software allows students the flexibility to edit, rearrange, highlight, and embed thoughts and ideas. This means that the students are actively engaged and can interact with the information over time. Just as with word processing programs, which enable highly flexible movement of text blocks and facilitate editing to create multiple versions of a piece of writing, the software gives students and teachers a common platform for revising information. They can continually return to expand the maps as they assimilate new content knowledge or to transform the maps as they reconceptualize ideas.

Figure 10.1   Thinking Maps Software for Mapping the Standards

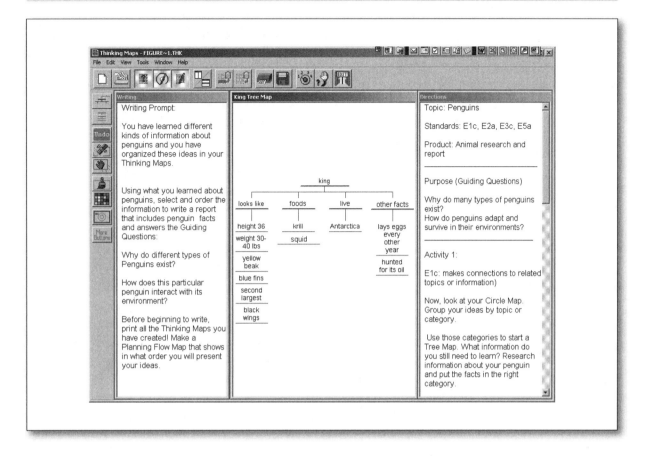

FROM THE INDIVIDUAL TO THE SYSTEM IN NEW YORK CITY

One inner-city school system took the step to unite teaching, learning, and state standards through Thinking Maps software. Community School District 27 in New York City was the largest of the city districts (before a recent reorganization) and was set in a diverse, low-socioeconomic-status area near Kennedy International Airport. Nearly 160 languages and dialects are spoken throughout this region. Many of the 37 elementary and junior high schools in the district were underachieving, and the standards movement was just on the horizon. During the 1997–1998 school year—after piloting and evaluating several approaches—the district adopted Thinking Maps as one way to help students, teachers, and schools through this process. With the support and guidance of Ken Grover, the deputy superintendent of Community School District 27, by the year 2000, most of the teachers had experienced Thinking Maps through direct training.

As an end-of-the-year assessment, all teachers were asked to submit examples of student work and their lesson design, with the New York City standards that were being met clearly identified on the top of each page. Lynn Kanter, a former reading specialist who became the district-wide Thinking Maps coordinator, produced a compilation of over 400 pages—all hard copy—of standards-based Thinking Maps lessons spanning all content areas and grade levels.

As teachers collected student work and designed engaging activities that integrated technology, the district team developed a database so that teachers in the district could tap each other's success and even see a sample of the type of work generated by a variety of students. *Mapping the Standards* (Curtis, 2004) was a pilot for the district, enabling it to continuously build an electronic database of successful learning experiences based on fundamental cognitive processes. The database of selected, high-quality lessons is searchable based on the standard(s) being met, grade, and curriculum area. Figure 10.1 is a partial example of how the three windows enable teachers to create standards-based essential questions, based on thinking processes and leading to the development of Thinking Maps, with a piece of writing as a final product.

The importance and implications of this project are multifold. As teachers experienced success, they were able to communicate the process they used to deliver the instruction, capture evidence of student work, and provide reflections or ideas about the learning they experienced. Within a school, teachers could build a dynamic library of successful lessons and activities. District 27 in fact began to share such lessons and maps with teachers throughout the district, and teachers began to dialog and discuss student work and pedagogy. Lessons could be opened up, adopted, modified, and exchanged, simply by using Thinking Maps software. This is not global "curriculum mapping" but detailed mapping of content-based thinking skills, units of study, and content standards.

EVOLUTION

Technology in the classroom is still in its infancy. For some teachers in District 27, this was the first time they had used a software program directly related to teaching practices and based on something that they were already using interactively in their classrooms. The software thus became a technology for learning, connected to the classroom and teaching experience, and not a disconnected process of learning a new technology.

Within our educational systems, advancements in the use of technology must combine with the necessary advancements in school climate, instructional practices, and instructional leadership. It will be in these high-functioning, well-coordinated environments that our students will have the greatest opportunity to succeed. Thinking Maps and Thinking Maps software compose a set of tools to integrate technology with pedagogy focused on higher-order thinking with the potential to create positive, systemic change in education. The dynamic visual circuitry of Thinking Maps creates an overlap between the human brain and the technology of the computer. These tools provide a crossroads—a nexus between brain, mind, and machine—for efficiently and effectively organizing, understanding, and communicating thinking within a classroom, across whole schools, and around the world.

REFERENCES

Bloom, B. S. (Ed.) (with Engelhart, M. D., Furst, E. J., Hill, W. H., & Krathwohl, D. R.). (1956). *Taxonomy of educational objectives: Handbook: Cognitive domain.* New York: David McKay.

Curtis, S. (2004). *Mapping the standards.* Raleigh, NC: Innovative Sciences.

Hyerle, D. (2000). *A field guide to using visual tools.* Alexandria, VA: Association for Supervision and Curriculum Development.

Hyerle, D. (2009). *Visual tools for transforming information into knowledge.* Thousand Oaks, CA: Corwin.

Hyerle, D., & Gray Matter Software. (2007). *Thinking Maps* (Version 2.0, Innovative Learning Group) [Computer software]. Raleigh, NC: Innovative Sciences.

McKenzie, J. (n.d.). *From now on: The educational technology journal.* Retrieved October 20, 2010, from www.fno.org

Moersch, C. (2002). *Beyond hardware: Using existing technology to promote higher-level thinking.* Danvers, MA: International Society for Technology in Education.

Section 3

Uniting Whole Learning Communities

11

A First Language for Thinking in a Multilingual School

Stefanie R. Holzman, Ed.D.

KEY CONCEPTS

- Results from an inner-city school with students learning a second language while differentiating instruction with a common language
- Moving expectations to a higher level across a low-performing school
- Changing school climate and culture toward higher-order thinking and literacy development

BREAKING THE RULES FOR CHANGE

"But I already use graphic organizers in my class," was the cry from my staff. As a first-year principal, I was breaking the most basic rule in the book for new administrators. I was immediately changing the mind-set of the culture—the way we do things around here—and I was making all these changes rapidly. A dynamic set of tools for activating the mind and directly influencing performance, Thinking Maps® were included in these changes. This was not an easy thing to do. Many of the teachers in this urban, inner-city, K–5 school of 1,200 minority students (85% of whom were entering with Spanish as their primary language) thought they were already getting the best out of their students. As the newcomer to the school, I had expectations that students should be achieving at higher levels than current test results indicated.

My high expectations are rooted in an understanding of what many of us who have attempted to learn a second language know: Learning content while learning a second language is a complex process. It is frustrating for a child to have ideas, vocabulary, and rich patterns of thinking in one language that are not immediately translated and understood by teachers in the context of the classroom. This is because the acquisition of a second language obviously gets in the way of students' thinking and learning. The Thinking Maps become a translator of language and thinking from one language-mind (Spanish) to another language-mind (English). Thinking Maps became our *first language* for thinking, thus supporting the languages, content learning, and cognitive development of our multilingual population.

My experiences from seeing the maps in use in other schools in Long Beach Unified School District made me believe that our students would learn the maps, and the result of all this would be higher academic achievement. This did happen. The numbers are in from the standardized tests given in California. The state has a very complicated formula to determine expected growth. Roosevelt Elementary School was expected to gain 11 points overall. We exceeded that goal with a 60-point gain. Not only did the school as a single unit make growth, but so did our significant subgroups: Hispanic students, English-language learners, and students of low socioeconomic status as determined by free lunches. In addition, with the implementation of the No Child Left Behind legislation, the expectation has been that 13.6% of the students in our school should meet the standards in language arts (including reading, vocabulary, spelling, grammar, and punctuation) and that 16% should meet the standards in math (including basic math facts and word problems). If a school does not meet the expectations, then it is identified as a program-improvement school and must take a number of corrective actions. As of this writing, and with two of our four tracks' test results in (including tracks with literacy classes for retainees and for students who entered school in fourth and fifth grade with no English skills), the results demonstrate that we are clearly not in program improvement.

Ironically, my intent as the instructional leader of Roosevelt Elementary School was initially isolated on these tools for a direct and immediate impact on student performance. What I did not realize and could not foresee were the deeper effects on the development of teachers across our year-round, multitrack school as a result of the use of Thinking Maps in their classrooms. I discovered that from an administrator's point of view, Thinking Maps did much more than what I had understood from both practical and theoretical points of view. First, there are changes in how teachers learn and teach and evaluate student work, especially with differentiated processes for our second-language learners. Second, there have been shifts in the culture and climate of our school, most obviously in the quality of professional conversations that now rise to the surface (see Chapter 17, "Mentoring Mathematics Teaching and Learning"). Third, there is a new level of access and discourse in the areas of teacher evaluation and accountability, which has led to a higher quality of teacher decision making. All of these changes—often referenced as keys to school change—will continue to have a long-term positive outcome on the academic achievement of the students at my school beyond the direct application of these tools by students to academic tasks and tests.

It is important for me to restate that I brought Thinking Maps into this school not for the purpose of bringing about change in these three areas but for an immediate shift of student performance that could cascade over time. Below are my discoveries about the interdependent ripple effects that I found in these other areas of teacher learning (including higher-order thinking for English-language learners), school culture, and accountability.

TEACHER LEARNING

The work of teaching is not only difficult, but it is also fast paced. It is the exceptional teacher who is self-reflective and aware of metacognitive processes (see Chapter 16, "Inviting Explicit Thinking"). Too often teachers are so focused on working with students that they rarely turn inward to notice what and *how* they are thinking. Yet I believe our students should be learning to do what we adults do as we internally process our experiences. Our internal dialogue and thinking are often hidden away, as are our emotional states, but teachers need to let students know what is happening in their heads; this can't happen if teachers are not aware of what they are doing. Once my teachers began learning Thinking Maps, they suddenly realized the types of thinking that were flowing through their minds and how the maps can show the students their adult thinking strategies and processes.

When my teachers became aware of their own thinking processes and how the Thinking Maps can communicate these to their students, they were so surprised that they had to check with someone to see if "they were doing it right." One very experienced teacher had an insight during a lesson about "the city and the country" in her first-grade class of English-language learners and came to me to check in. Lots of conversation had happened during her lesson, but at the end of the lesson, she realized that she could have organized this information into a Tree Map.

An example of this is the Tree Map created by a cooperative group about an emotion that surfaced during the reading of a Junie B. Jones book (see Figure 11.1). These five students were able to use the map to organize their thinking about anger: what it is, references to characters in other books who show anger (text-to-text connections), what it looks like, and, then, things that one would say when angry. "Mr. Angry" is at the top of the tree. By visually modeling a process for thinking through ideas, and even working through the content of emotions, a teacher can let her students know how she had organized this information in her head. The students *see* thinking evolve and then use the tools independently and in cooperative groups. Language and cognitive development then go hand in hand.

Figure 11.1 "Angry" Tree Map for Writing

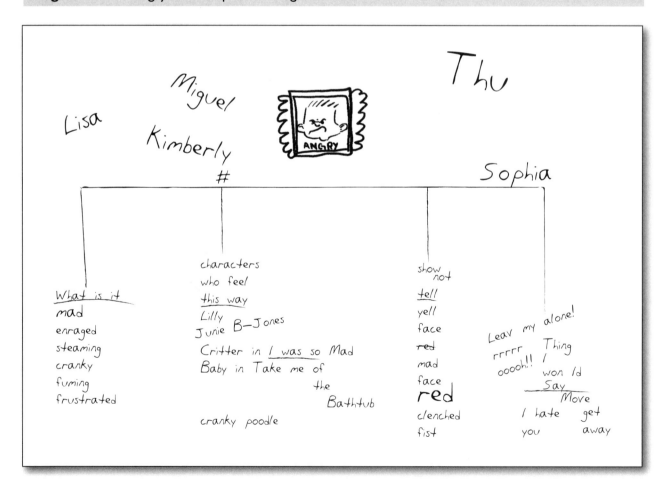

TEACHERS TEACHING AT A HIGHER ORDER

The capacity for students to be able to apply higher-order thinking skills is referenced everywhere as an ultimate goal of school outcomes in content standards, in textbooks, and on standardized tests. Most teachers are aware of a hierarchy of skills as referenced in Bloom's (1956) Taxonomy of Educational Objectives. For example, they know that synthesis-level questions are more complex than knowledge, or fact-based, questions. However, many teachers are not as cognizant of the kinds of thinking associated with higher-level thinking skills. For many, learning the Thinking Maps was the first time teachers actually had a clear understanding of specific types of thinking skills, how the skills interrelated and transferred across disciplines, and, most important, how the skills worked together to engage and sustain higher-order thinking on a day-to-day basis in classroom settings.

After the training, the positive energy from the teachers from this new understanding and related tools immediately transferred itself to the students in their classrooms. This is because these teachers realized that the focus was on immediate use and translation for students. When I walk into classes and I want to know what kinds of thinking the students are learning about and how they are applying these foundational skills to content learning, my teachers can now identify this because they know Thinking Maps. They can also tell what kind of thinking the students are expected to use. Importantly, Thinking Maps were used to promote critical thinking skills even for students who were still acquiring English.

All students in Grades 1–5 were tested on a standardized test in reading and math, and students in Grades 2–5 were also tested on the California standards test. Much of the math section includes reading. The teachers taught students to analyze the type of math question they needed to solve—for example, comparison, whole to part/part to whole, relationships, patterns, and so on—and the map associated with each. Once the students understood the five kinds of "story problems," they were able to tease out the critical attributes of these and apply them to the test. For example, in response to the word problem shown in Figure 11.2,

Figure 11.2   Math Problem-Solving Flow Map

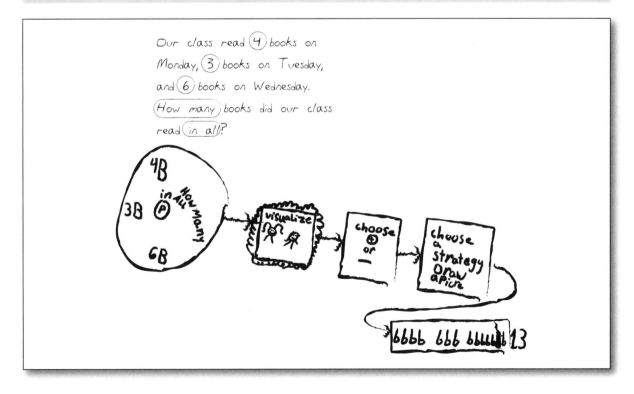

one first-grade student selected the key information from the problem using a Circle Map and then used the Flow Map to show the steps and the strategies involved in solving the problem based on the information in the initial Circle Map. The change in students' ability to do these problems made a significant difference between last year's and this year's school scores.

Each year in our district, students are also required to take a writing test that is scored on a holistic scoring rubric. The task is response to literature, which parallels one of the state's required tasks. Although primarily a reading task, students must read a passage and then respond to a prompt. In Grade 1 at my school, students had to read a story and then demonstrate their understanding of the text by using a Thinking Map to demonstrate the sequence of the story and then show how the characters changed over time. Most students used a Flow Map and then a Bubble Map as their response to the task. This type of task gave us insight into the students' comprehension both at a knowledge level (the sequence) and at deeper levels (how the character changed over time), without burdening them with having to write a complex essay.

This was especially helpful for teachers in analyzing the understanding of the English-language learners. The use of the Thinking Maps for this task also enabled the students to read more critically on the standardized test. Kristin Tucker, a first-grade teacher, reflected that "the Thinking Maps took the English-language learner to the highest level of thinking . . . in a very simple way. I didn't have to explain in words what I was doing; instead I just exposed the students to the maps, and the students just 'got' them very easily. It was so easy that students quickly learned to combine maps by themselves." This facilitated student learning of content, and the explicit transfer of thinking skills by students also provided her with additional time to teach!

Other teachers commented on how they noticed that the type of thinking used in one curriculum could be used in another. Because the teachers were able to make these connections, they were able to help students make the same connections. The results were that students were able to more quickly learn the content once they understood the underlying types of thinking they needed. Instead of teaching specialized skills and strategies particular to one content area, teachers began to generalize these deeply within and across disciplines.

DIFFERENTIATION OF INSTRUCTION AND ENGLISH AS A SECOND LANGUAGE

Over 85% of the students who enter kindergarten in our school speak Spanish as their primary language. By law, we are required to differentiate the instructional practices based on the level of English-language proficiency of students. Theoretically, differentiation seems so simple: Teach differently to different students based on their individual needs. Easier said than done. However, one of the differences that Thinking Maps has made at my school is that teachers teach the same content to various groups in their classroom, but they have begun to provide alternative means for students to access the content and show what they know. For example, some teachers expect students to use the Thinking Maps as processes to a final product, while others expect students to use the tools as a final product to demonstrate their thinking and comprehension of the content.

In one of the third-grade classes, the students were expected to understand the similarities and differences between two planets. All students were required to complete a Double Bubble Map comparing and contrasting the two planets, which was the stated outcome of the lesson. However, to differentiate the lesson, students who were fluent in English were also expected to write a report that contained this information. Students less fluent in English needed only to create the Double Bubble Map. The teacher was able to evaluate the factual and conceptual learning by every student using either strategy (the map alone or the map and writing). With fluent English speakers, she was also able to evaluate their ability to communicate their learning in writing, something she already knew the less fluent English speakers would not yet be able to do. Of course, it is also essential to have the students who are not fluent in English begin to write from the Thinking Maps, as this provides the bridge from their primary language to the mainstream spoken and written form. As a first language for thinking, the maps became vocabulary builders, visible organizers, and starting points for writing in a second language.

The important point here is that the teachers are able to assess content learning and use student maps as data points to see whether or not language is getting in the way of understanding or if there are content misconceptions that need reteaching. It is often difficult to determine how much limited English-proficient students understand of what is taught. If a teacher wants to know what a second-language learner has learned, does the teacher ask the student to use the second language if the student does not have verbal or written fluency? If assignments ask them to write what they know, these students often drown in the English language. They have to figure out the vocabulary, the syntax, the spelling, and the punctuation of English and at the same time remember the content they have learned. The results are that teachers often evaluate the students' English skills and sentence construction and not their content knowledge or their reasoning. However, when teachers ask students to use Thinking Maps to demonstrate what they know, the students do not have to focus on English and can use their mental energies to communicate what they know about the content. They do not even have to use words to convey this information. In most cases, Thinking Maps lend themselves to visuals (e.g., drawings or pictures from magazines) to communicate the content.

EVALUATION OF STUDENT WORK

One of the key components of the changes I focused on in my first year as principal was to insist that teachers be able to evaluate the degree to which students learned what was taught. In some cases, such as in mathematics, which has its own universal symbol system, this was easy to do with a pre- and posttest. We did not wait until the results of the state's standardized tests to determine if students achieved growth. Thinking Maps became a powerful strategy that teachers used to evaluate student learning. The results provided teachers with information that was used to monitor student growth and to adjust teaching.

Teachers used Thinking Maps in various ways to determine the quantity and quality of what students learned. Some used Circle Maps as pre- and posttests to determine what they learned. Other teachers gave students an assignment that required them to demonstrate their thinking. For example, one first-grade teacher asked students to retell a story. She was able to evaluate the students' comprehension based on the Flow Maps they created. A third-grade teacher asked students to determine the causes and effects of pollution on the ocean. It was quite evident who "got it" and who didn't. The teacher was able to quickly reteach those who needed it. In all these cases, our English-language learners were able to participate fully in the core curriculum.

CLIMATE AND CULTURE CHANGES

During this initial phase of training, I was impressed by the rapid, contagious nature of the spreading of these tools. The Thinking Maps kept "bobbing up" into other classrooms, even though not all teachers got trained immediately. It appeared that teachers were sharing ideas in the lounge, during grade-level meetings, or wherever they met. Teachers actually met on their own time to talk about professional concepts.

I realized that one of the unplanned benefits was that because Thinking Maps were so easy to implement, they could easily become the topic of professional talk. This occurred not only between pairs of teachers but between teachers who rarely had occasion to share ideas, such as a kindergarten teacher and a third-grade teacher. Suddenly, teachers had a first language for thinking in which to talk about student learning, one that was not dependent on grade level or content area.

Another change that occurred was that the teachers realized that the culture of the school was going to be one in which lifelong learning was not reserved just for students. The expectation was that teachers should be learning new strategies that help accelerate student achievement and that "doing things as we've always done them" was no longer acceptable. The difference between learning the maps and participating in other staff development was that these tools emulated adult thinking and strategies. These were then shared with students. Thus, the strategies were authentic. Rather than teachers learning a "canned program" that did not reflect what they as adults did and did not give them what their students needed, teachers were learning lifelong strategies for themselves and then teaching them to their students. As teachers began to experiment with the Thinking Maps in their own lives—such as making Tree Map shopping lists—they developed into the learning community that I was trying to foster at my school but never expected to get from these tools.

Another benefit I was surprised and pleased to see was that new teachers could participate in the discussions about high-quality tools as equals. The visual language and common vocabulary were not a mysteriously complex formula that created a wall between veteran teachers who had internalized a thoroughly unique and idiosyncratic teaching style and the new teachers and instructional aides who were just learning the ropes. With a common language, veteran teachers could model expert applications along a continuum—one rope—that novice teachers could easily grab onto and make their own (see Chapter 17).

TEACHER EVALUATION AND ACCOUNTABILITY

Not only can teachers use Thinking Maps to determine the depth of learning of their students, but this language also creates an easy opportunity for an administrator to determine teachers' depth of learning and implementation of Thinking Maps. This is because these tools are visual and become a running record of application, and because the ultimate end user is the student, not the teacher. Often teachers go to staff development workshops and come back excited about what they have learned. However, it is difficult to determine the quality and consistency of the applications over the short and long term.

A quick walk through a classroom looking for evidence of the Thinking Maps and talking with students gave me a good feel for how well, in what context, and at what level of thinking the maps were being used. However, the evidence became much more clear as I looked at student work, especially in writing.

As a school, we analyze student writing once a month. Teachers from the same grade level get together, score student work against a district-created rubric, and then analyze the work as to what the students do well and what still needs to be taught. Teachers who taught Thinking Maps to students as aids in writing found that the quality of student writing improved (see Chapter 7, "Empowering Students From Thinking to Writing"). These results were similar for students in kindergarten and in Grade 3. Teachers used these data to make professional decisions as to how to adjust their teaching to better meet the needs of their students. This was done without any intervention or pressure on my part. Teachers made these types of professional decisions based on the results from the student work—the holistic thinking translated into linear writing—from their class.

IMPLICATIONS FOR IMPLEMENTATION

The implementation of Thinking Maps at my school has brought changes that affect not only student performance as shown in the results presented above but also the quality of instruction and the culture of the school. I know that over time, I will continue to have the same high-level results as other schools in terms of academic performance for my students. I also know that the changes I see as Thinking Maps become a regular part of the instructional program will also become more deeply embedded in the culture of the school.

There are several dramatic changes I put forward during my first year as a principal that I regret. The implementation of Thinking Maps was not one of them. I asked my staff what they thought accounted for the growth in student achievement. Obviously, I wanted to make sure that we repeated these successful strategies. Every member of my staff responded that it was the implementation of Thinking Maps that made a significant difference in student outcomes. When we analyzed exactly how teachers used the maps, we found two patterns throughout the school. First, Thinking Maps were used across the curriculum in all grade levels including kindergarten. Second, Thinking Maps were used to promote critical thinking skills even for students who were still acquiring English.

Heather Krstich (who taught the third-grade combination literacy class with all the third-grade retainees and fourth-grade very limited English-language learners) suggested that the reason the Thinking Maps helped was that they gave the students a cohesive feeling across all the curricula. "The students did not feel [that the curriculum] was so segmented. They were able to focus on their thinking instead of on individual activities in each of the curricula. Thinking Maps gave the students a systematic approach to thinking that they can use over the years." She added that the English-language learners in her classroom had a cohesive strategy built on the language of the maps. "The maps have such a consistent language that students were able to concentrate on their thinking rather than what they were doing."

With this experience of implementing Thinking Maps, I also now have a standard by which I can compare other professional development trainings and other changes I plan to promote at Roosevelt Elementary School. This standard includes implementing changes that successfully affect student academic outcomes, teacher learning, reflection, accountability, and the school climate as effectively as this common language for learning, teaching, and assessing.

We now have this new standard in our school—including for our students—because we have a first language for thinking, whether it be in a first or second language for speaking and writing. This language will help us to think and act on complex problems—such as how to transform and continually grow in an inner-city environment—with the confidence that we will be able to see more clearly each other's thinking.

REFERENCE

Bloom, B. S. (Ed.) (with Engelhart, M. D., Furst, E. J., Hill, W. H., & Krathwohl, D. R.). (1956). *Taxonomy of educational objectives: Handbook: Cognitive domain.* New York: David McKay.

12

Feeder Patterns and Feeding the Flame at Blalack Middle School

Edward V. Chevallier, M.Ed.

KEY CONCEPTS

- Uniting students from an elementary feeder pattern using a common language for thinking and learning
- Using Circle Maps and Frames of Reference for identifying author's tone, mood, and style
- Note-taking and thinking skills development using multiple Thinking Maps®

After 10 years as a classroom teacher, I was offered two wonderful and challenging experiences, first as an elementary principal and then as a middle school principal. Through these positions I deepened my understanding of the complexity of instruction. I watched teachers lay a foundation for learning for elementary students, and as I entered my present position, I also saw that many of our middle school students needed a stronger foundation in skills to improve their learning that would stay with them throughout their educational and work careers.

My awareness of this deeper need grew over time from my classroom visits, walk-throughs, and supervision processes. I frequently heard frustrated teachers directing students to "take notes" as they were introduced to new information. I also heard my teachers lament that students didn't know "how to think" when they were challenged with new information and concepts. Over time I realized I couldn't recall any clear examples of explicit instruction in those two important areas—note-taking skills and thinking skills—even though teachers could well identify and articulate these problem areas.

It became clear that the very core of learning that I began to seek out was rarely found in these classrooms. I came to believe that the issue was larger than the individual teachers: They had never had a unified, consistent way of addressing thinking skills for learning that required sustained, consistent, direct, and differentiated instruction in these skills for all students across multiple years. The absent foundation was missing not because of isolated negligence, but because of an institutional blind spot that so many schools inherit from a structural problem of schooling. We have focused on content knowledge and content-specific processes in schools. The missing piece is a quality mental resource for explicitly addressing transferable learning-processing skills that transcend any one teacher's curriculum or the set, vertical path in a content area.

Through an event that can best be described as good fate, at a time when I was seeking solutions to these problems, I was introduced to Thinking Maps. This solution has been not a quick fix, but a systematic implementation over the past six years that has brought a unified language to this school. This is underscored by the successes I see on a daily basis and at the end of each year in test scores. In advocating for the adoption of Thinking Maps, my goal was to give individual students a set of tools they could learn as they came from different elementary school experiences and take with them as they continued their educational careers. What I did not foresee was that over the long term our campus would experience a less obvious, school-wide benefit: the development of a community language through which all of us could mature as individuals into a learning organization.

LIGHTING THE FIRE IN A MIDDLE SCHOOL SETTING

Blalack Middle School is a campus of approximately 1,100 students in Carrollton, Texas, a city just northwest of Dallas. As the city of Dallas continues to grow, Carrollton-Farmers Branch Independent School District has been quickly changing from a suburban, middle-class district that was once predominantly Caucasian to a diverse school district serving many different ethnic groups and a range of socioeconomic levels, with students in the district speaking 46 languages and dialects and representing 53 countries. Four very different elementary campuses feed into Blalack, creating a diverse mix across socioeconomic, racial, and cultural groups.

When the approximately 400 new students enter sixth grade at Blalack every year, our challenge is immediate: We must provide opportunities that allow all students to become a cohesive group—ready to learn and ready to succeed. We must help our students respect diversity and appreciate the strengths of their new classmates. Thus one characteristic of Thinking Maps that became an immediate enticement was the opportunity to develop a common language for our students. The phrase "and many shall become one" is incredibly apparent to a middle school educator. In *Leadership for Differentiating Schools and Classrooms*, Tomlinson and Allan (2000) identify a stark reality: Every three years, middle schools have a nearly complete turnover of their student populations and families, and thus new challenges for parental involvement.

My participation in an initial Thinking Maps training, before my faculty was trained, was an eye-opening experience. Three specific outcomes of using these tools were identified, and each has proven to be true over our years of implementation. I believe that these three outcomes have significant answers to many of the needs we have at our middle school and possibly most middle schools around this country:

• *Thinking Maps help students actively process information.* The use of the maps creates immediate and specific questions. In a middle school classroom, the constant challenge is maximum engagement. Used in even their most limited form, Thinking Maps ensure eight "ready" questions—questions associated with each of the eight thinking skills. Thinking Maps build a bridge from concrete knowledge to abstract concepts.

• *Thinking Maps bridge the divide between concrete facts and abstract thinking as a developmental necessity for adolescents.* Thinking Maps give students a flexible structure for creating their own vision of knowledge as they create their own maps from blank paper. Because no map is ever complete, this flexibility ensures that students at all levels of growth can be consistently challenged in their thinking, building from concrete information to concept formation.

• *Thinking Maps work as teaching, learning, and assessment tools.* The flexible configurations of the maps allow all teachers to contribute to creating applications within and across content areas. Students can successfully use maps as independent learners and thinkers to organize their thoughts for note taking, on formative assessments, and on summative assessments. Many of my teachers regularly ask students to create one or several Thinking Maps to show what they know as they are developing ideas, structuring an essay, or responding to the typical questions that appear at the end of most chapters.

EARLY LEVELS OF CHANGE AND CONCERN

In *Taking Charge of Change* (Hord, Rutherford, Huling-Austin, & Hall, 1987), considered by some to be the seminal work on change in education, the authors introduce the concerns-based adoption model (CBAM). In this model, a levels-of-use continuum gauges how people are using an innovation, from nonuse and orientation, through the middle stages of preparation and mechanical and routine use, to the upper stages of refinement, integration, and renewal. Our implementation of Thinking Maps has followed such a pattern.

In the early stages, the comfort level and range of implementation varied. Some teachers jumped in with full excitement and energy, while many teachers quickly moved from a level of orientation to a level of refinement and even integration within a very short period of time. Others were more reluctant. Their inconsistent use caused them to remain at the routine level. Nonetheless, as the implementation was campus-wide, all teachers incorporated the maps into their classrooms in varying degrees because of the training that was focused on students' developing automaticity with the tools.

The student-centered dimension of implementing the maps was never more evident than when one of our administrators confiscated a "slam book" early in the school year. A slam book begins when middle school students identify their "best friend for life." Using a notebook, the students begin corresponding on a regular basis, usually passing the notebook to one another in the cafeteria or hallway. At one point, an administrator came into possession of a slam book and found three high-quality examples of Thinking Maps as shown in Figures 12.1a–c. The student had begun the process of planning a party by identifying her "perfect circle" of friends by using a Circle Map and then used two Tree Maps to organize couples. As an administrator

Figure 12.1a Slam Book Circle Map for Automaticity

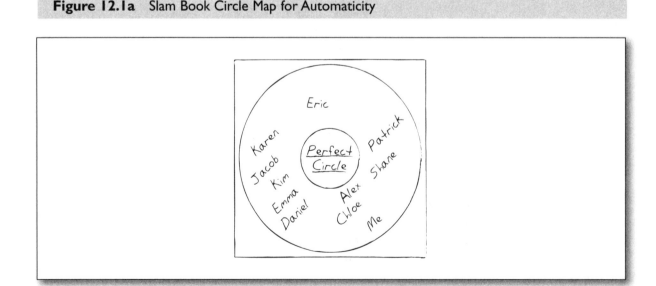

Figure 12.1b　Slam Book Tree Map for Automaticity

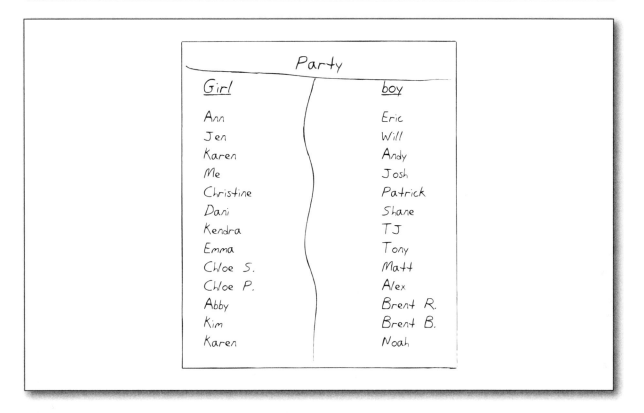

Figure 12.1c　Slam Book Tree Map for Automaticity

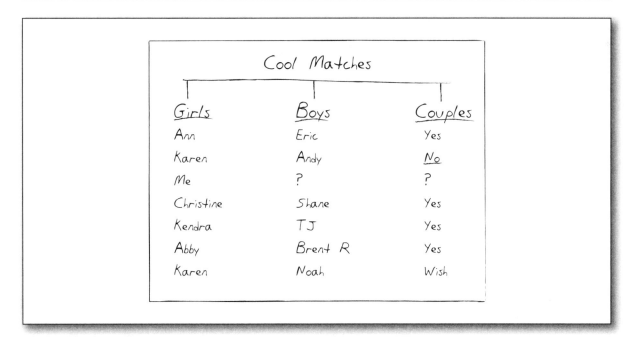

I could not have been more excited. I had been seeking an initiative through which adolescent students could learn tools for independently organizing notes and applying thinking skills, and I had found these tools.

COMMUNICATION FOR DIFFERENTIATION

All of these early events helped us to shift to the real challenge of implementation: moving from igniting the fire for a new initiative to fanning the flame. To increase effectiveness, the fanning process had to be ongoing, promote excitement, and document successes. In *Leadership for Differentiating Schools and Classrooms*, Tomlinson and Allan (2000) address the importance of communication as a factor in sustaining change. The issue of communication is addressed as it specifically pertains to parents and the public. The five qualities of effective communication are that communication should avoid jargon and focus on effects for students, be consistent, be persistent, be interactive, and take many forms. An exemplar of these interdependent qualities is clearly shown through the sustained efforts of implementing Thinking Maps at our school.

I. Avoid Jargon and Focus on Effects for Students

In this era of standards-based, test-driven education, it is important that we not lose sight of the fact that students must be given opportunities to be successful and leave us prepared to be successful at the next level. Educators in Texas and around the country are often driven by concerns about test results and the No Child Left Behind initiative. It is reassuring that we support our students to use Thinking Maps, knowing that these skills enable them to deeply process information and ensuring that these same tools directly impact their performance on state and other standardized tests. To verify this understanding with our staff, we used a professional development opportunity to review specific state curriculum standards and identify specific Thinking Maps that can be used to teach and assess each standard.

Teachers were asked to review the curriculum for the subject and grade level that they teach. For each curriculum indicator (or standard), teachers were asked to identify the underlying thinking skill and Thinking Map(s) that would be helpful in ensuring that students mastered the indicator. One example comes from Jennifer Farlow, a sixth-grade social studies teacher, and her students. By using the Tree Map as presented in Figure 12.2, students were

Figure 12.2 Social Studies Developing Countries Tree Map

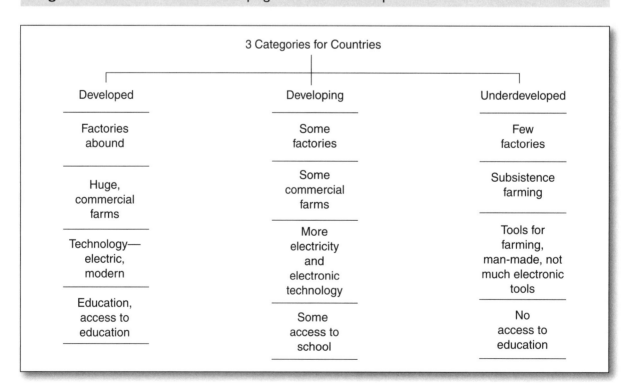

able to categorize information and get a visual depiction (and understanding) of three stages of economic development as they apply to countries. They were also able to clearly see specific factors of production as they apply to these stages. Using Bloom's (1956) Taxonomy of Educational Objectives as a guide, teachers were also able to identify the kind of thinking required by students in test questions and the direct application of the maps by students to the curriculum indicators that must be mastered.

2. Be Consistent

While we encourage creative use and flexibility of the maps, we also ensure that the common visual language has the consistency that enables complex applications. For example, when a question concerning sequencing is asked in a test situation—such as "What are the steps in the process of a bill becoming a law?"—we want students to identify the Flow Map as a common tool for understanding this process.

Brittnie Bragg, a language arts teacher, shared two examples that she regularly uses in her classroom. As students come into her room each day, they are asked to complete a warm-up Thinking Map on something they learned, read, or did in the previous class period. Over time, the directions progress from her assigning a specific Thinking Map to her instructions to "use any of the eight Thinking Maps to show me something you remember from the story we read last class period." These warm-up activities provide opportunities for practicing the maps and for practicing fluent, autonomous transfer of thought processes.

A second example stretches the students to even higher levels of thinking. In teaching and reviewing the challenging concept of recognizing the author's style, tone, and mood, Mrs. Bragg asks students to create a Circle Map divided into three parts as shown in Figure 12.3. In the center circle, the students write the title of the story. One third of the circle is segmented for style, one for tone, and one for mood. The students are directed to define each of the three

Figure 12.3   Tone, Mood, and Style in Language Arts Circle Map

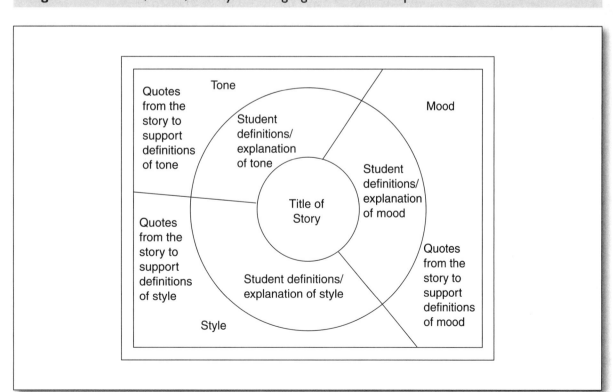

components as they are used in the story and, in the Frame of Reference, prove their definitions by identifying direct quotes or examples from the story to support their thoughts. Such an example underscores the importance of developing a common and consistent vocabulary in a middle school setting for foundational thinking skills and tools. Even with a common district curriculum, the abstract concepts of author's tone, mood, and style lend themselves to a variety of instructional interpretations across the four elementary schools that feed into our community.

3. Be Persistent

Persistence as a habit of mind (Costa & Kallick, 2000) for improved thinking and communication has been vital to the success of our campus implementation. Our efforts with Thinking Maps have been sustained over a period of six years, and to achieve this, several publicly stated expectations are emphasized and acted upon each year.

First, implementation is school-wide. All students, Grades 6 through 8, are reintroduced to the eight cognitive skills and maps during the first six weeks of every school year. Second, all teachers new to the campus are required to complete the introductory "Day One" Thinking Maps session conducted by a certified trainer. Third, the campus principal participates in all training. As active participants in training, campus administrators are positioned to serve as coaches in supporting teachers to sustain implementation.

4. Be Interactive in Implementation

The quality of implementation is sustained by interaction among all stakeholders in the process. Over the past six years, discussions have occurred within departments, in leadership teams, and in planning groups regarding the effectiveness of the maps. Teachers have assumed ownership of the implementation as they have created activities for classroom instruction. A yearly campus improvement plan, developed by a team of teachers and parents, includes specific references to the use of the maps throughout the instructional program.

In recent years, map activities have been used for our own leadership and professional development tools. For example, we have used the tools for a study of current professional literature, data disaggregation of state test scores, and school-wide goal setting. In the past few years, an ongoing process of "plan, implement, study, and revise" resulted in the adoption of the Thinking Maps language by the elementary campuses that feed into Blalack. Each year, a transition meeting of elementary fifth-grade teachers and middle school sixth-grade teachers is held, and Blalack sixth-grade teachers excitedly share the benefits of the Thinking Maps and the contribution they make to helping students achieve at higher levels. As a result, all of the feeder elementary campuses moved toward implementation, and now almost all students entering Blalack as sixth graders are Thinking Maps veterans.

5. Use Many Different Forms for Sharing and Celebrating

A visitor to our campus cannot leave without seeing the maps affixed to classroom bulletin boards, sprinkled throughout student notebooks, and displayed throughout the hallways. The integrated use of Thinking Maps software (Hyerle & Gray Matter Software, 2007) ensures that students can apply their knowledge in new ways and save an electronic portfolio of their thinking and content knowledge. Parent newsletters are another form of communication that is frequently used.

The power of sharing with parents surfaced during a Thinking Maps training I conducted for paraprofessionals who assist at-risk students in our inclusive classrooms. One of the Learning Center managers, who happened to be the parent of a former Blalack student, came to ask for a clarification of something that was discussed. During the conversation, she asked me if her daughter would be able to tell her what Thinking Maps were. Being a proud principal, I assured her that that would be the case. A few days later, I happened to see this parent again, and she excitedly shared with me that her daughter could indeed identify the maps as well as the thinking process for each map. My confidence in these maps as tools that would stay with students beyond our school was cemented.

FEEDING THE FIRE: CONFIDENCE AND CONTINUED SUCCESS

As our campus population has continued to change and our challenges have grown, the success levels of our students have continued to rise. This feeds the fire and our confidence as teachers, students, and administrators. Our teachers are ensuring that every child is challenged to succeed and is given the internal, intrinsic mental resources to contribute to that success. Mary LeRoy, a math teacher at Blalack and a Thinking Maps trainer, expressed this belief:

> When I see a student who has had a history of struggling with math attack a problem with confidence, both the student and I feel the success. Thinking Maps have created this confidence in many of my students. The maps have given my students a means of organization and a strategy to set up and solve a multistep problem, outline a project, and much more. Once upon a time, a struggling student would see a math test as a white sheet of paper with black letters and numbers and an automatic failure. Now, the same student sees the same test as separate problems, each giving a clue to the map to be used.

From that day, over seven years ago, when I realized that the twin problems voiced by teachers about the lack of note-taking and thinking skills by students might be resolved through Thinking Maps, I never imagined that this focus on fundamental thinking processes as tools could, from the ground up, help transform our school into a much richer learning organization. It took perseverance as educators to see the forest of diverse students also as individual trees growing with common needs. This common language enabled a student with special needs, who was struggling with a task assigned by his teacher in another math class, to finally look to the teacher with a simple question: "Can I use a Thinking Map to get started?"

REFERENCES

Bloom, B. S. (Ed.) (with Engelhart, M. D., Furst, E. J., Hill, W. H., & Krathwohl, D. R.). (1956). *Taxonomy of educational objectives: Handbook: Cognitive domain*. New York: David McKay.

Costa, A., & Kallick, B. (2000). *Activating and engaging the Habits of Mind*. Alexandria, VA: Association for Supervision and Curriculum Development.

Hord, S., Rutherford, W., Huling-Austin, L., & Hall, G. (1987). *Taking charge of change*. Alexandria, VA: Association for Supervision and Curriculum Development.

Hyerle, D., & Gray Matter Software. (2007). *Thinking Maps* (Version 2.0, Innovative Learning Group) [Computer software]. Raleigh, NC: Innovative Sciences.

Tomlinson, C., & Allan, S. (2000). *Leadership for differentiating schools and classrooms*. Alexandria, VA: Association for Supervision and Curriculum Development.

13

Becoming a Thinking School

Gill Hubble, M.A.

KEY CONCEPTS

- The 10-year development of a whole-school, integrated thinking-skills approach in New Zealand
- Using multiple maps for scientific problem solving
- How Thinking Maps® changed collaboration, communication, and performance across a K–12 single-sex girls' school

I have always thought that all schools could become "thinking schools"—schools that consciously and systematically focus on the development of cognitive and critical thinking for all students—via various pathways. St. Cuthbert's College in Auckland, New Zealand, the girls' school described in this chapter, piloted and evaluated a range of thinking strategies and approaches as a first stage, before finally realizing that doing a thorough job of introducing, training, and implementing Thinking Maps would actually provide a basis of understandings about cognitive strategies in general. When I was the associate principal and later researcher and consultant for the school, I became aware that this foundation allowed other strategies to be used and in fact strengthened various combined approaches. Over time this allowed for autonomy for both teachers and students as they selected the best strategies to fit particular purposes. Students using Thinking Maps on their own is a start but is not the end point or long-term goal of becoming a thinking school. This has been witnessed over the past three years as Thinking Maps have been integrated into dozens of schools in England (in coordination with the Cognitive Education Centre at the University of Exeter) that are refining their own evolving definitions toward schools in the 21st century focused on the wide-ranging processes of thinking.

St. Cuthbert's has developed many learning approaches, but a solid understanding of the basic thought processes gained through Thinking Maps has been crucial. The other approaches that have been complementary are Costa and Kallick's (2000) Habits of Mind in the behavioral domain and a focus on Bloom's (1956) Taxonomy of Educational Objectives to explain to students the steps that can be taken to think in more complex ways. In addition, this school has a focus on philosophy. Originally this was developed through the Philosophy for Children program developed by Dr. Mathew Lippman, but now questioning, building arguments, logical and lateral thinking, making assumptions, generating concepts, and ethical thinking are all given significant curriculum time. Time is also deliberately given to the teaching of various skills using mobile phones and Internet blogs, which allows students to use Thinking Maps and other strategies outside the classroom. This has resulted in a huge expansion of the information-technology department, which services student responses and links both teachers and students together in a sophisticated, flexible thinking community, responsive to and respectful of others' ideas.

The pathway this school has taken has resulted in learning and *thinking* being central to the way everything is done. The school community sees itself as a thinking school because all the opportunities provided by the school are in some way designed to extend students' thinking outcomes.

BEGINNING THE LONG PROCESS

In the later part of the 20th century, our school began an evolutionary process that finally envisioned a community of learners who could move beyond "tacit use" of thinking skills. Through research, practice, personal discoveries, and many rich conversations, we made a multiyear commitment to integrating the Thinking Maps language into our community. Over the recent years, we believe that our school has achieved "reflective use" of these tools—a sophisticated metacognitive use involving reflection and evaluation (Swartz & Perkins, 1989). We have come to believe that if our students functioned as reflective users of Thinking Maps, this would increase their thinking-skills repertoire and encourage autonomy of thinking and collaboration, certainly important if not essential outcomes for every school in a democratic society.

An assumption underlying the explicit teaching of thinking is that instruction in thinking skills can enhance the development of a student's thinking-skills repertoire (e.g., you can identify and teach the skills required for conscious decision making). In a narrow sense, it is always possible to teach thinking-skill strategies and tools and to test a student's cognitive comprehension of these skills or even his or her ability to apply these skills to a given problem. In a broader sense, the vision of many educators and researchers of the thinking-skills movement of the past few decades has been that the direct teaching of thinking is possible and is a necessary next step in the evolution of teaching and learning toward transfer of thinking skills across—and deeply into—content areas, for interdisciplinary problem solving and lifelong learning. Our story is of a school wanting it both ways: direct, formal teaching of thinking skills and explicit transfer into content areas.

St. Cuthbert's College is a unique, single-sex, independent school spanning the K–12 grade levels, with a student population of 1,500 girls aged 5–18. The college is expected to provide an outstanding education that not only encompasses academic, sporting, and cultural excellence but also adds the dimensions of character and values education. Thus, the long-term development of a systematic, fully integrated use of thinking skills, ultimately leading to our use of Thinking Maps, took a continuous focus and persistent attention to the goal.

There is a high expectation of all involved that we must provide for individual needs and produce graduates who can gain entry to the universities and courses of their choice and approach tertiary studies, and life, with the attitudes and skills that encourage success and personal fulfillment. Parents expect of the school that it retain its traditions and at the same time be innovative. Through the process of our evolution, we have moved from being a high-quality school with strong academic outcomes to being a true learning organization unified by a focus on developing high-quality thinking. Along the way, our academic results have moved us to the top rungs of the educational ladder in New Zealand, but this seems a sidebar to our evolving capacities to seek deeper understandings of how our minds work and to treasure the intrinsic rewards gained from becoming a school as a home for the mind.

PHASE 1: DISCOVERING TOO MANY POSSIBILITIES

In 1992, staff and management began this process by reviewing the school philosophy guided by the following questions: What kind of learners do we want to produce in this college? What behaviors, attitudes, skills, and knowledge would they have? We agreed that we wanted our students to become adults who were lifelong, independent learners, who approached life's situations and problems positively and persevered to find resolutions and answers. It had been the norm in schools such as ours for teachers to be responsible for writing superb lessons. They were expected to supply students with books of resource notes and to test, train, and, in general, provide opportunities for students to learn. The focus was on disseminating information and expecting students to study and memorize all this valuable knowledge so they could have success in national examinations.

While our school did well in the national rankings of senior secondary examination results, there was a nagging feeling among some staff that our teaching methods were producing graduates who were dependent learners: students who had excellent recall skills, who were prepared to read and study hard, but whose work was careful, methodical, and pedestrian rather than original, inventive, and risk taking. This idea was supported by the fact that many good students gained fine marks of around 75%–85%, but relatively few broke into the 90th percentile at the university scholarship level. We decided that we had a responsibility to make a change for our students. We embarked on a project in 1992, which we hoped would lead our students toward being autonomous learners.

First, we made a list of all the qualities such a learner would have. What developed from this was the conviction that effective learners are good thinkers who have a range of internalized strategies they can use to do their work. Then we debated these questions, to achieve the changes required to create the learning community we had described:

- How would this change our teaching practice?
- How would this change how students apply themselves to education?
- What skills or strategies would they need, if "better thinking" were our goal?
- From the range of theorists and practitioners who wrote on thinking, learning, and best educational practice, which should we use as our models, and which of the many strategies should we choose?

By 1992, a range of exciting strategies, methodologies, frameworks, and programs was becoming available for teachers who were interested in encouraging their students to think deeply and independently. A group of our staff read through the available literature and attended courses on best practices. The problem soon emerged: too many possibilities. Everyone who went to a course or read one of these books came to school converted and full of enthusiasm to try out the new ideas. We were all over the place. Across our K–12 school could be found pockets of teachers "doing" such processes as Edward de Bono's CORT program, mind mapping, multiple intelligences, and learning styles.

This was all terribly exciting to those of us involved. We held many personal development–training sessions for the whole staff between 1993 and 1994, and some of us became specialists in one process or another. However, by 1994 it became obvious that we had made a great change to individual teaching practice, but done nothing that made a school-wide impact for students. An individual student could have had some very good lessons from innovative teachers but not have recognized the strategies used or their application elsewhere. In addition, students' thinking patterns or habits would have remained unchanged, and students would not have developed a set of strategies they could regularly use to do their work more meaningfully. We were also quite aware that there was very little conceptual transfer or internalization of the strategies.

PHASE 2: FOCUS ON TRANSFER AND "DOUBLE PROCESSING"

As a staff, we decided to focus on transfer: We would all focus on a selection of strategies, teach them across all disciplines at the same time, practice them, and explicitly identify them, so students could see the transfer links and how useful they could be in different situations. We selected some of the lessons from several programs and had developed the firm belief that students who processed work in a number of different ways gained a deeper understanding of the content. We called this "double processing": If a lesson involved written notes in linear form, then homework could be to talk to parents about it. If a graphic organizer was used in class, then linear notes could be used for follow-up. At this stage, the graphic organizers we used were such things as the fishbone, the Venn diagram, sequence boxes, and mind mapping (or concept mapping). None of us had really associated these wide-ranging, disconnected graphics with a cognitive function as they were used by staff to sort content information given in class or for homework. They were prescriptive: Students were told to fill them in.

In 1998, we again reviewed our thinking program. So much had been done, but somehow it still seemed more like a personal development program for staff to improve teaching strategies than for the explicit development of autonomous learning for students. Had we gone wrong? Better teaching had led to better marks for all, but it seemed to us that we were not making enough of a difference for *all* students. We referred again to Costa's (1991) vision of a school as a home for the mind as a reference point. Here was a vision of everybody in a school community working together to make thinking central to the way everything was done. What we needed was a common, school-wide language that we could all use, which could be built on from age 5 to age 18 in greater depth. We had a unique opportunity to introduce good thinking skills early and develop them over the years so they really made a difference, but which approaches were out there that could do this?

PHASE 3: UNITING THE SCHOOL WITH A COMMON LANGUAGE

In 1999, we decided to have a research year where interested staff would examine the various approaches, programs, and strategies that could form the basis of an effective thinking program. We focused on the primary elements of thinking from the critical, creative, and caring/affective domains. Thinking Maps appeared to be an excellent way to focus on eight basic cognitive processes and the use of the Frame of Reference for metacognitive development. The challenge for us was to get both staff and students to see these as effective thinking processes, united together as a language, rather than as isolated graphic organizers. Our goal was to gradually teach and implement these over three to five years so students would have a range of strategies to employ.

YEAR 1: INTRODUCING THINKING MAPS IN 1999

To introduce a common visual thinking language to the whole K–12 continuum of St. Cuthbert's teaching and learning needs was an ambitious undertaking. We chose to introduce Thinking Maps through a three-year implementation cycle, by first teaching the use of Thinking Maps explicitly within noncurricular contexts. We chose this method of introduction since research (Perkins & Salomon, 1989) revealed that cognitive skills are not automatically acquired unless they are taught explicitly. This was a formal approach carried out by everybody: expected, planned, and agreed on by staff. Following the initial training, teachers were grouped into departments to find applications within subjects and units and were supported by follow-up sessions as they gained confidence. They began with a narrow view of what an isolated map could do—and what the maps could do together—and we encouraged them to focus on students gaining confidence and experience in use across the curriculum.

We also established a Department of Thinking and employed a thinking coordinator to manage the program and write the lessons using a six-step methodology: Label the strategy (the cognitive skills and map), explain the purpose, practice (provide practice experience and feedback), transfer (put into different content contexts), evaluate, and reflect. Teacher attitude was crucial, and where the teacher was confident and prepared, the lessons proved very successful in teaching the strategy.

While the primary school staff and students had a positive attitude toward the Thinking Maps approach, some secondary staff expressed reservations. Secondary staff had concerns about teaching skills in noncurricular contexts; they disliked the imposition of creating "artificial or forced" opportunities for conceptual transfer. In turn, some secondary students questioned the need to learn about the maps separately because "the teacher shows us how to do them in class anyway." These older students said, "We already know how to think, and we don't need you to tell us." Generally, this is a situation easily overcome by confident, persuasive teachers who believe that the processes they are teaching can make a difference, but it is very difficult when the teachers themselves are unsure as they integrate the tools into their repertoire.

Despite these difficulties, we achieved our goal of having every child in the school introduced to the maps in an explicit way. Students are able to use all the maps as required in a range of situations and when use of the maps is genuinely integrated and flexible. Most staff members model metacognitive processes by saying, "I need to analyze this information—which maps do you think would be useful here?" Consequently, we see much greater choice and flexibility of use, including the use of a range of maps to reach a decision or to extend an idea.

We believe that our earlier work of encouraging teachers to get students to doubly process notes also paid off: During some lessons, students were to take notes only in map form and then for homework write up the information in linear form, and vice versa. We saw excellent collaborative work develop, as some groups elected to take class notes in map form and work as teams to develop the ideas as fully as possible. It is much easier to see ideas being extended when they can be presented visually, and students enjoy adding to a collaborative map.

We also had considerable success in working meaningfully with departments to help them create units and lessons that used the maps in subjects. These "transfer" lessons were almost always valued highly by staff and students. The goal was to demonstrate how a thinking tool could be used right across the curriculum—how it could be used for homework and study, in assessments, and to help make real-life evaluations of problems in context and make decisions.

Teachers began to see how useful a map was in eliciting prior knowledge. Students are now often asked to draw a map early in a lesson and then at the end of the lesson. By comparing the maps, students see and evaluate their own progress, thereby developing a sense of personal efficacy of themselves as learners. Metacognition and evaluation! Students also feel positive as they choose which maps to use when given a task. Secondary school staff members who initially were not enthusiastic about the maps because they said they had their own subject-specific processes became more positive when they saw that the maps could clearly reveal where thinking had gone wrong. All students benefited from this opportunity to analyze the merits of each other's thinking processes.

YEAR 2: EVIDENCE OF INDEPENDENT USE IN 2000

In the second year, we were confident that students knew what a Thinking Map was (tacit use), but we were uncertain of the degree to which students used the Thinking Maps independently.

We wanted to know the extent to which students had moved from tacit use of Thinking Maps, to aware use or even strategic use. Students could use the maps when asked, but we suspected that they did it without clear intent. The challenge for the year 2000 was to gather evidence of the existing students' independent use of the Thinking Maps.

To determine the extent to which a fluent and "reflective" student use of maps occurred in problem-solving situations, we had students use their 20-minute thinking-skills time to collaboratively solve a long-term problem using Thinking Maps. For example, one teacher created a challenging activity on endangered animals playfully presented through a Gary Larson cartoon:

> Imagine you are a member of a team of researchers charged with reversing the population decline of the endangered "balloon" animals that have a hard time surviving in a harsh landscape. Use Thinking Maps as tools for generating, organizing, and assessing factors that might affect the population size of the balloon animals (e.g., physical factors, catastrophic events, food supply, disease, competition, ecotourism). Develop an action plan, based around your Thinking Maps, to help reverse the population decline.

The students' efforts were assessed, and prizes for fluent and flexible use of Thinking Maps were awarded. One group of four students created the example, shown in Figures 13.1–13.5, of using multiple maps to analyze this problem.

Figure 13.1   Factors Affecting Size of Population of Balloon Animals

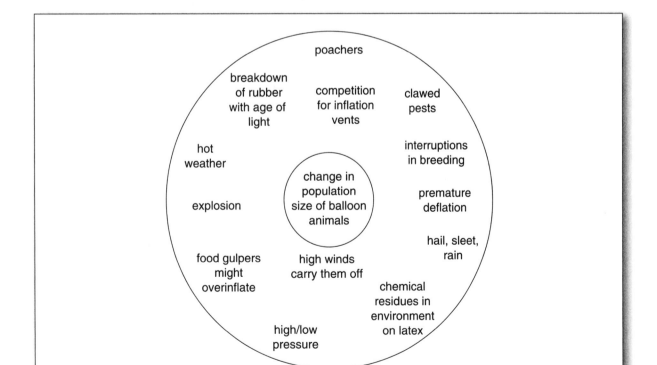

Figure 13.2 Categorizing Factors Affecting Size of Population of Balloon Animals

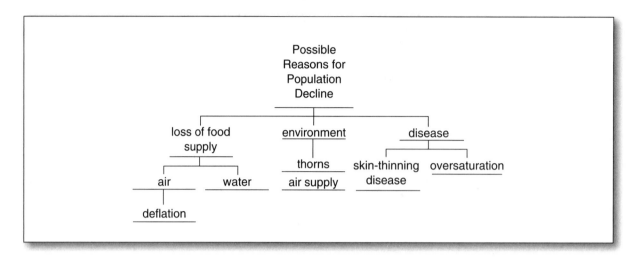

Figure 13.3 Causes and Effects of Population Decline of Balloon Animals

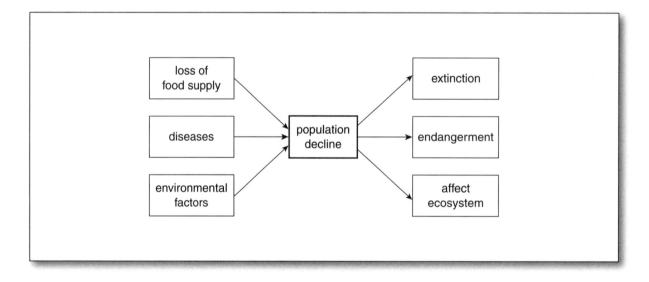

The purpose of the activity was to evaluate how students, working in cooperative groups, could apply multiple thinking processes via Thinking Maps to gain a solution to the scientific problem found in cartoons and nature. This sample of student work is representative of the quality of work received and reveals how these students could employ the tools for multistep problem solving and decision making. Although some students showed strategic and even reflective use of maps, the majority still struggled to show the fluency we expected in their map use.

Figure 13.4 Comparing Possible Solutions to Population Decline

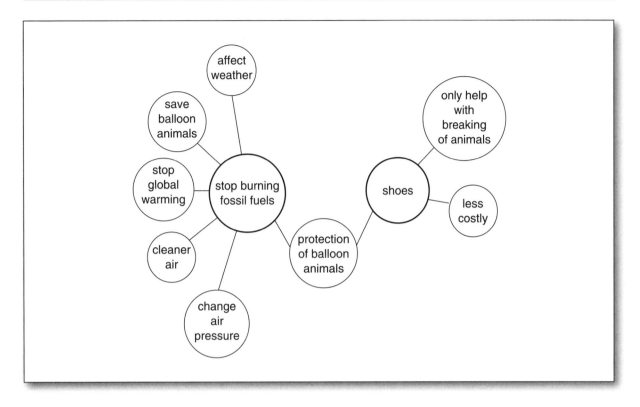

Figure 13.5 Making an Analogous Relationship With a Possible Solution

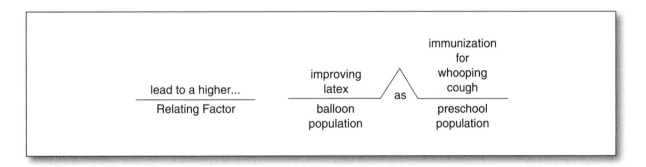

YEAR 3: REVIEWING AND MOVING FORWARD IN 2001

Our review of student applications revealed that there was still a need for more explicit teaching of these tools. The development of autonomous transfer of thinking skills does not happen over just a year or two. It happens during the evolution of a student's educational career and lifetime. Our evaluation of student map use in the year 2000 indicated that many students and some staff were not as confident or competent in the use of Thinking Maps as we believed possible and necessary to reach the goal of being authentic, independent thinkers. We needed to revisit individual maps for fluency.

Though there was a risk of repetition for both teachers and students—the risk that many schools do not take for long-term change—we created a more authentic, thematic learning experience for senior students based on their reflections on the "Big Day Out," a 12-hour music festival that many students and their friends had attended. We also carried out in-school research during the year using a questionnaire to ask students about the maps they had used, about the subject areas in which they used different maps, if they had used maps to organize their thoughts in situations outside of school, and whether they believed their thinking had been developed through learning about Thinking Maps.

In the junior school, students were positive about Thinking Maps, had experienced their use in many different settings, and almost uniformly enjoyed using them to enhance their thinking both at school and at home. In the senior school, the results were predictable: Students who had experienced staff who valued the maps and provided opportunities for transfer into several different curriculum areas were positive about the usefulness of the maps and optimistic about map-related improvements in the way they solved problems or sorted issues. In contrast, students who had been provided with few opportunities to use the maps in curriculum areas or who had had teachers who avowed "grudging compliance" saw the maps, and the thinking-skills lessons, as "boring and a waste of my time." Without opportunities for transfer, senior students marginalized the maps and considered them pointless.

Once again, it was evident that teachers make the difference to the implementation and effective use of a learning strategy. In 2001, in the senior school, we also moved toward more departmental autonomy. Secondary departments were asked questions such as the following: What kinds of thinking do you most value in your department? What are the most powerful experiences to encourage this thinking for students? What Thinking Map activities will you use to develop these skills? How might you show the effectiveness and value of your thinking-skills focus for students' learning?

Departments were required to add their "thinking focus" to their departmental plan, and staff could choose to be apprised of this thinking focus. Individual departmental choice was interesting. The technology department chose to improve its students' metacognitive thinking through developing links between sequencing (Flow Maps) and the design process. The art department wanted to use maps to strengthen problem finding and metaperception. In social sciences, pattern finding was valued, with a focus on Flow Maps for sequencing and Double Bubble Maps for comparing and contrasting, and in the music department, there was exploration of the use of Brace Maps to better teach musical notation and intervals.

YEARS 4–5: A COMMON LANGUAGE IN 2003

Through our continued focus and retraining, by 2003 we had achieved a common visual-thinking language across the school, with staff and student competence with the maps much increased. The Department of Thinking expanded to two full-time teachers supported by a team of staff. Examples of student use of Thinking Maps continued to be displayed in every teaching space. They were regularly used in assessments and curriculum lessons. In the secondary school, we saw more experimentation in flexible map use than in the early years, with several maps being linked and used to process a task. In the junior school, the majority of students showed fluent map use by Year 6, and students were adept users of the Thinking Map software (Hyerle & Gray Matter Software, 2007; see Chapter 10, "Thinking Technology").

Thinking Maps continued to be explicitly introduced in the junior school. However, after three years' implementation, the map knowledge base in the senior school was considered to be such that teaching of individual maps was only required for new students. Flexible catch-up training for new students and new staff was provided each year, and ongoing support from the thinking coordinators was provided on an individual and departmental basis.

By 2003, we were able to recognize some significant advances in the way the maps were being used, especially since St. Cuthbert's College had expanded its professional development time to one and a half hours a week. There was planned training for teachers in how to link the maps to other thinking or learning strategies. This encouraged students to use a wider range of strategies together to engage with the content knowledge. When several approaches are used together—such as linking Costa's 16 Habits of Mind with Thinking Maps—the emphasis on isolated tools lessens and changes to an emphasis on whole thinking and learning processes. It also extends the quality of the thinking involved. Here is a sampling of some of the spin-off benefits of our evolution. Teachers have been experimenting with the following:

- Developing a metacognitive lesson plan, where teachers identify a specific learning goal, and the questions they can ask students that will allow them to identify for themselves appropriate Thinking Maps to use.
- Encouraging greater infusion by creating intranet-based learning activities. Students can call up a page of lesson activities available for a task, click on a hyperlink, and be presented with a range of links to higher-order thinking, Thinking Maps, and multiple intelligence–differentiation activities. They can then download these directly into their responses.
- Encouraging flexible use by having a school-wide focus on "applied thinking," where a philosophical real-life problem is analyzed using the maps and inquiry techniques.

These examples reflect the inherent rigor and flexibility of Thinking Maps and the empowering nature of the change process that was allowed to mature naturally over time. The learning outcomes for our students based on fundamental thinking processes and learning approaches have been remarkable. Academic results in New Zealand's national league tables have risen consistently, with the college a national academic leader, placing 1st or 2nd in New Zealand in every senior external examination category for the past five years, up from 12th at the start of our evolutionary process. We have also seen improved results on international tests and PATs (reading, listening, and comprehension tests), the high level of acceptance and approval from students and parents, and the continued use of double processing using the maps and linear writing from our students who now attend universities.

Yet the most powerful outcome has been the move to collaborative and interactive classrooms where students—and teachers—are confident to discuss their learning and to learn from each other. We now know that students are much more willing to share their work with the class when it is developed visually, collaboratively, and through a flexible, common language for thinking that is the foundation for the evolution of our community. And, as teachers and school leaders, we are able to work deeply in our own content areas, with focused collaboration in teams. After 10 years, we are still living the never-ending ebb and flow of change and thriving as an evolving school as a home for the mind.

REFERENCES

Bloom, B. S. (Ed.) (with Engelhart, M. D., Furst, E. J., Hill, W. H., & Krathwohl, D. R.). (1956). *Taxonomy of educational objectives: Handbook: Cognitive domain.* New York: David McKay.

Costa, A. L. (1991). *The school as a home for the mind.* Palatine, IL: IRI/Skylight.

Costa, A., & Kallick, B. (2000). *Activating and engaging the Habits of Mind.* Alexandria, VA: Association for Supervision and Curriculum Development.

Hyerle, D., & Gray Matter Software. (2007). *Thinking Maps* (Version 2.0, Innovative Learning Group) [Computer software]. Raleigh, NC: Innovative Sciences.

Perkins, D. N., & Salomon, G. (1989). Teaching for transfer. *Educational leadership, 46*(1), 22–32.

Swartz, R. J., & Perkins, D. N. (1989). *Teaching thinking: Issues and approaches.* Pacific Grove, CA: Midwest.

14

Stories From Mississippi

Results From College to Kindergarten

Marjann Kalehoff Ball, Ed.D.

KEY CONCEPTS

- Research and significant reading test score results at the community college level
- "Eureka" moments of students and teachers to empirical research and test results
- Thinking Maps® as a common language—from college to preschool throughout the state

The source of the mighty Mississippi River is Lake Itasca, a small glacial lake in Minnesota. Upon exiting the lake, a shallow area of rapids approximately 2 feet deep allows individuals to wade across the river using stepping-stones to guide and assist them. As the river continues south, it picks up speed, running more quickly with less resistance, and becomes wider and deeper. All along the way, the flow is fed by tributaries that make it an even more powerful force to be reckoned with. Upon reaching New Orleans, the river is 200 feet deep and half a mile wide. The river continues its journey into the Gulf of Mexico.

From the Mississippi Delta to the Gulf Coast and across the state, Thinking Maps have been spreading wider and deeper from district to district, teacher to teacher, and student to student. Over the years, as districts begin the implementation of the maps, they are, as we call it, "wading in the water." If during that first year they stumble, there are stepping-stones offered by educators from schools around the state upon which to rely and receive help. Using Thinking Maps effectively and over multiple years, teachers begin to move with greater ease from map to map, all the while adding depth to the content they are teaching to students. During this journey, educators are given assistance in connecting maps with grade-level objectives, writing processes, reading comprehension strategies, state standards, and a variety of creative ways to use these valuable tools with their students. As teachers continue to use Thinking Maps, the ownership transfers to students whose thinking becomes deep and expansive, enriched and powerful.

The results offered here range from prekindergarten to college classrooms. At the end of this chapter a story is told by middle school teacher Suzanne Ishee about an educational community, the Pass Christian School District, physically wiped off the map by Hurricane Katrina on August 29, 2005, and then rebuilding, rising up again to the highest levels of success.

THINKING MAPS AT THE COLLEGE LEVEL

In 1981, I joined the faculty at Jones County Junior College in Ellisville, Mississippi, as a reading, study skills, and English instructor. I was faced with the challenge of how to address the individual needs of students, transcending their differences while maintaining the purported integrity of the college curriculum. The setting is a melting pot for ability levels, a range of potential courses, and advanced educational plans. Because most community/junior colleges are committed to the open-door policy of admitting students regardless of their ability, age, experiential background, or career aspirations, they are faced with the profound problem of how to treat such diversity. ACT composite scores may range from 8 to 32, while a profile of personal characteristics of these students presents a new, less traditional type of student clamoring to be taught. Supported by civil rights litigation and generous government and scholarship aid and buttressed by a prevailing confidence in the efficacy of advanced education as well as the demands of a complicated technological society, these students have come in unprecedented numbers.

When I began teaching at Jones County Junior College, I was baffled by the apparent failure of the students to transfer thinking skills taught in my classes to other academic areas. After nearly 10 years of frustrating efforts to find more effective strategies, I discovered Thinking Maps, which produced significant results. As I began using the maps, my colleagues from other academic areas informed me, "Your students are doodling in my class. They are drawing circles and squares while I am lecturing." "Oh no," I confidently replied. "They are not doodling—they are thinking!" I realized that I had a set of visual tools for learning, a vehicle I needed to help students develop and transfer critical thinking skills to various academic areas.

As the use of Thinking Maps continued, a change occurred in the way students approached learning. They no longer looked at the magnitude of their textbooks, but instead they organized and simplified the material by mapping assigned readings. They began to recognize patterns of organization in paragraphs and passages by applying the appropriate Thinking Map to specific reading selections. Making further connections of the thought process to Thinking Maps enabled them to see the type of thinking required to complete a particular task. One of my college students had been diagnosed with attention deficit disorder as a young girl and had been sent to numerous tutors who equipped her with a variety of study strategies that did not work. After being taught Thinking Maps, she commented, "I like Thinking Maps because they are how I think anyway; now I have ways to organize all that information." She proceeded to make a perfect score on her first American History test after mapping the material.

RESEARCH FINDINGS: READING COMPREHENSION AT THE COMMUNITY COLLEGE LEVEL

After I used the maps for several years in my college classes, I believed it was important to determine whether or not Thinking Maps, interwoven with an existing college reading course, would have a significant effect on reading scores or be affected by the status (traditional/nontraditional) of the student. The investigation was conducted over two semesters with a sample of 92 students forming the control and experimental groups. An analysis was made as to whether the treatment of mapping had resulted in a significant difference between the Thinking Maps control groups and "no-mapping" groups in reading scores as well as the variables of fast reading, phonics, comprehension, scanning, structure, vocabulary, and word parts. The necessary calculations were made using the multivariate analysis of covariance

(MANCOVA) using the Wilks's lambda criterion. Follow-up univariate analyses were used to clarify any significant multivariate results.

Statistically significant main effects were found for the treatment of Thinking Maps on reading comprehension. Significant differences at the .01 level were found for 5 out of 7 subtests of fast reading, comprehension, structure, vocabulary, and word parts, with the Thinking Maps group outperforming the no-mapping group on each of the five variables. The findings of the univariate treatment by status analysis of covariance were consistent with the results of the multivariate analysis, which found that only the main effects of treatment were statistically significant. The main finding reflected on what I saw happening in these college classes: *Thinking Maps made a significant difference in reading test scores.* Whether a person was characterized by age, social roles assumed, or other criteria such as being traditional or nontraditional had no significant impact on reading test scores.

These findings were published in my dissertation at the University of Southern Mississippi (Ball, 1998). The research findings along with improved student performance and satisfaction reinforced my confidence in Thinking Maps as an indispensable visual language for teaching and for learning. Each semester I surveyed my students at the end of the term as to which strategies used were most beneficial, and 90% of the students chose Thinking Maps as most helpful in studying textbooks, organizing material, retrieving information, and taking tests. Their responses included the following: "Why did I have to be in college before I learned about Thinking Maps?" "Thinking Maps are really useful and have brought my grades up." "Thinking Maps move me right into what I am doing."

BEYOND EXPECTATIONS

I will always remember the day Diana entered my reading and study skills college class at Jones County Junior College with all the reservations of an older, returning student. She appeared bright but unsure of her ability to do well after being out of school for many years. At 16 years of age she had been diagnosed with arthritis, and by her late 20s she had been diagnosed with multiple sclerosis. Diana had been told she could never be an effective learner because of her disabling conditions, but despite the time lapse since her previous formal education, and her lack of confidence, she excelled in the activities in my class. Through the use of Thinking Maps, she was able to organize content material for discussions and tests. As time passed, Diana shared her joy from successes experienced as a result of using Thinking Maps, not only in my class but also in other areas. She believed she had found a set of visual tools by which her limitations and negative predictions could be overcome.

From her achievement in the basic classes, she set a goal of becoming a licensed practical nurse and entered the nurse's aide program. However, after only two weeks into her new endeavor, she sadly informed me that she was withdrawing from college. Surprised, I questioned why, and she answered, "I failed my first nurse's aide test. Now I realize the predictions have come true—I am too limited to meet college requirements." I was not as convinced as she for I had seen her potential. Answering my question about which technique she was using to study, she said, "The Notetaking System of Learning, SQ3R (Survey, Question, Read, Recite, Review), and Thinking Maps." "How often have you used Thinking Maps?" I asked, to which she replied, "A little." My response was, "Don't use them a little—use them a lot!" She left my office that day with her spirits lifted and a promise to apply Thinking Maps to her studies.

After two weeks, she appeared with a smile on her face and the declaration that she had decided to stay in college. When asked what had changed her mind (and hoping it was success), she replied, "I have been using Thinking Maps daily." As a result, she had made an A on her last nurse's aide test. She was absolutely elated, and from that day on, she experienced success on tests in that program, leading to her entry into the Licensed Practical Nursing (LPN) program, where she excelled. As she progressed in her studies, she began assisting her peers in learning how to organize their material. Not only did she win the gratitude of her fellow students, but the instructors were impressed with Diana's outstanding performance on tests, class work, and state board examinations. Diana completed her LPN training as an outstanding student and quickly secured a position in a hospital as an LPN. As a result, the nursing staff proposed and established a pilot program in which all entering LPNs would learn how to use Thinking Maps.

NURSING: A PILOT PROGRAM SET UP AT THE COLLEGE LEVEL

The ripple effect from the utilization of Thinking Maps was impressive. Based on the success of students in my college classes as well as the achievements of my student Diana and the interest of other nursing students and the nursing instructors, a pilot program was set up in spring 2002 at Jones County Junior College (JCJC) by which entering LPN students would be instructed in the use of Thinking Maps in their nursing courses. Upon taking the exit exam at the conclusion of the structure and function course, 100% of the students passed the exam, the first time this had occurred in 17 years. Another group of entering LPN students was taught Thinking Maps in spring 2003, with a 100% passing rate on the comprehensive Fundamentals of Nursing exam (Educational Resources Inc.) given at the end of the semester. Sandra Waldrup, the director of practical nursing, said, "The practical nursing faculty is constantly trying to identify methods which would make learning and retention easier for our students. The volume of information they need can be overwhelming. Thinking Maps provide a consistent way to organize and link related concepts into a manageable system. Our students benefit from Thinking Maps as indicated in their evaluations."

As I began the fourth semester of Thinking Maps training for LPNs in fall 2003, one of my students remained after class to say, "My mother is working successfully as an LPN after completing the course at JCJC. When I told her you were teaching me about Thinking Maps, she shared with me that she had profited from using Diana's nursing notes, which were all in maps. I feel confident that I will make it using the Thinking Maps, which my mother passed on to me."

Another student in the fourth-semester training, Heather Lewis, wrote, "I am using Thinking Maps for the LPN program, and wanted you to know that my grades have gone from Cs and Bs to high Bs and As. I'm so glad, and now I am using the maps in everything."

FROM COLLEGE TO PRESCHOOL

After using Thinking Maps in my classes and seeing positive results from their application, I felt compelled to share these visual tools with others. I thought that if college students who believed they could not perform satisfactorily were succeeding with the help of Thinking Maps, could not this tool also make a difference in the lives of prekindergarten through 12th-grade children *before* they became frustrated and deemed themselves failures?

My outreach began as I presented the results I had experienced from the use of Thinking Maps at conferences and workshops across Mississippi. I contacted school districts from which many JCJC students come, discussing the benefits of teaching Thinking Maps to their students before they enter college. Jones County, a district I call "the pioneer of Thinking Maps in Mississippi," indicated its willingness to introduce the tools to its K–12 teachers. Located in a largely rural area of the state, the Jones County School District, composed of seven elementary, three middle, and three high schools, piloted Thinking Maps across the district in Grade 4. Twenty-five fourth-grade teachers utilized the maps, and after one year, the district's score increased from level 3.5 to level 4.3 (with 5.0 being the highest), with the fourth-grade's scores increasing most significantly. Thomas Prine, former superintendent of Jones County School

District, states, "Thinking Maps allow children when confronted with a problem to have a process that they can use to organize their thoughts, enabling them to solve that problem. As a result, the students in our district have excelled district-wide."

By the mid-1990s, as the successful use of Thinking Maps became better known, interest grew. During the 1995–1996 school year, Dr. Susan Rucker, principal at Brandon Middle School, implemented Thinking Maps in Grades 4–8 in her school. Dr. Rucker states, "As former principal of Brandon Middle School, I saw the use of Thinking Maps as a way to help students organize their thinking processes. The program proved to be a success for students who had difficulty with performance-based thinking skills. Students of all ability levels showed improvement."

Throughout Dr. Rucker's school, maps were evident everywhere: on the floor, on the ceiling, in display cabinets, in the hallways, in the classrooms, even in the cafeteria. After the introductory Thinking Maps training, Dr. Rucker's expectations included having teachers explain in their lesson plans how the maps would be used and show evidence of dialogue between teacher and student, teacher and teacher, and student and student on Thinking Maps as well as evidence of student and teacher utilization of the maps. When the statewide performance-based scores were published that year, Brandon Middle School students had significantly increased their score by 10 performance-based points in all but one grade level, leading Brandon Middle School to be named one of only five Blue Ribbon Schools in the state that year.

Dr. Penny Wallin, former superintendent of the Picayune School District, was one of the first teachers to be certified by the National Board for Professional Teaching Standards in Mississippi and in the nation and used Thinking Maps when she was a classroom teacher. She states, "In my roles as National Board Certified Teacher and administrator, I understand the importance of equipping learners with pathways to learning. Although all students do not learn in the same way or at the same rate, they must think and process. Thinking Maps are truly useful for a lifetime, providing consistent, common visual tools that support the eight thinking processes as identified by research."

Pass Christian, a small school district (two elementary, one middle, and one high school) located on the Mississippi Gulf Coast, began training its middle school teachers in the use of the maps. After a year of Thinking Maps implementation, the writing scores of seventh-grade students on the state writing assessment increased from level 2.2 to level 3.0 (with 4.0 being the highest level). Only 2 students received level 4 in 2002, while 40 students attained level 4 in 2003. Upon investigation of what had made such a difference, it was noted that most of the students achieving level 4 had been instructed in Thinking Maps and had been using them in their classrooms. As a result of these successes, additional training took place in both elementary schools and the high school to ensure district-wide immersion in Thinking Maps for all levels. Later in the chapter, the use of the maps in this district over a nine-year period will be reviewed.

The impact Thinking Maps have had on the education of Mississippi's students is impressive. To date, approximately 350 schools (234 elementary, 69 middle, and 47 high schools), 15,000 teachers, and 429,000 students have been exposed to the maps.

THE RIVER RUNS DEEP AND WIDE

It appears that one of the reasons for the outstanding results and longevity of Thinking Maps in Mississippi schools is the depth of training followed by the degree to which the maps are implemented. After a school has used Thinking Maps for one year, teachers from each school are selected to become expert trainers for their school. Criteria of selection include expertise in the use of the maps, the employment of innovative methods, and the ability to communicate and collaborate effectively with colleagues. A network of Thinking Maps trainers across the state has been established, and meetings are conducted to keep these individuals updated and to provide additional curriculum ideas for their schools.

As an extension of the development of an expert teacher-based training group, the first annual Thinking Maps Conference was held at JCJC in October 2002. This gathering brought together over 300 educators, from kindergarten to college, from all over the state to experience the power of these common visual tools. Keynote addresses were given, but most important, teachers presented a range of Thinking Maps applications in breakout sessions. The "Thinking Maps Gallery" highlighting student and teacher projects provided an opportunity for educators to share ideas and to see integration of the maps with all levels and areas of curriculum.

This gallery of work from K–12 schools from across the state showed that this common visual language has the capacity to connect all learners. Much like the examples shown in the gallery, the examples shown in Figures 14.1a–d illustrate the developmental range of the use of just one tool, the Brace Map, focused on only one piece of content knowledge, the structural parts of the eye.

Figure 14.1a Kindergarten Brace Map of the Eye

Figure 14.1b Fifth-Grader Brace Map of the Eye

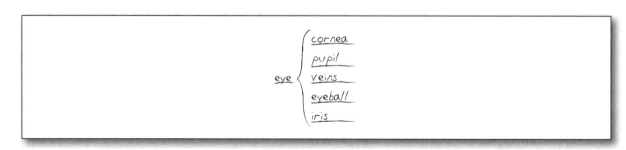

Figure 14.1c Eighth-Grader Brace Map of the Eye

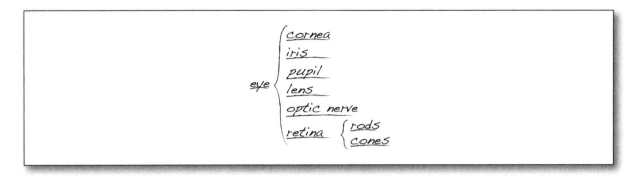

Figure 14.1d College Nursing Student Brace Map of the Eye

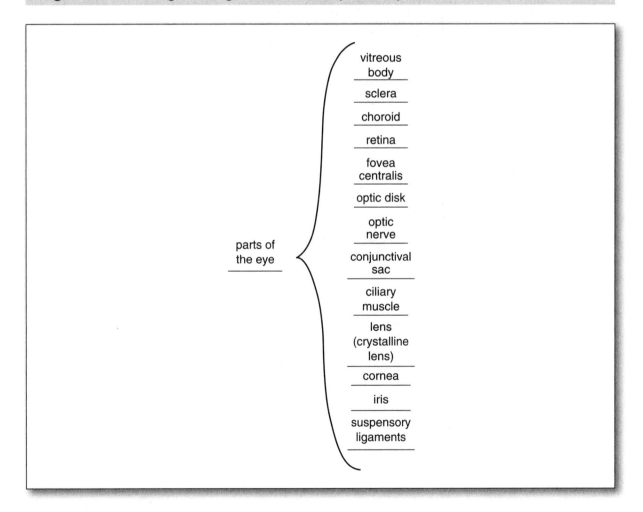

These examples show how the same concept created at varying levels of vocabulary and difficulty may be presented using Thinking Maps as a common visual language to enhance depth of learning, bonding students from kindergarten, to fifth and eighth grade, to the college levels.

As a professor and now as a change agent in schools, I am continually made aware of the far-reaching implications and possibilities of the maps for students and teachers. Traveling to numerous school districts across the state, I have seen Thinking Maps used in classrooms from preschool to 12th grade. Not only do I share with these teachers what I have learned about Thinking Maps, but I also take away many new and exciting ways to use maps in my college classroom. Throughout my 25 years of teaching, I have tried many interventions to help students become more successful learners and have often changed strategies and texts. One thing, however, has not been altered—use of Thinking Maps. When my students ask, "May I take these home to my children?" or say, "I helped my child with his Bubble Map last night and he helped me with mine," I am certain that Thinking Maps are the bridge not only from subject to subject but also from generation to generation.

It is gratifying to know that Thinking Maps are credited with student successes and teacher satisfaction throughout the state. Over the past year I have asked educators in several school systems to give me feedback on what they have seen happen in their schools, and for their analysis of the results on standardized tests. Of course, because schools and school systems are complex and performance changes have many dimensions, it is difficult if not impossible to demonstrate a direct correlation between the implementation of Thinking Maps and changes in standardized test scores without a refined research design.

Given this frame of reference, it is still important for educators to discuss their observations from the field, as Thinking Maps are implemented across all grade levels in each school over many years. Descriptions of how the maps have been implemented and the perceptions of the effectiveness of Thinking Maps from educators in some of the districts that have implemented Thinking Maps over one to nine years are helpful for our understanding of the effectiveness of these tools over time. These educators give voice to what is a complex shift in performance by teachers and students.

Pascagoula School District 2010

By Ann Parrish, Curriculum and Instruction Specialist

In 2009, the Pascagoula School District implemented Thinking Maps in two of our elementary schools and both of our sixth-grade schools. Each school has a trained trainer, and the four curriculum specialists are trained as trainers as well. As the year progressed, we saw more and more evidence of growth in teachers as they utilized the maps. Trainers presented staff development mini sessions in after-school meetings, and we were able to give teachers suggestions as we observed lessons and reviewed lesson plans. Thinking Maps are an excellent way for our students to organize their thoughts and facts for later applications. They are wonderful for teacher introduction of a new skill or concept and for extension and student applications by using multiple Thinking Maps. During the 2009–2010 school year we saw student work displayed in classrooms and hallways, as well as school displays, which used Thinking Maps to share information for visitors, and we looked forward to starting the next school year with full implementation beginning on day one. We were so pleased with the first year of implementation that we decided to add four more schools for the second year. In a year of budget cuts, this speaks volumes. Our goal is to eventually have total immersion in our district.

Tupelo City Schools 2010

By Diana Ezell, Assistant Superintendent

In July 2009, the Tupelo Public School District (TPSD) administrative team was trained in Thinking Maps, while the district's 20 instructional coaches were trained as trainers for Thinking Maps. The district plan had been for the administrators to use Thinking Maps during meetings and team planning throughout the 2009–2010 school year, and at the same time the instructional coaches would integrate Thinking Maps in their coaching sessions.

During the training of administrators and instructional coaches, a unanimous decision was made not to wait but to begin training all teachers in the district in the fall of 2009. Collectively, they identified a need for a common language from prekindergarten through 12th grade and did not want to wait a year. The trainers worked with Dr. Ball to develop a plan for introducing and reinforcing the use of Thinking Maps in the classrooms. On the first day of school, Thinking Maps were displayed in the hallways, and the excitement continued throughout the year. The TPSD lesson planning elements include Thinking Maps as a requirement so that Thinking Maps are used in every subject. The district scores on benchmark assessments improved throughout the year across the district.

Gulfport School District 2010

By Carla J. Evers, Director of Instructional / Federal Programs

Because of the professional learning experiences that our teachers in the Gulfport School District have had with Thinking Maps and *Write . . . from the Beginning* (Buckner, 2000) since 2003, we have been better able to prepare our students to use the maps to organize their thinking and process information at deeper levels. Students at all levels routinely use multiple Thinking Maps to help them structure their writing and thought processes in cross-curricular applications. The maps have been particularly helpful in schools with higher poverty rates in that their use has encouraged vocabulary development and improved composition skills.

MINDS OF MISSISSIPPI

It now has been over five years since Hurricane Katrina came ashore. The city of New Orleans, Louisiana, was a tragic and unbearable center of destruction, with the winds and water penetrating the city and destroying lives and neighborhoods. Little known to the outside world, just up the Gulf Coast was where Katrina actually made landfall: along the stretch of land of the small coastal towns of Pass Christian and Gulfport in Mississippi. For several years before the devastation of Katrina, Pass Christian had brought Thinking Maps to its community of learners with great success. As you will find out below in the personal and professional reflections from Suzanne Ishee, facing the trauma and the challenge of rebuilding a community and its schools from the ground up to becoming the top-performing school system in the state was propelled by an enduring focus on student thinking.

THE PASS CHRISTIAN SCHOOL DISTRICT STORY
PASS CHRISTIAN SCHOOL DISTRICT 2010
BY SUZANNE ISHEE, PASS CHRISTIAN MIDDLE SCHOOL TEACHER

In every teaching environment, educators look for the "magic bullet" that will open up their students' abilities to access and process information in such a way as to invite application in all areas of life.

(Continued)

(Continued)

Often overlooked is the innate ability that all learners have to think about and focus on information presented to them on a daily basis. When given the opportunity, no matter what the circumstances are, people of all ages and positions in life will grow and come together, as long as there is a common language to link them to their experiences. This is a story that begins in a small town in southern Mississippi along the Gulf of Mexico. It explores the ability of a people to survive and thrive in spite of the direst of circumstances—Hurricane Katrina.

Thinking Maps were introduced in the middle school of the Pass Christian School District in 2002. After data collection of student progress on standardized tests, it was found that the district was in the middle of the continuum on statewide test scores prior to the implementation of the maps. After the first year of applying the Thinking Maps to students' learning, the results were amazing! When the seventh-grade writing assessment results were released, we were elated to see that the students had jumped from 3% to 30% achieving a perfect score of "4." The only variable in the before and after scores was the use of Thinking Maps in the classrooms.

From 2002 to 2005, student achievement increased dramatically in all areas of assessment. From kindergarten to high school, scores rose to the top levels across the state of Mississippi. Although the demographics of the district did not fit the statistical data of how students should perform, student achievement continued to climb. Over 60% of the students were on free or reduced lunch prior to Hurricane Katrina. The high school was recognized as a national Blue Ribbon School, and the two elementary schools and the middle school commanded great respect for their achievements. Success was expected and became a point of pride among the learning community.

As students traveled from classroom to classroom, teacher to teacher, and school to school, they were able to use a common language for learning as introduced by Thinking Maps. Learning looked the same and sounded the same no matter where the students found themselves. The Pass Christian School District became the place to visit for other districts in the state and served as a model for continued excellence. Over a few short years the district had reached the top level of achievement as measured by the state—a level 5.

Everything Changed

On August 29, 2005, everything changed. The small town of Pass Christian, as well as many other towns and cities along the northern Gulf of Mexico, was virtually wiped off the face of the map. Hurricane Katrina roared ashore with an unprecedented tidal surge and changed the way the community, as well as the school district, looked at the world. In a matter of 12 horrendous hours, people, places, and things disappeared into the Gulf of Mexico. The Pass Christian School District staff members, *85% of whom became homeless themselves,* had to clear away the debris and discover what was left to re-create the learning environment for their students. Stripped of its entire physical community, the educational community came together with the sole purpose to survive and thrive. There were no books. There was no technology. Only one building remained, and even that structure had been damaged by 4 feet of water that traveled inland from the highest storm surge ever recorded.

Daily survival was uppermost in everyone's minds. Finding food and shelter for the homeless, locating missing persons, and identifying the dead became the "new normal." School and learning could have become mere distractions to the populace. However, the Pass Christian School District became convinced that the loss of the learning community would mean the loss of the entire community. Recovery was only possible if a common thread could be used to connect everyone— students, staff, and parents. That common thread was the language of metacognition—the ability to think and to evaluate those thoughts. Thinking Maps were there before the storm, and they were there after the storm, providing continuity in the midst of chaos.

The Pass Christian School District was faced with what appeared to be the insurmountable task of rebuilding a learning community when virtually all was lost. Students and staff came together to continue their pursuit of excellence by using the common language of Thinking Maps! This common language for learning, this metacognition, allowed the entire community to rise above circumstance and to heal and prosper in the face of a national disaster. The district was able to derive meaning from incredible loss.

Staff came together to begin rebuilding a school district, piece by piece. In a world that was out of control, it became a matter of necessity to give the students and staff a means of gaining control over the overwhelming task set before them. One of the most critical factors in the district's survival was the awareness of a common frame of reference—the use of Thinking Maps district-wide. This became the starting point of the realization that although Pass Christian, Mississippi, was literally removed from the face of the political map, students and staff still had their "mental maps." Instead of dwelling on what was not, individuals and groups could focus on what was.

For seven weeks, staff worked diligently to prepare a site for the district to return to the business of educating its children. Trailers were brought in to serve as classrooms. As students and staff entered their new environment, it became evident that the definition of school had changed. It was no longer the brick-and-mortar buildings with orderly hallways decorated with the work of diligent students. School became "people" and shared memories of survival. It was a place to vent and deal with emotions that would unexpectedly rise to the surface with very little provocation. Nothing looked the same. Even the makeup of individual classes was altered due to the loss of students and staff, many of whom had moved to other states and schools as a result of losses from Hurricane Katrina. Where and how could the school district begin to put the pieces together to ensure that the students did not lose what they had already acquired? The answer was apparent in what was already there—the "comfort zone" of Thinking Maps.

Beth John, director of curriculum and testing in the Pass Christian School District, said, "Thinking Maps are not a school tool. They are a life tool." In this context, staff and students began the journey back to a cohesive learning environment. They drew on what they knew about thinking and learning and charted a course to achieve even greater things than had been accomplished prior to Hurricane Katrina. They were determined to not let the storm define who they were as a community of learners. It was through this process that the real essence of learning stood out so dramatically. Learning became the application of the processes that were inside the students and the staff. Although much had been lost in the physical realm, every individual still had all that was needed to move forward. The Pass Christian School District quickly identified Thinking Maps as a key component to recovery.

The commitment to excel and thrive was not limited to the classroom. Each staff member of the district bought in to the premise that it would take everyone to re-create a community. Thinking Maps played a strategic role in daily planning and assessment and in establishing long-range goals. Individuals and groups were on the same page because of a common language established before the storm. This commonality extended into the community as a whole. Things began to come together. As the debris from the storm was slowly removed from the streets and areas where buildings and homes once stood, the emotional clutter was peeled away by the thought processes of individuals and groups. Continuity provided control. Control brought peace of mind. The impossible became the improbable.

Today, four and a half years after Hurricane Katrina forever changed the community's perspective, the Pass Christian School District has made tremendous strides in rebuilding all that was lost. By entering the post-Katrina world and surviving and thriving, the Pass Christian School District's story became "everyman's" story. Returning to learning was the one component of normalcy that reflected what was before the storm and helped bridge the gap to the future. In time it became apparent that the Pass Christian School District story was one to be shared with the world. The Pass Christian School District decided to document its journey through video.

The Pass Christian system applied for a grant from the Thinking Foundation to tell this story and was awarded the grant in 2009. Interviews with administrators, teachers, and students became the oral history of how Thinking Maps provided the impetus for recovery. Students were filmed in their

(Continued)

(Continued)

classrooms using the maps for continued success. Dr. David Hyerle conducted question-and-answer sessions with staff. Out of the many hours of footage the concept became reality, and *The Minds of Mississippi: The Pass Christian School District Story* was born as a film documentary and was released in January 2011, more than five years after Katrina made landfall. Through the process of documenting where the district had been and where it was going, the documentary became more than a story. It became affirmation and absolution for all involved in the production.

As one member of the Pass Christian School District said, "For the rest of the world Hurricane Katrina is over. For the staff, students, and community of Pass Christian, Katrina will forever remain a part of our hearts and a part of our past." Thinking Maps continue to play a huge role in continued excellence in the Pass Christian School District. In the yearly evaluation of school districts in the state of Mississippi, the Pass Christian School District is ranked number one in the state based on empirical evidence referenced to national norms as reported in November 2009.

Moving Beyond the Pain

The state of Mississippi has adopted a much more stringent testing model designed to rank students with the rest of the United States of America. The QDI (Quality of Distribution Index) is a representation of the distribution of student test scores across the various statewide assessment instruments. The scale of 0–300 (300 being the highest ranking) indicates where a school district performs against other districts in the state as well as on a national level. For the 2008–2009 yearly assessments the Pass Christian School District achieved a score of 203 as opposed to the state average of 149. As illustrated by the figure below, the Pass Christian School District performed far above the average school district in the state.

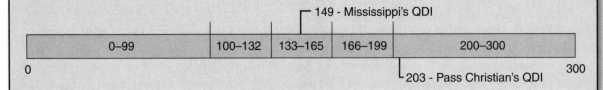

This evidence is a strong indicator of the effectiveness of the Thinking Maps in maintaining the recovery from loss to acceptance to progress as a district and as a community. A walk through classrooms today reveals students and teachers actively engaging in the learning process and dialogue through the use of Thinking Maps.

The Thinking Maps also are used to plan student interventions in the tier process to help students overcome deficits and to promote an across-the-board approach to intervention. Dr. Peggy McCullough, intervention strategist at Pass Christian Elementary School, created a Thinking Map to ensure that all students are correctly placed in the tier process and to guide the teaching staff throughout the process.

The Pass Christian School District is looking forward to the release of the documentary *The Minds of Mississippi: The Pass Christian School District Story,* as a way to share with the world its success and struggle to keep a community together during the aftermath of Hurricane Katrina. The experience of this district can be applied universally to any community, culture, or people trying to survive crises of any magnitude. If a system of order and familiarity can be established to bring a common way of evaluating and planning in any difficulty, then survivability becomes a realistic goal. Thinking Maps provide a common language to break down barriers and give continuity to process. Through process, order is established, and common goals are achieved.

The common language for learning introduced to the Pass Christian School District almost eight years ago has proven to be one of the threads that held the community together under the direst of circumstances. Thinking Maps helped the Pass Christian School District in its journey to recover, revive, and rebound after almost total destruction. The journey continues today.

THE RIVER KEEPS MOVING FORWARD

It is gratifying to know that the deep integration of Thinking Maps into schools and classrooms throughout the state is thriving with improvement of student performance and positive feedback from teachers and administrators. It should not take a catastrophic event to sharpen our view about what is important for students living in the 21st century. Thinking Maps, by providing a common language in a variety of settings from the delta to the coast, keep Mississippi moving forward. Thinking Maps are woven throughout the educational community much as the Mississippi River winds its way through the geographical landscape. The stories of Mississippi, like the river, do not stop here. They continue to flow into the what-ifs and possibilities of the vastness of the mind.

REFERENCES

Ball, M. K. (1998). *The effects of Thinking Maps on reading scores of traditional and nontraditional college students.* Doctoral dissertation, University of Southern Mississippi, Hattiesburg.

Buckner, J. (2000). *Write . . . from the beginning.* Raleigh, NC: Innovative Sciences.

15

The Singapore Experience

Student-Centered Fluency

Ho Po Chun, M.Ed.

KEY CONCEPTS

- Thinking Maps® in a multilingual country focused on thinking processes and information literacy
- Using Chinese language characters within a Multi-Flow Map for facilitating cause-and-effect reasoning
- Bringing students to fluency through direct instruction in Thinking Maps and software

Singapore is a small city-state nation with a rich, diverse history as a major trading center in the heart of the Asian oceans. As a crossroads island for commerce, it has been conquered and colonized many times over hundreds of years, with the British relinquishing authority to Singaporeans just a few decades ago. Understandably, it has a diverse population with many cultures and languages, from Chinese, Indian, and Malaysian to British influences. Singapore is just four times the size of Washington, DC, with a population of approximately 4 million. Our main language is English. Our country has also become one of the Asian economic powers in the past decade, mostly through finance and technology, not through its natural resources. Unlike its Asian neighbors, Singapore has no significant stores of natural resources from which an industrial, manufacturing economy can thrive, even needing to import fresh drinking water from Malaysia. It is understandable, then, that in the 21st century, our only true natural resources are the minds of our citizens. Singapore is quickly becoming an information nation.

With this background, it makes sense that the Singapore government hosted the fourth International Thinking Conference in 1997. This conference is convened every two years in locales from MIT in Cambridge, Massachusetts, to Auckland, New Zealand, and has been coordinated by leaders in the field of thinking-skills development. The theme of the Singapore conference was appropriately "Thinking Schools, Learning Nation." This event has been used as one leverage point for shifting the mind-set of our educational system—and country—from a more traditional focus on rote learning to including the facilitation of thinking as an integral part of learning.

At the opening ceremonies of the conference, the president of Singapore spoke eloquently about the need—the necessity—for Singaporeans to reinvent themselves in pursuit of the highest-quality education based on consciously and systematically developing the creative and analytical thinking of Singapore's people. While the conference participants from all over the world, including over 400 Singaporean principals, listened, it became clear that the speaker could have been any president of any country in the world, as the world now turns on the capacities of its citizenry to think, problem-solve, use technology, and collaborate effectively across the globe.

Aziz Tyebally, a teacher and head of the Department for Humanities at Chung Cheng High School, a school that has successfully implemented Thinking Maps, recently delivered a research paper at a nationwide symposium that revealed this need: "In a knowledge-based economy, information is abundant. What made one person more successful than the other was not the information alone, but rather how effectively he made use of the information. Therefore, our program is designed to prepare the pupils for the economy of the future."

Both the president and this teacher made the point that all Singaporeans, including parents of the future workers and citizens of the country, need to improve their thinking. This focus became our entry point into directly training students to become fluent in the use of Thinking Maps.

THINKING MAPS IMPLEMENTATION: STUDENT-CENTERED TRAINING

Presenters at the conference such as Peter Senge (systems thinking), Edward de Bono (lateral thinking), and Art Costa (Habits of Mind) spoke, respectively, about the need for systems thinking, approaching problems from multiple points of view using lateral thinking, and activating Habits of Mind such as reflectiveness and metacognition. The Thinking Maps model was also presented by David Hyerle as a way to integrate thinking-skills instruction with content learning, Habits of Mind with technology, and teaching and learning with assessment. By the end of the conference, many educators in Singapore were excited about many new directions and processes, including Thinking Maps. As one first step, the Singapore branch of the Association for Supervision and Curriculum Development invited Dr. Hyerle to return the following year to present the theoretical and practical foundations for using visual tools, generally, and Thinking Maps, specifically, to about 400 teachers from primary and secondary schools and junior colleges over three days.

While our early results of implementation a year later in a few pilot schools revealed that the Thinking Maps were effective, the model of whole-school training and follow-up with teachers that is used in the United States for implementing Thinking Maps did not mesh with the existing organizational structures in Singapore. The schools and class sizes are large, the time-sensitive curriculum is well defined, and the teachers are focused on the continuing efforts to achieve consistently high content-based test score results, placing Singapore very high on international rankings in mathematics and science. So we went in a significantly different direction than most professional development designs: We focused on students as the first target population for training. We also proceeded to draw on the strength of our country that the president had pointed to in his opening address: the complete commitment by every parent to give his or her children a world-class education.

In most countries, professional development focuses on the training of teachers first, who then use new instructional methods with their students. However, because Thinking Maps are also student centered—and given the structure of our schools and funding—we offered a unique plan: Our consultants would directly train classrooms full of students in how to use Thinking Maps and Thinking Maps software (Hyerle & Gray Matter Software, 2007) on a weekly basis over one or two semesters. Schools are given $160 per student annually that they may use for enrichment courses for students. However, a school has to seek the approval of the parents before signing a student up for a course. Each school is also allotted $80 for each student. This money is to be used solely to meet students' particular learning needs. The funding was available, and many parents enrolled their students in our Thinking Maps courses.

Through our targeted training courses, students become fluent with the maps much more quickly than if teachers had to integrate the approach into their day-to-day lessons. This is much like the use of computers: Often students may be more open to new technologies, as they don't have to consider what they need to change or replace in a complex and content-laden curriculum. In addition—and this may seem odd to an outsider—unlike teachers in other countries, where the students move from classroom to classroom at the secondary level, here, the teachers are the "rovers" and the students stay in the home base for most of their lessons, except perhaps for Mother Tongue (Chinese, Malay, or Tamil), Music, Art, Computer, and Physical Education. This means that a teacher does not have the exclusive use of a particular classroom and the students remain the center of attention.

At this point, 11,594 primary school students and 1,629 secondary school students have gone through direct training by our consultants, and a total of 730 teachers have gone through an intensive course of 12 hours over 3 days to become experts for their schools. Through this whole process, we have learned that the ultimate power of these tools lies in the hands and minds of the learner.

STUDENT WORKSHOPS

The student workshop model turned out to be every bit as successful as we had envisioned. After every course, we would ask students to fill out an evaluation. Below are the comments of some Primary 6 students who have attended our workshops:

"Thinking Maps help me in my Reading Comprehension. I'm able to sequence ideas in a passage."

"In Composition, using the Multi-Flow Map helps me look at the bigger picture."

"Thinking Maps help me expand my vocabulary."

"Thinking Maps help me keep to the point—no 'straying.'"

"The use of Thinking Maps helps me save time."

"My vocabulary has improved after using Thinking Maps."

These comments came from students actively integrating Thinking Maps into their daily work in school through activities that we used to develop fluency of thinking processes. Explicit, systematic, developmental, and content deep, the activities directly train students how to independently apply multiple maps to products such as essay and creative writing that are required by their teachers. The infusion activities that we created are on a continuum, building from introduction to each cognitive skill, the respective map, and multimap use toward products in every content area. Importantly, these levels of fluid, flexible, and novel applications demonstrated by our students exceeded our expectations. We believe this is because we started our work in Singapore focused on student fluency and not on teachers becoming slowly comfortable with sharing the maps with students over months and years.

An example of an infusion activity that we developed to scaffold student thinking and bring fluency to students is shown in an abbreviated form (see Figure 15.1). This activity is conducted in Session 10 with Primary 4 students. The previous nine 1-hour sessions introduced students to each of the eight maps and the Frame of Reference. This lesson is designed to support students in generating their own story using multiple maps of their choosing. The lead activity in this lesson is to show four pictures of the process of burglars breaking into an apartment, with the final panel showing the family coming home to find the house a wreck and a beautiful vase shattered and in pieces on the floor. The defined outcomes of this activity are for students to be able to independently develop ideas and suitable phrases using the Circle Map, become fluent in developing descriptors of emotional responses of characters using the Bubble Map, and then create a logical progression of events with a surprise using the Flow Map. The product was the use of the maps to write a story about the events.

Figure 15.1   Lesson Planning

Session 10

Theme: A Burglary

Primary 4 Lesson Plan

Picture Composition

Objective: To revise the use of Circle, Bubble, and Flow Maps

1. Pupils to study the pictures and come up with different scenarios. (5 Mins) (Robbers are not necessarily strangers. May be an inside job)

2. Pupils brainstorm for ideas and write in Circle Map. (5 Mins) (broke into the house, wore black outfits, would not be seen in the dark, ransacked the house, sound of the breaking vase woke the family, armed with baseball bats and brooms)

3. Pupils use Bubble Map to describe the scene and feelings of the characters. (5 Mins) (Remember to use the Frame of Reference)

Example

Scene—late night, quiet house, messy, broken vase, loud crash, thorough search

Feelings—burglars: nervous, disappointed, scared, panic, alarmed, frantic, daring, physical appearance: black outfits, suspicious-looking; family: shocked, puzzled, angry, suspicious, nervous, scared, worried

4. Pupils sequence the story using the Flow Map. (5 Mins)

5. The conclusion can be a surprise ending. (5 Mins)
   • Something left by the robbers, whom they knew
   • Discovered that she had found something in the vase that she had forgotten
   • Invaluable vase
   • Found long-lost heirloom

(35 Mins)

Pupils write out the maps on their own.

Pupils write draft 2. To be handed in next session.

This lesson was followed in Session 11 by a creative writing assignment using the setting of a conflict in which students are involved. The students were told that they did not have to replicate the use of three maps from the three lessons, nor were they expected to use the maps in the same way. Figure 15.2b shows a piece of writing about an imaginary situation in which a boy is with his brother, who decides to tear up a neighbor's garden. The page of pre-writing using five different maps in very unique ways is an exemplary use of the tools (see Figure 15.2a). As you can see, information is actually scaffolded in the maps, moving from a general Circle Map on "vandalism" to focusing in on the crime "scene." The emotional state of having a brother involved in such an escapade is described in a Bubble Map, using revealing adjectives such as *afraid, worried,* and *unhappy.* The next shift is to a Tree Map for organizing the details of each paragraph. The prewriting process is completed by using a Multi-Flow Map to think about the causes and effects of this event. The final essay directly reflects the culminating Tree Map, where everything is put together in detail and information is grouped by paragraphs.

If you look closely at the prewriting and the product (see Figure 15.2b) it is easy to see that not all of the information in the maps makes it into this story. This is because we trained students not to merely replicate the information from their prewriting maps in a formal way, but to use the maps as a grounding for the essay. Often when students use static graphic organizers for writing, the writing becomes static. In this case, the writing flows nicely, even without a Flow Map, because the author has generated the rich, holistic ideas and vocabulary that enable flexible and creative writing.

TEACHER TRAINING

Of course, to give this attention to student fluency and transfer in the classroom, we knew that our model had to target teachers as well as students. While our initial focus was on the students, we did not neglect the training needs of the teachers. As mentioned above, many teachers went through 12 hours of professional development, but often class teachers would be observing and learning along with the students during our student workshops. This supported teachers' understanding of the tools in real time, using the deep examples and modeling shown above, rather than sitting through long hours of workshop trainings. The teachers are happy that they are able to teach with the Thinking Maps as soon as they are trained because their students already know the maps. Many teachers initially believed that there was no need to take the extra time in teaching the maps to their students, so our work offered them dual support. By taking over one of their classes, we not only taught the maps to the students, but the teachers were able to learn the maps at the same time.

Our consultants also conducted follow-up visits to the school to offer advice and support in the school's implementation efforts in integrating Thinking Maps into the curriculum. The number of visits and the kind of help offered depend on the needs of the school. This ensures that the school is continually supported in its implementation process. During these visits, issues such as monitoring of student work, provision of assistance to the heads of departments, and any other matters related to learning and teaching with the maps are addressed. Below are comments by teachers who have used Thinking Maps in their lessons:

"My pupils are better at organizing their writing. I see more descriptive words used in their writing."

"Excellent! They can control their time better in the sense that they can complete a story within the composition time limit. This must be due to their efficiency in their organization skills."

Figure 15.2a   Student Maps

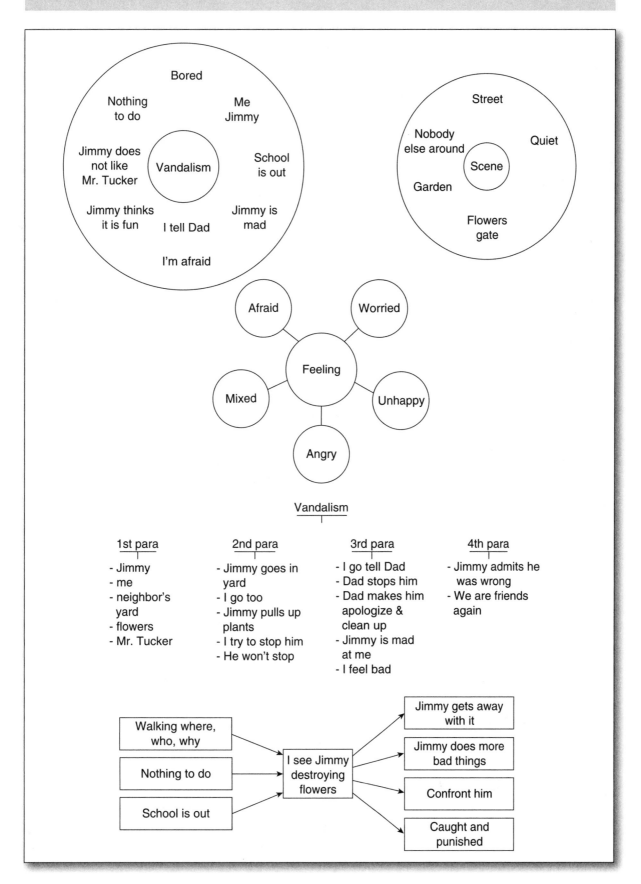

Figure 15.2b   Story Writing to Accompany Maps

Vandalism

School was over for the day. Jimmy, my brother, and I were bored. We wandered down the street looking for something to do. We were the best of friends and always did things together, sometimes with some other kids, too, but today nobody else was around.

"Hey, look! There's Old Man Tucker's garden. Looks like he's not home. Let's go see it." Jimmy pointed down the street. Mr. Tucker was very old and lived alone. He loved working in his garden and had a lot of flowers and potted plants.

Jimmy ran through the open gate and I followed, hesitantly. Our parents always told us not to go on other people's property without being invited. Jimmy went over to a large bush with bright red flowers. With a sly grin, he pulled off a handful of flowers and threw them over his head, laughing.

"Jimmy! Don't do that! You know not to do things like that!"

"So? I'm just having fun. The flowers will die and fall off anyway."

"But you shouldn't tear them up. Mr. Tucker will be mad with you."

"Yeah? Well he won't know who did it. Unless somebody tells him. And nobody knows except you, and you never tell on me for anything."

He was right. I had never told on him before, since most of the stuff we did together wasn't bad. Maybe annoying, but nothing like stealing or wrecking somebody's else's property. I watched him for a minute as he pulled up some green leafy plants and tossed them around. I just couldn't let him continue.

"Jimmy! Stop it!"

"You gonna make me?" he said.

I turned and ran home. Dad was in his study reading the newspaper. "Dad, you better come see what Jimmy's doing." I felt bad by telling on him, and was worried that he would be mad and not be my best friend anymore. But I just couldn't let him get away with it. If he got caught, Old Mr. Tucker might call the police, and that would be worse than telling Dad.

Dad brought Jimmy home and told him that when Mr. Tucker came home they would both go over and Jimmy would apologize and clean up what he had done, and then he would work for Mr. Tucker helping him in his garden for two weeks after school to pay for his mischief.

Jimmy scowled at me angrily. I wanted to sink through the floor. But the next day he admitted that I had done the right thing, and he felt bad about what he had done. We were pals again.

"The pupils are more confident and are able to use the Thinking Maps to generate ideas in some activities. In Comprehension, pupils are able to pick out/highlight important ideas and not lift out sentences from the passage."

"Thinking Maps helped students to focus better."

"Pupils are more aware of flow of ideas."

"Pupils have improved in ideas and vocabulary. Pupils are attempting to use newly acquired vocabulary."

"They are more confident in the use of it as a thinking tool, and showed better organization of ideas as they have a standard framework to work on."

THOUGHT AND LANGUAGES

In response to the call from our Ministry of Education to systematically support creative and analytical thinking, many teachers, for the first time, have a flexible structure that enables them to develop their students' thinking processes. Aziz Tyebally, quoted earlier, describes how his department used the high level of student fluency with the maps to engender a new way to assess students:

> The pupils are required to use Thinking Maps to represent the development of their group discussions as well as their individual thought process. The Thinking Maps are dynamic, as they can be constantly built upon over a period of time; hence, a measure of their development of thought could be seen. The school has also incorporated a write-up on Thinking Maps in its Humanities Handbook and uses it as a means of assessment. The maps were simple enough to learn, so the opportunities for use in complex situations were immense. This was further supported by user-friendly software, which the students could use to enhance their projects. The feedback from students, using a feedback form, was highly positive from the first course conducted. We noted that the number of times per week students say they use Thinking Maps in class and on their own has increased over the years. This seems to indicate that Thinking Maps are becoming more extensively used as a common visual language.

The ease of use, the fluid quality of students' use of the tools, and the flexible structure leading to a new way of assessing thinking and learning have all been essential to the use of Thinking Maps across subject areas and grade levels. The metacognitive skills of the students in these schools are also more evident when the teachers are more fluent in each of the maps, and in particular the Frame of Reference. When teachers systematically keep a portfolio of their students' work using the maps, they are better able to track the development of their students' thinking processes.

There is something powerful as well as subtle about this common visual language for learning that transcends other models of thinking and best practices. We have found that these tools are not bound by language or culture. There were some initial concerns voiced by some principals that the Mother Tongue (Chinese, Tamil, Malay) teachers would not adapt to the use of Thinking Maps as well as the other subject teachers. Just the opposite transpired. We see examples all the time of Chinese characters and other languages embedded naturally within the patterns of thinking represented in the maps. For example, a student has created a Multi-Flow Map showing the causes and effects of throwing things from tall buildings (see Figure 15.3), a real concern in Singapore since many families live in high-rise apartment buildings. These second-language, Mother Tongue teachers have surpassed all expectations by demonstrating how innovative and creative they are in integrating the maps into their lessons.

We believe that this is because the cognitive patterns such as sequencing, categorization, and analogies are universal processes of humankind and of the human mind. The visual maps become a common reference point for communicating, expressing, and uniting thought and language. In a country such as Singapore, where East *has met* West, our island culture may be best understood as an embodiment of layers of languages and cultures from generations. We need common tools such as Thinking Maps that help us communicate through the often impenetrable barriers of language and culture that have the potential of separating us. There may be a lesson here for every country at the beginning of the 21st century. We, as global citizens, are increasingly in need of common ways of communicating as our world becomes ever more connected and globalized, as technologies web us together, and as we seek to find common ground through understanding about how different people think around the world. As many have said, we may have much more in common than we think.

Figure 15.3 Chinese "High Rise" Multi-Flow Map and Translation

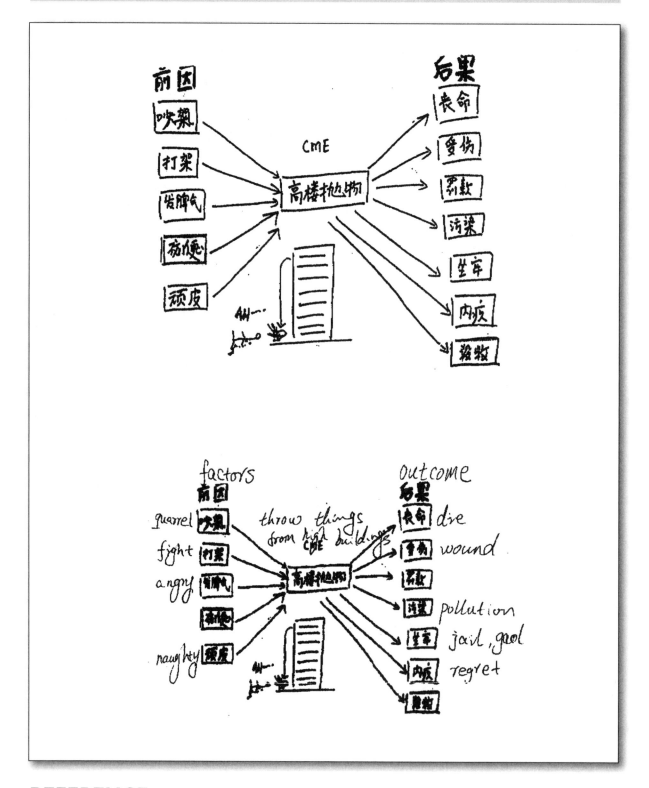

REFERENCE

Hyerle, D., & Gray Matter Software. (2007). *Thinking Maps* (Version 2.0, Innovative Learning Group) [Computer software]. Raleigh, NC: Innovative Sciences.

Section 4

Transforming Professional Development

16

Inviting Explicit Thinking

Sarah Curtis, M.Ed.

KEY CONCEPTS

- Facilitating reflective practice by teachers through a Training of Trainers model
- Using student-centered work to heighten teachers' understandings of teaching, learning, and assessment
- Flexibility with Thinking Maps® for planning and in-the-moment teaching

RESPONSIBLE AND RESPONSIVE PROFESSIONAL DEVELOPMENT

Reacting to the urgency to improve student performance, schools have implemented program upon program and offered workshop after workshop with few opportunities and insufficient time for teachers to deeply learn, integrate, or reflect upon these approaches. Educators of the early 21st century face a daunting challenge in trying to meet the needs of all students, of all languages, ethnicities, abilities, and socioeconomic backgrounds, while being held to new standards of achievement. An increase in accountability and a leveling of support leave many educators feeling overwhelmed, undirected, and unprepared. Michael Fullan, a researcher of change processes, states that "the greatest problem faced by school districts and schools is not resistance to innovation, *but the fragmentation, overload and incoherence resulting from the uncritical acceptance of too many different innovations*" (Sparks, 1997).

As a teacher, I felt burdened and exhausted because everywhere I turned it seemed like I had to teach one more unit of content, administer another test, or address the state standards. Buried under district initiatives, school memos, the new math program, and a recently adopted curriculum, I could barely see through to the real purpose for all these improvements: student achievement. After spending weeks wading through a topic-driven curriculum and figuratively traveling the globe and spanning centuries of time to reteach myself Renaissance history, the ancient cultures of Meso-America, and the principles of force and motion, I wondered, how could I integrate these isolated topics, and how would my students be able to jump from stone to stone constructing a pathway of understanding?

My unsettling experience with fragmentation was transformed as I began to apply Thinking Maps as learning and thinking tools for myself and for my students. While constructing a whole from the pieces, it became apparent to me that educators need tools and processes to meaningfully translate these initiatives into practice and to support and engage teacher thinking through the implementation process. As a result of my experiences with Thinking Maps, engaging educators in reflective thinking about teaching and learning through the use of this language became the focus of my professional inquiry and practice.

With the goal to improve teaching for student improvement, educators are now seeing that there must be a systemic plan in place for school improvement. Schools need to engage in professional development that really develops the professional so that teachers, just as students, have time to reflect on their own learning processes. Donald Schön (1983), a leading author on reflective practice, describes expert practice as "an artful inquiry into situations of uncertainty." Reflective practitioners ask themselves, "What am I doing and why? What worked and what didn't and why?" Providing occasions for teachers "to reflect critically on their practice and to fashion new knowledge and beliefs about content, pedagogy, and learners" is a key component of a new vision for staff development (Sparks, 1997). In its standards, the National Staff Development Council recommends "organizing adults into learning communities," "guiding continuous instructional improvement," and emphasizing collaboration with colleagues to engage the entire school culture in reflections about teaching and learning. Defining the broad goals of professional development is one component of this new vision, but we also need to identify best models, not merely a laundry list of best practices, that will explicitly integrate theory, practice, and reflection and directly impact student learning.

THINKING MAPS: A MODEL FOR REFLECTIVE PRACTICE

As my teaching progressed in the early 1990s, my school in Lebanon, New Hampshire, as a whole faculty began to implement Thinking Maps as tools for learning, planning, and instruction. Our principal was very interested in the facilitation of metacognition over the long term, not just for students, but also for teachers and administrators. As the first year of using these tools progressed, I began to see student discourse and meaning making reflected in the types of thinking inherent in the Thinking Maps. These tools also helped me reflect on the content in a holistic and connected way and design units of study focusing on threading concepts rather than streaming content. Simultaneously, I gained insights into student learning and my own instruction. Students who previously had trouble learning new and difficult content now had a means of connecting new information, processes, and interactions with prior knowledge. They were very capable of thinking deeply about the subject matter but needed an explicit way to examine it and express their thinking. I realized that instead of modifying the content, I needed to fortify their tools for learning.

The students were not alone in their growth. When I used Thinking Maps in planning and instruction, my own patterns of thinking improved. The avalanche of curriculum, assessments, district programs, and school memos that buried me in September now seemed more manageable. I could understand and articulate concepts more coherently, synthesize the fragmented curriculum, and feel confident about my ability to help students be successful learners. My professional and personal experiences applying Thinking Maps fueled my curiosity to see what happened in other classrooms and, more specifically, what happens in the minds of teachers as they use Thinking Maps with their students. How do Thinking Maps, tools that facilitate both continuous cognitive development and explicit visual representations of metacognition, promote teacher reflection?

After leaving the classroom to begin providing in-depth Thinking Maps professional development training and follow-up, I wanted to examine these issues in depth. My teaching experiences were exclusively in rural settings in New England, so I also became interested in how this model would work in inner-city classrooms with teachers who worked with diverse populations, in low socioeconomic neighborhoods, and in schools with historically low achievement. I conducted action research as part of a master's project during the 2000–2001 school year, working with two groups of 15 educators: one group from the Syracuse City School District in Syracuse, New York, and another in Community School District 27 in Queens, New York.

What I found mirrored my experiences; not only did the Thinking Maps improve teaching and student performance, but the model itself deepened teachers' reflection on their own teaching and instruction and produced richer reflections about their students' thinking. For one fifth-grade teacher of particularly challenging students in Syracuse, Thinking Maps were tools that linked together student and teacher success: "I was teaching a lesson in social studies, and I must have asked a question every conceivable way I could think of. Nobody participated. So I drew a Multi-Flow Map on the board and got where I wanted to go! Thinking Maps not only seized the teachable moment; they *created* the teachable moment." Ultimately, I came to see that these deeper levels of reflection and performance changes developed because the Thinking Maps invite explicit thinking and thus reflection, bringing a clarity that inspires confidence and competence.

RESULTS OF TEACHER-REPORTED REFLECTIONS

My study focused on those teachers who participated in the Thinking Maps Training of Trainers professional development sessions. Although I was primarily interested in how teachers created Thinking Maps for the purpose of engaging in reflection about learning and instruction aside from their daily classroom interactions with students, I also found that teachers used students' Thinking Maps examples and teacher-generated Thinking Maps lesson plans as visual references that generated reflection about student learning, instruction, and planning. Teacher-reported data revealed positive changes in both student behavior and performance and teacher curriculum and instruction as a result of Thinking Maps implementation.

Figure 16.1 shows the categories of what teachers most frequently identified as having improved as a result of Thinking Maps implementation. Data collected about student performance focused on themes regarding improvement in students' thinking, particularly relating to task persistence and organization in writing; improvement in student behaviors including attention, motivation, and participation; and an increase in student-directed learning. Teachers reported greater clarity in instruction, increased awareness of purpose in lessons, and a greater degree of effectiveness in teaching. These student and teacher findings, separately and collectively, demonstrated how all learners in the classroom used the same set of tools, Thinking Maps, to visually represent their thinking, which led to a greater level of understanding and efficacy.

The qualitative findings offer valuable information about the climate and creation of classroom environments in which teachers design and present clear and meaningful instruction and students can understand, attend to, and participate in learning tasks in challenging urban settings. It was through teacher reflection about Thinking Maps experiences that these urban educators gained insight into student learning, teacher instruction, and curriculum planning.

REFLECTIONS ON STUDENT LEARNING AND BEHAVIOR

Being able to see their own and others' thinking afforded students and teachers new understandings about themselves and each other as learners. Having a visual representation

Figure 16.1 Teacher Reflection Results Tree Map

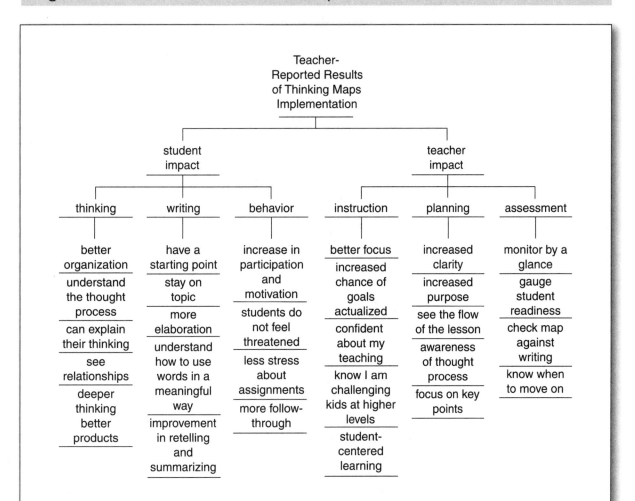

system for knowledge created confidence and competence for the learner (see Chapter 5, "Closing the Gap by Connecting Culture, Language, and Cognition"), whether that person was a student or a teacher. A third-grade teacher from Syracuse shared a story involving a child who frequently misbehaved in class, didn't finish his assignments, and totally avoided writing. He loved Tuesdays because the school counselor visited with him during the writing period on that day. Every Tuesday, the child glanced at the door, eagerly anticipating the counselor's arrival and his free ticket out of the writing assignment. However, one particular Tuesday, following a Thinking Maps training session, his teacher used a Circle and Flow Map to explain the assignment to the class and to demonstrate how to organize ideas on the way to a piece of writing. Focusing intently on the lesson and adding his ideas to the class map, the boy hadn't noticed the counselor entering the room. The student explained that he was busy working on something and couldn't leave right then.

Observing the student's level of engagement encouraged the teacher to examine why this lesson was effective and what caused inattention with this student and others in the classroom. The teacher thought the lesson was successful because using the maps in her lesson gave students a cognitive and visual cue to follow the process of writing. As the teacher used the Flow Map to organize and sequence the ideas in the story, her verbal explanations of processes were supported by the visual representation of the map, thus making the thinking processes explicit to the students. Students could follow not only the steps but also the mental dynamics of idea formation. Teacher clarity and a concrete model of the abstract thinking processes invited this student's participation and understanding.

What does an improvement in motivation and the level of engagement tell us about learning? One Training of Trainers cohort group noted how often negative behavior is a defense mechanism for confusion or fear, or the result of frustration with traditional models of instruction and production of work. Perhaps, group members posited, this student wanted to participate in writing but couldn't organize his ideas or sequence his thoughts. These improvements in behavior might indicate that students have the ability but not the means to represent ideas clearly and proceed to writing.

During one training session, in the middle of a discussion of the success stories about students with behavioral issues and attention problems, one participant exclaimed, "Thinking Maps can replace Ritalin!" (see Chapter 3, "Leveling the Playing Field for All Students"). After the initial laughter died down, the teachers began to seriously explore the plausibility of this exclamation. One teacher stated that Thinking Maps would be a viable alternative therapy:

> Thinking Maps work for these kids because they are consistent when nothing else in their life is. They go home to a place without rules, responsibility, and consequences. Their home life is chaotic. No routine, no schedule. Sometimes Mom is home, sometimes not. No one is looking out for them. They can do whatever they want, whenever they want. Although they might like the freedom, they don't have a sense of order or control. They come to school wanting that power and sense of control. The consistency of Thinking Maps can give them a sense of ownership. "I can do this. I know how to do this." They feel like they are good at something.

In her reflections, this teacher considered from within her own cultural experiences and assumptions aspects of how the familial and socioeconomic context of the students might surface within this learning community: consistency, control, and ownership. She was sensitive to the underlying emotional currents in the classroom and understood how Thinking Maps could alleviate the tension. As she examined the effectiveness of Thinking Maps, she identified permeating, perhaps universal, needs.

Other teachers remarked how Thinking Maps had supported the emotional as well as the cognitive development of students by appealing to students' sense of safety. "They [students] feel comfortable, not confined to a certain number of responses . . . add to them as lessons progress . . . and use them on their own as well as in a group." Another teacher noted, "If I reflect for a minute, I think it [using the Thinking Maps] has widened our horizons because kids are empowered over their learning. They are more willing to take risks because with a map nothing is wrong. You can show your thinking how you want. It doesn't have to be the same as the next person's."

Listening to these observations, there was a common recognition that one's knowledge and its expression don't necessarily coexist. Just because students knew information didn't mean they would share it. In the complex climate of preadolescent, urban classrooms—where the culture of the students does not necessarily match the cultural background of the teacher—the expression of knowledge by students may be double-edged, as their ideas are subject to outside expectations and scrutiny. The Thinking Maps, a flexible, consistent, common visual language, supporting both the process and the product of thinking, were understood by these teachers as a safe venue for students to show what they know (see Chapter 5).

TEACHER INSTRUCTION AND PLANNING

Although a considerable amount of teacher-reported data focused on student learning, teachers discussed some of the same ideas of competency and confidence surrounding their own instruction and planning. Teachers' reflections about Thinking Maps integration identified that Thinking Maps helped them to become more flexible, responsive, clear, and purposeful in their instruction and planning.

In-the-Moment Instruction

At the third Training of Trainers session, a kindergarten teacher couldn't wait to share what she had learned with the group. In preparation for a lesson comparing and contrasting two books about George Washington, she had drawn a Double Bubble Map with four bubbles for the similarities and three bubbles on each side for the differences. During the lesson, she recorded the children's responses, but within moments, they had exhausted her template. "You need more bubbles!" they chorused. Their powers of observation and attention to detail astounded her. She learned how attentive her students were and planned to use those responses as a rubric by which to judge their future work. The map was an unexpected assessment tool. Moreover, her students reminded her not to predetermine their capacity for information. "My thinking could have limited their thinking!" she realized. Reflecting about this experience led her to question her expectations of her students and their proficiency with observation and comprehension skills.

Whereas the kindergarten teacher used the Double Bubble Map to facilitate comprehension after reading, a second-grade teacher applied the Thinking Maps to support students' thinking during math computation. Working at a low-performing elementary school, this teacher found herself in an anxiety-producing situation when an outside group of consultants selected her for observation. The school had purchased a very specific program aimed to improve mathematical computation skills and hopefully release the school from the state's probationary status. To guarantee results, the company structured quality checks at participating sites. This teacher was slated to teach a lesson on subtraction and feared the consultants' presence because the children were having a difficult time with subtracting two-digit whole numbers. "I was thinking what the kids had problems with," she says. "In the middle of the problem, they seemed to forget the next step."

She decided to use a Flow Map to show the sequence of steps in subtraction. The next day, the students accurately completed the problems using the Flow Maps at their desks. The observer thought the lesson was sensational and asked if she could keep a copy of the Flow Map. "The Thinking Map helped me get my ideas in order and really think about subtraction," the teacher says. The Flow Map clarified her own thinking as well as that of the students. Relating to the sharing of this example at the training session, another teacher later reported in the postsession survey nearly exactly the same sentiment: "They [Thinking Maps] help me organize, and lessons involving the use of Thinking Maps have a far greater chance of reaching their objective."

Planning

Reaching her objective, rather than repeating last year's abysmal performance, was exactly what a sixth-grade teacher was determined to do with her unit on fairy tales (see Figure 16.2). Unlike the previously mentioned situations, this teacher used the Circle Map during the initial planning stages as a reflective tool to help her analyze the unit and plan for success. First she brainstormed all the tasks, materials, and understandings necessary for students to be able to write the final product, an original version of "Cinderella." Looking at the Circle Map while simultaneously recalling the problems from last year's narratives, she anticipated some obstacles and consequently selected the most important ideas, including defining elements of a fairy tale that would support students in the development of their final piece. She asked herself, "What do I want them to learn? Which Thinking Maps would help them notice the patterns in various versions of 'Cinderella'?" She selected the multitiered Bridge Map (see Figure 16.3) as the tool to isolate the elements of a fairy tale and help students see the pattern of elements across many versions.

She then used a Flow Map (see Figure 16.4) to sequence the progression of tasks to ensure that students actively processed the material. She decided to have students apply specific Thinking Maps at different times during the reading process to scaffold their comprehension. In her planning, she became very animated, discussing how she could incorporate cooperative learning and sharing among groups. Her work demonstrates her understanding of the learning process of her students and the need for students to first deconstruct fairy tales during reading and later reconstruct the elements in their own fashion while writing their own original Cinderella story. With the maps, she had a built-in, ongoing assessment of their comprehension and could adjust her instruction accordingly. As she decided about both the progression and the nature of instruction for this unit, she had to adopt the learner's perspective

Figure 16.2 Cinderella Lesson Planning Circle Map

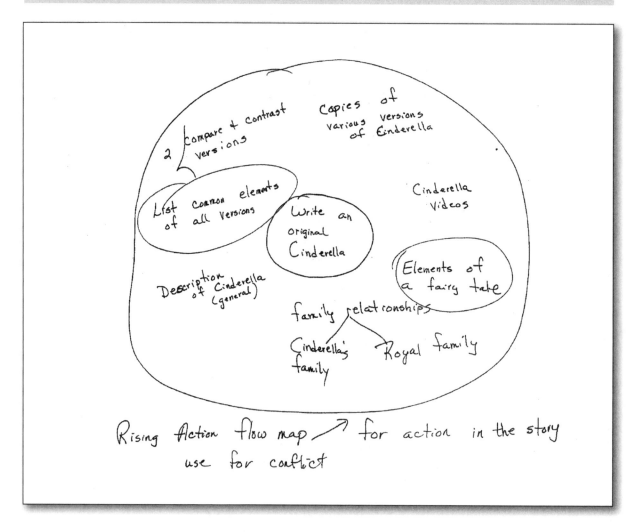

Figure 16.3   Elements of a Fairy Tale Bridge Map

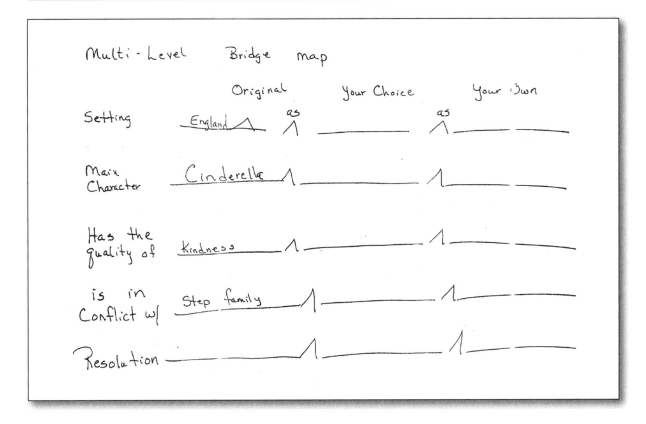

Figure 16.4   Cinderella Unit Plan Sequence With Multiple Map Integration

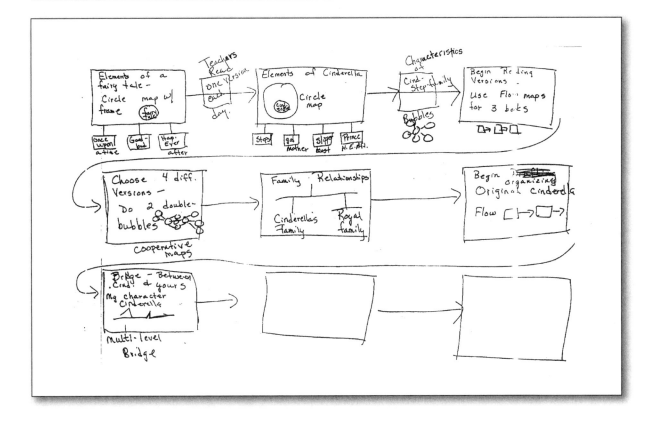

and anticipate where her students might have difficulty. Applying the maps as both a lesson-design technique and a student tool, this teacher was deeply reflective, shifting her perspective from the end product to the processes required in her students' minds. As she left the training session that day, she felt very confident in her ability and in her students' abilities to find the essentials within a Cinderella story.

This teacher's mapping of her Cinderella unit exemplifies how Thinking Maps aid teachers' understandings of the topics they teach and how using the maps promotes reflection about instruction. To effectively plan a unit, teachers need to clearly articulate their outcome and decide on an effective course of instruction. For example, they need to anticipate how students would know what the elements of a fairy tale are and identify the variations in elements due to the geographical and cultural background of particular tales. Thinking Maps thus provide teachers with a means of questioning themselves to look for certain patterns of knowledge.

Beyond the Classroom

In addition to their teaching positions in the classroom, these Training of Trainers participants used Thinking Maps to help in their other roles within the school organization. As curriculum coordinators and teachers on special assignment, half of the educators were responsible for evaluating, presenting, or integrating new programs into current practice. Under the pressure of time, money, test results, and district demands, these educators had to present ideas to administrators and faculty members who were at times highly skeptical about new approaches. To understand and present the key points clearly, concisely, and convincingly, these educators used the same tools that fostered understanding and participation in the classroom to communicate their ideas. One teacher remarked, "Thinking Maps were most helpful in creating a clear and concise outline for staff of the requirements and concepts to be covered in the New York state core curriculum."

It is interesting to note that at the beginning of the sessions the participants were constantly asking how to integrate the Thinking Maps with the New York State English Language Arts assessment. They wanted to know how they could immediately use Thinking Maps to support the writing process and other comprehension skills tested on the assessment. If they didn't teach writing, they asked, "How does this help math problem solving?" or "How can we make this work with our reading framework?" or "What maps would you use with conflict or equality?" Initially, the stress wore a *V* in their brows as they worked hard to bring the Thinking Maps onto their overcrowded plates, because previous professional development experiences had brought another program to implement rather than tools for integrating what was already on their plates.

Over the course of the training, they learned how the Thinking Maps would actually help students learn the patterns of thinking embedded in reading and writing across all subject areas and existing in programs they were using. The discussions and feedback changed from knowledge questions about the maps to understandings about effective integration of the maps into existing programs and processes. "Now I am much more aware of the thought process I am working on with each assignment," said one teacher. "I know I am reaching higher levels of thinking." Another teacher remarked, "The *thinking* is the process, and the *maps* are the language." So by the end of the training process, the maps were an effective and efficient set of tools for integrating layers of instruction.

In the same way the participants' students had taken ownership of the maps and become fluent with the tools, the educators I followed had become more fluent and reflective thinkers. They seemed much more capable and confident about asking and answering questions about learning in the context of their complex, challenging, and often changing educational environment.

CREATING A CULTURE OF CHANGE THROUGH INVITING EXPLICIT THINKING

When I consider the layers of pressures placed upon teachers in the classroom—and the shifts made by these educators I was able to observe and question during this study—I think about the intrinsic personal and professional rewards of working in a school in which faculty members are reflective practitioners. Imagine whole schools in which students, teachers, and administrators use tools to understand content, context, their colleagues, and themselves. As demonstrated in this study, Thinking Maps implementation and the Training of Trainers process provided both a language and a model for thinking deeply and reflectively about student learning, teacher instruction, and planning. "Thinking Maps," observed one of the participants, "ensure that thinking is the focus of teaching." This focus on inviting explicit thinking through Thinking Maps animates reflective practice—the process of thinking about the complex nature of teaching and learning—and ensures that responding, relating, and renewing are at the center of creating the unique culture of schools.

REFERENCES

Curtis, S. (2001). *Inviting explicit thinking: Thinking Maps professional development: Tools to develop reflection and cognition.* Unpublished master's thesis, Antioch New England Graduate School, Keene, NH.

Schön, D. (1983). *The reflective practitioner: How professionals think in action.* New York: Basic Books.

Sparks, D. (1997). Reforming teaching and reforming staff development: An interview with Susan Loucks-Horsley. *Journal of Staff Development, 18*(4), 20–23.

17

Coaching and Supervising Reflective Practice

Kathy Ernst, M.S.Ed.

KEY CONCEPTS

- Using Thinking Maps® to improve supervision, coaching, and teaching
- Using Thinking Maps for lesson observation and collaborative reflection
- Using Thinking Maps to facilitate lesson study in mathematics

Milo Novelo and I walked briskly through the corridors of the New York City public school. Milo was one of my advisees in the Leadership in Mathematics Education program at Bank Street College of Education, and the purpose of my visit on this blustery November day was to supervise him in his role as mathematics coach. He looked forward to these site visits because they enabled him to do what an effective, skillful educator *must* do but is rarely supported in doing: reflect on, question, analyze, and improve his practice. As Milo put it, "When you spend a day walking in my shoes, you put a mirror to my work so I can stand back and look at it. You challenge me to examine what I'm doing and to question *why* I do what I do." I looked forward to these visits because they gave *me* an opportunity to learn—to deepen my own understanding of mathematics teaching and learning and to reflect on and improve my skills as coach and supervisor.

On the day of the visit, Milo informed me that our destination was a fourth-grade class, taught by Anna, a novice and struggling teacher. Unfortunately, given the constraints of the school schedule, he was unable to have a planning meeting with Anna. This is often the case in schools around the country as *time* is one of the most significant barriers to the improvement of teacher quality through the completion of the full cycle of supervision or coaching. It was only this morning that he had touched base with her, introduced himself, and arranged for us to come into her class during the math lesson. Observations and consultations by several curriculum "experts" with disparate directives had failed to yield improvement in her ability to manage and teach her students. The little self-confidence and joy she once had about teaching was rapidly eroding. As we entered her room, Milo tried to put Anna at ease by introducing me with his usual line: "Kathy's my advisor from Bank Street. She's here for the day to observe *me* and to help me do a better job as math coach."

Until that day, I had been dissatisfied with my techniques of scripting observations and my process of analyzing the observation data with teachers. At the beginning of each postconference, typically I would ask the teacher for his or her input: "What stood out for you regarding the children's work and thinking? What aspects of the lesson were you pleased with?" Although I was often successful at building upon and deepening the discussion with references to the teacher's observations and samples of children's work, there existed an uncomfortable disconnect between my observations, written in the moment, and those of the teacher, recalled after the fact. Upon further reflection, I discovered some unsettling patterns in my work.

In spite of the fact that my classroom observations often yielded pages of descriptive and accurate accounts of meaningful dialogue and action, they were not readily accessible to me, or to those I was coaching or supervising. There was little *transparency* or visible access by teachers to my notes, which, in turn, often led to a subtle loss of trust. Professional trust in the context of coaching and supervision is essential to the development of teacher improvement. Pragmatically, whenever I needed to retrieve an anecdote that was relevant to my debriefing conversation with a teacher, the flow of our discussion was usually interrupted while I hurriedly scanned pages of my notes, searching for the "gem" I knew was buried somewhere between the mountains of lines. There sat the teacher, passively, while I sat in control of the data (after all, they were written in my own "chicken scratch"—who else could make sense of them?). All too often these awkward interruptions gave rise to a cloud of tension that threatened to inhibit our conversation. I'd occasionally notice the teacher glancing uneasily at my notes, trying to decipher what I'd written. In these situations I tried to reassure the teacher that my purpose was not to evaluate his or her performance but to facilitate reflection and improvement in his or her practice. It was evident that *my* practice needed to improve. How could I more clearly and efficiently document events that I observed in the classroom? How could the retrieval of observation data and conversations about them be more inclusive and democratic for teachers? And how could my use of the lesson data facilitate inquiry and analysis focused on student learning and the *teaching*—not on the teacher?

TOOLS FOR FOCUSED OBSERVATION AND REFLECTION

The breakthrough occurred for me that day when Milo and I entered Anna's classroom. I began using a simple visual tool to help me graphically represent the flow of the lesson. As I settled into a chair at the back of Anna's class, I took out my clipboard and oriented it in a different way—horizontally rather than vertically. Today I was going to record my observations of Anna's teaching while also capturing Milo's coaching moves with a Thinking Map—a Flow Map—used to sequence events. I had recently been introduced to Thinking Maps, but I had not yet perceived them as tools for supervision.

It was evident from the beginning that Anna was not only unsure of the mathematics and the purpose of the lesson, but she lacked assertiveness and control of the class. As I watched her unsuccessfully lead the students through an introductory activity of identifying multiples of 8 on the hundred chart, I asked myself, "What's *important* to document? What questions, comments, prompts, and actions have the potential to stimulate conversations that can lead to improvement of her teaching?" I tentatively lowered my pen to the paper, wondering, "*How* do I document what I see and hear? Where does one event end and another begin? Is an action or a dialogue a new event or a *substage* of the previous event?" Trusting that there are multiple ways to map a lesson, I cast aside my uncertainty and dove in. My pen flew across the paper as my questions guided me to make split-second decisions about *what* and *how* to document. Curiously, I discovered that the simple act of drawing rectangles around events as they unfolded brought visual clarity to my thinking, which, in turn, enabled me to focus on the essence of the teaching and learning. As the lesson ended and Milo arranged to meet with Anna at a time later in the day, I looked over my Flow Map. In spite of my "chicken scratch," the representation of my observation was so visually clear that the classroom dialogue and action nearly jumped off the page. At long last I had data that were *readily accessible!*

Milo's eyes widened as I laid out the Flow Map of the lesson on the table in front of us (see Figure 17.1). He and I sat side by side as I began to retell the story, pointing to each event as we went along. At times, it was Milo who deciphered my writing and joined in the storytelling. What amazed both of us was the ease with which we could retrieve events of the lesson and the comfortable, collaborative nature of this process. There was none of the anxiety or defensiveness characteristic of some debriefing conversations I facilitated in the past. Instead, our focus was on the map in front of us, with its clear, descriptive evidence of the teaching, coaching, and student learning.

We read the Flow Map of the lesson and discussed how Milo could rephrase some of the questions he had posed to students and the modeling he had done for Anna when he stepped in to give specific directions to the students. Then we examined the Flow Map through a different lens: We looked at how he could support Anna in her mathematics teaching. Anna had gotten off to a rocky start, failing to engage her students in the launch of the lesson, so we examined Event #1: *Anna in front of class using pocket 100 chart to help students find multiples of 8* and Event #2: *Students are inattentive.* I asked Milo, "What do you think *caused* the kids to be inattentive?" As Milo talked, I realized the type of thinking that we were both doing: cause and effect reasoning. I simply shifted to the use of the Multi-Flow Map and began recording his responses in a form that first showed the possible causes of the difficulties (see Figure 17.2). Milo proceeded to reflect on the possible reasons: Anna had not given the students a clear sense of the purpose of the lesson; as Anna highlighted multiples of 8 on the hundred chart, she used a yellow marker, which made the resulting pattern difficult for students to see; it was apparent that many of the students lacked prior experience in exploring patterns of multiples on the hundred chart—perhaps they should have begun with multiples of a number smaller than 8, such as 2 or 3.

Later in the day, Milo and I met with Anna to talk about the lesson. Knowing how disheartened and overwhelmed she was feeling in her role as a new teacher with no prior training in this mathematics curriculum, we decided to focus only on the beginning of the lesson. Milo opened the conversation by asking, "How do you think things went?" Anna responded, "I don't really get the point of this lesson. . . . The kids had a hard time getting started, and when I gave them the activity sheet, they were confused. It helped when you stepped in and gave them directions."

Moving his chair next to Anna, Milo said reassuringly, "We noticed some of the same things you did." At this point, Milo re-created the partial Multi-Flow Map he and I had constructed earlier in the day, starting only with Event #2: *Students are inattentive.* He reiterated a cause that Anna herself had just identified—*purpose of lesson not clearly articulated*—and added it to the map. Milo then explained to Anna how an exploration of multiples on the hundred chart enables students to see visual and numerical patterns, which are essential to building a deeper understanding of multiplication and division. He suggested a way to introduce the activity to students. As Anna seemed to grasp the purpose of the lesson, Milo continued. "Something else we noticed was that the kids couldn't really see the highlighting of the multiples of 8, so it was hard for them to find *other* multiples of 8." Milo added another cause of students' inattentiveness to the map: *patterns on the hundred chart not visually clear.* As he elaborated, Anna nodded in agreement, offering suggestions about how she could use colored

Figure 17.1 Flow Map: What was the sequence of events observed and documented in the lesson?

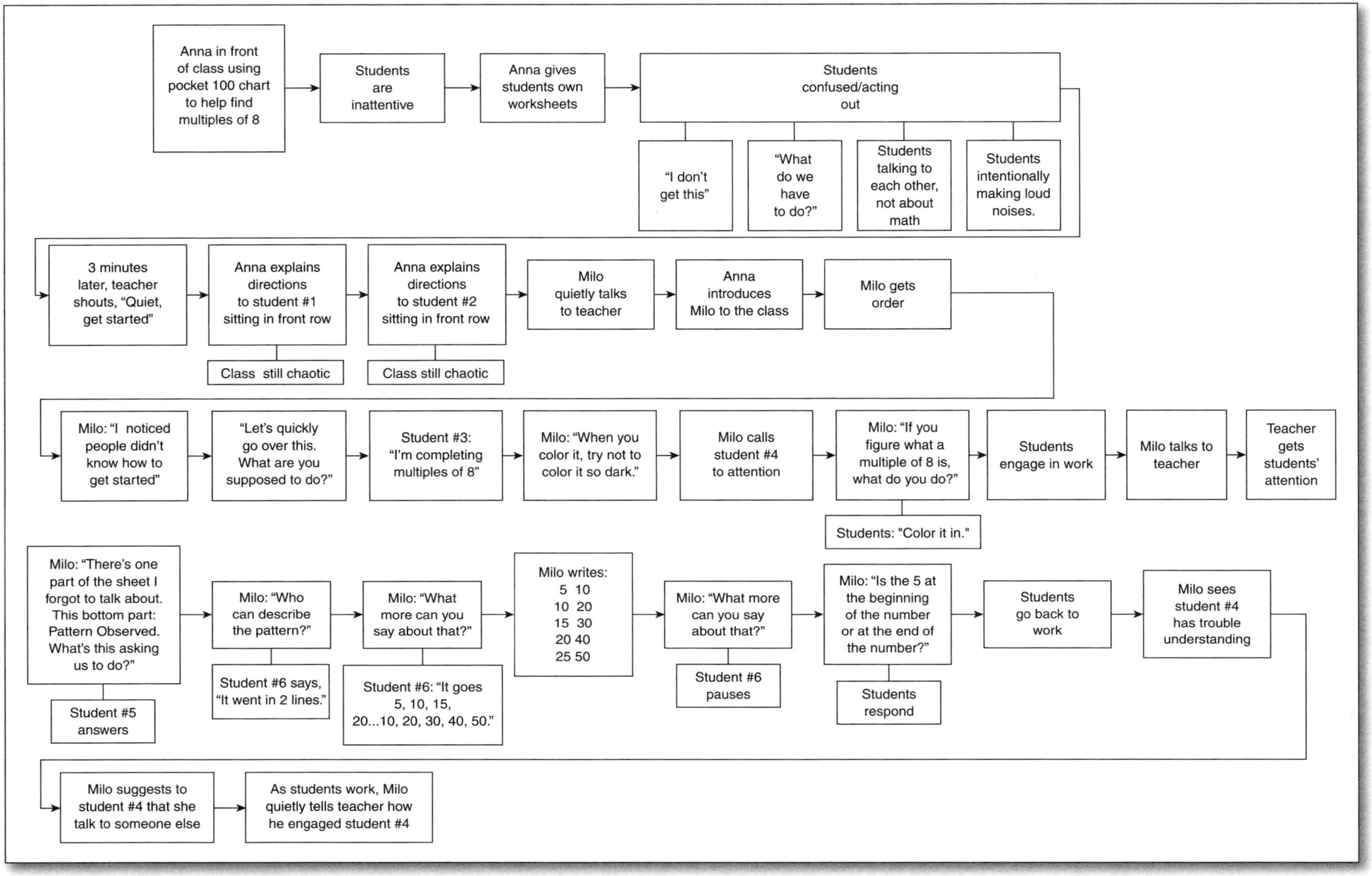

Figure 17.2 Multi-Flow Map: What caused students to be inattentive?

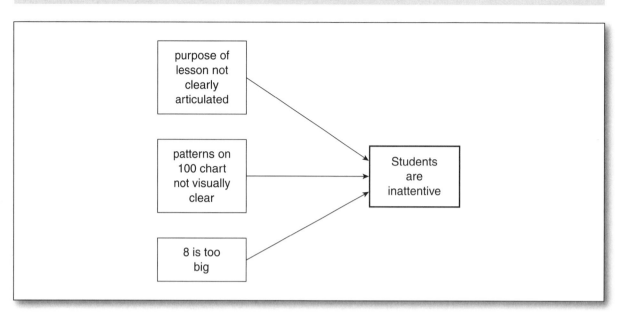

acetate squares to more effectively highlight the multiples. Finally, Milo shared his assessment of the students' relative lack of experience with the activity, and the ensuing difficulty they had with identifying patterns for such a large number. After adding this third cause (*8 is too big*) to the map, Milo engaged Anna in an exploration of multiples of 2 and 3 on the hundred chart, modeling the kinds of questions she could later pose to her students. At the end of our conversation, Anna looked at the partial Multi-Flow Map Milo had constructed and said, "So many people have come into my classroom with vague advice and comments that have just made things worse. This is the first time anyone's given me concrete suggestions about what I can *do*. This has been really helpful—thank you." The map in front of us, elegant in its simplicity, had not only facilitated clear thinking in our process of reflection, dialogue, and inquiry, but it was an immediate document of our conversation and a springboard for further action.

I had experienced something very powerful that day—the discovery that the use of Thinking Maps could so efficiently and effectively cause a qualitative shift in my postobservation conversations with teachers about their instruction and student learning. The visual representation offered a coherent cognitive map from which verbal inquiry could emerge. The Flow Map of the lesson had given Milo and me an explicit and immediate record of the class dialogue and actions that we could readily access and discuss *together*. The Multi-Flow Map had enabled us to analyze, together and later with Anna, the causes of student inattentiveness, which led to deep conversations about the mathematics, the mathematical thinking of the students, and ways in which Anna could engage her students and support their learning. Most important, the maps served as a third point—visual patterns of thinking before us—so that we could focus our attention on the *teaching*, not on the *teacher*. This shift, so difficult to attain in debriefing conversations, was naturally mediated by the visible representation of the lesson flow and the collaborative inquiry invited by the use of the Multi-Flow Map in the lesson analysis. The use of the maps had enabled Milo and me to do our best thinking, and as a result, the time we spent together was the most productive it had ever been. We also had an explicit, visual document of our work and thinking during the supervision process, which could be readily accessed and reflected on in the future. As I left Milo's school that day, I was struck by the realization that I could use Thinking Maps to significantly advance another aspect of my work—school-embedded professional development incorporating an adaptation of lesson study.

TOOLS FOR EXPLICIT LEARNING IN LESSON STUDY

A plethora of articles, research, and literature reveals the significant influence Japanese lesson study has had on practice-based mathematics professional development in the United States. As Stigler and Hiebert (1999) assert, "The premise behind lesson study is simple: If you want to improve teaching, the most effective place to do so is in the context of the lesson." Japanese lesson study has indeed improved instruction (Fernandez & Yoshida, 2004; Lewis, Perry, & Hurd, 2004; Stigler & Hiebert, 1999), and teachers and researchers in the United States have implemented various adaptations of lesson study with similar results (Jalongo, Rieg, & Helterbran, 2007; Lewis et al., 2004; Watanabe, 2002; West, Hanlon, Tam, & Novelo, 2005; Willis, 2002). As I experimented with the use of Thinking Maps in my own facilitation of lesson studies, I discovered that the maps maximize opportunities for teachers to deepen their understanding of mathematics, mathematics teaching, and learning. Like no other tools or techniques I had used in the past, the maps brought increased depth and rigor to teachers' conversations about lesson planning, teaching, and improving the quality of their instruction to more effectively meet the learning needs of their students. Thinking Maps have brought to the lesson study process a level of explicitness, effectiveness, and efficiency that I experienced that day supervising Milo.

Let me take you through a lesson study cycle of planning, observation, and debriefing I recently facilitated with a team of 5 first-grade teachers in a New York public elementary school. On the first day, in a two-hour session, we surfaced and addressed the team's questions about math teaching and learning and collaboratively planned the lesson goals, activity, and the sequence of lesson events. The next day, I taught the lesson as the teachers observed, and we met for almost 90 minutes to reflect on and debrief the lesson. The results of our work follow.

Part 1. Surfacing Questions: Framing the Lesson Study With Teachers' Questions

It had been three months since I last worked with the first-grade team, and after spending a few minutes getting reacquainted, I asked, "What questions do you have about math teaching and learning?" At the time of my visit, teachers were ready to introduce their students to solving and representing subtraction removal problems in a variety of ways, so their questions reflected this topic. I used a Circle Map (see Figure 17.3) to record their questions, which enabled me to determine the models, contexts, and strategies they used in their teaching and also to assess what support they needed from me. As we discussed their questions, we explored the mathematics and approaches to teaching and learning subtraction in the context of their observations of their students' work and thinking. The teachers were frustrated by a common phenomenon: Young children often solve a problem one way but choose a method of representation that is familiar to them but doesn't reflect the approach or strategy they used. As we delved more deeply into the problem of how to teach students to show *how* they solved a problem, it became evident that we lacked a coherent understanding of the differences among approaches, strategies, and representations. To clarify our thinking, I constructed a Tree Map, and asked, "What *tools* do children use to solve subtraction removal problems? What are the *strategies* they might apply? How might they *represent* their solutions?" As teachers shared their ideas, I recorded them in the appropriate categories (see Figure 17.4). Teachers were delighted by how the simple yet elegant visual clarity of the map enabled them to *see and understand* the differences among tools, strategies, and representations. This understanding subsequently sharpened the group's thinking about the planning, teaching, and assessment of student learning throughout the lesson study process.

Figure 17.3 Circle Map: What questions do we have about math teaching?

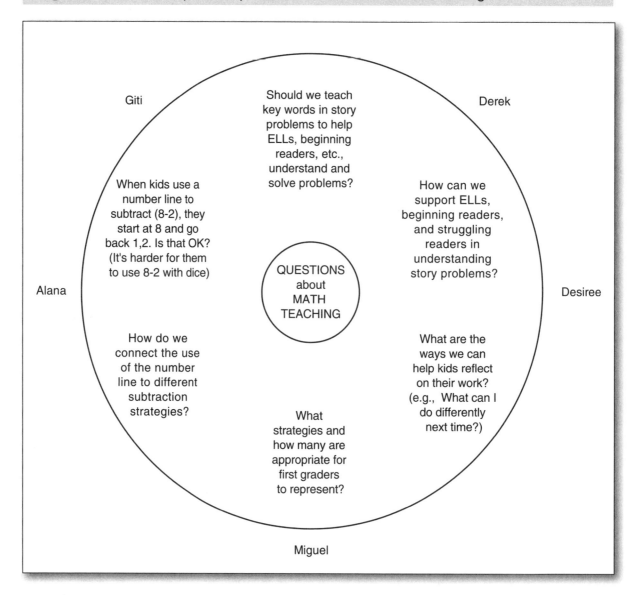

Part 2. Lesson Planning: Defining the Lesson Goals and Sequencing the Lesson Events

To define learning goals for students, we constructed a Circle Map (see Figure 17.5). We used the metacognitive frame to discuss and explore questions such as the following: What do students know and understand about subtraction? What tools do they use to solve subtraction problems? What subtraction strategies do they know and use? What are their misconceptions? What is their prior knowledge and experience in representing their solutions? Where does this lesson fit in the unit? How can the lesson engage students? What difficulties do you anticipate students will have? What extensions or modifications might students need? How do the lesson goals align with New York State standards? (Corresponding state standards are included in italics in the frame of the Circle Map.) These questions enabled us to define, with more specificity, what we wanted students to learn *in this lesson,* and they also focused our thinking on how to meet the diverse learning needs of students.

Figure 17.4 Tree Map: What are the differences among tools, strategies, and approaches in subtraction removal problems?

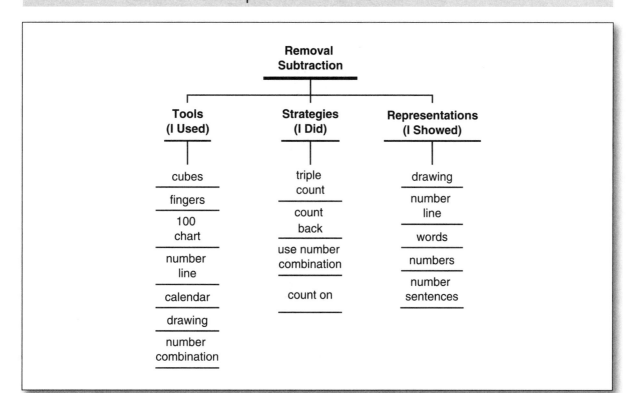

We then discussed a problem context that would engage students and developed a problem for students to solve and represent during the math workshop (student work time). Using a Flow Map, we sequenced the questions and prompts I would use in the lesson launch (introduction; see Figure 17.6). We also discussed what would be important for teachers to observe during this part of the lesson; observation prompts were embedded as substages so teachers would remember to record what they saw and heard.

What was important for teachers to observe as children worked independently on the problem? How could teachers support children who were struggling or in need of a challenge? We examined the Tree Map (see Figure 17.4) to anticipate the range of tools, strategies, and representations the children might use and then scanned the Circle Map defining the learning goals (see Figure 17.5) to determine the levels of support students might need. This information, so visually explicit and accessible, enabled us to efficiently construct, in a relatively short time, a Tree Map (see Figure 17.7) as a tool to categorize and focus our lesson observations.

Part 3. Lesson Experience/Observation

The next day, I met with teachers for about 15 minutes prior to the lesson to review the maps representing our work and thinking of the previous day. We reiterated expectations of what to observe during the lesson launch, workshop, and lesson summary (class discussion/ wrap-up). The Flow Map served as a visual observation tool of the lesson launch. Teachers used their Tree Map to focus and record their observations of children at work. At the end of the lesson, we brought our lesson artifacts—student work, class charts constructed during the lesson, and teachers' Flow and Tree Maps filled with descriptions of what they saw and heard—to our debriefing meeting.

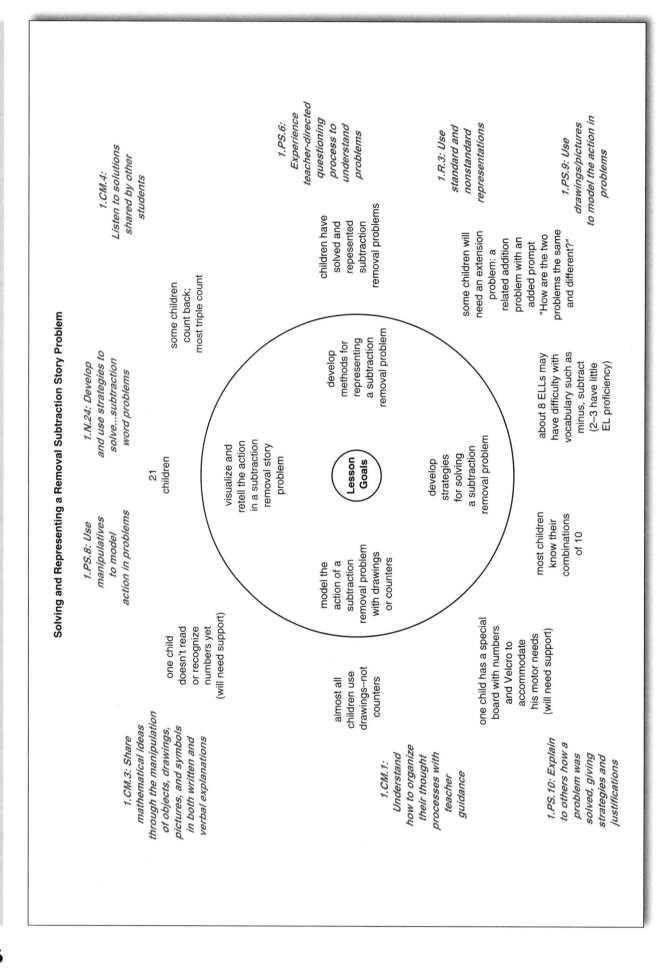

Solving and Representing a Removal Subtraction Story Problem

1.CM.4:
Listen to solutions shared by other students

1.N.24: Develop and use strategies to solve...subtraction word problems

1.PS.8: Use manipulatives to model action in problems

1.PS.6: Experience teacher-directed questioning process to understand problems

1.R.3: Use standard and nonstandard representations

1.PS.9: Use drawings/pictures to model the action in problems

21 children

some children count back; most triple count

children have solved and repesented subtraction removal problems

some children will need an extension problem: a related addition problem with an added prompt "How are the two problems the same and different?"

Lesson Goals

develop methods for representing a subtraction removal problem

visualize and retell the action in a subtraction removal story problem

develop strategies for solving a subtraction removal problem

model the action of a subtraction removal problem with drawings or counters

about 8 ELLs may have difficulty with vocabulary such as minus, subtract (2–3 have little EL proficiency)

1.CM.3: Share mathematical ideas through the manipulation of objects, drawings, pictures, and symbols in both written and verbal explanations

one child doesn't read or recognize numbers yet (will need support)

most children know their combinations of 10

almost all children use drawings--not counters

one child has a special board with numbers and Velcro to accommodate his motor needs (will need support)

1.CM.1: Understand how to organize their thought processes with teacher guidance

1.PS.10: Explain to others how a problem was solved, giving strategies and justifications

Figure 17.6 Flow Map of Lesson Launch: What will the teacher do and say to engage students in the lesson?

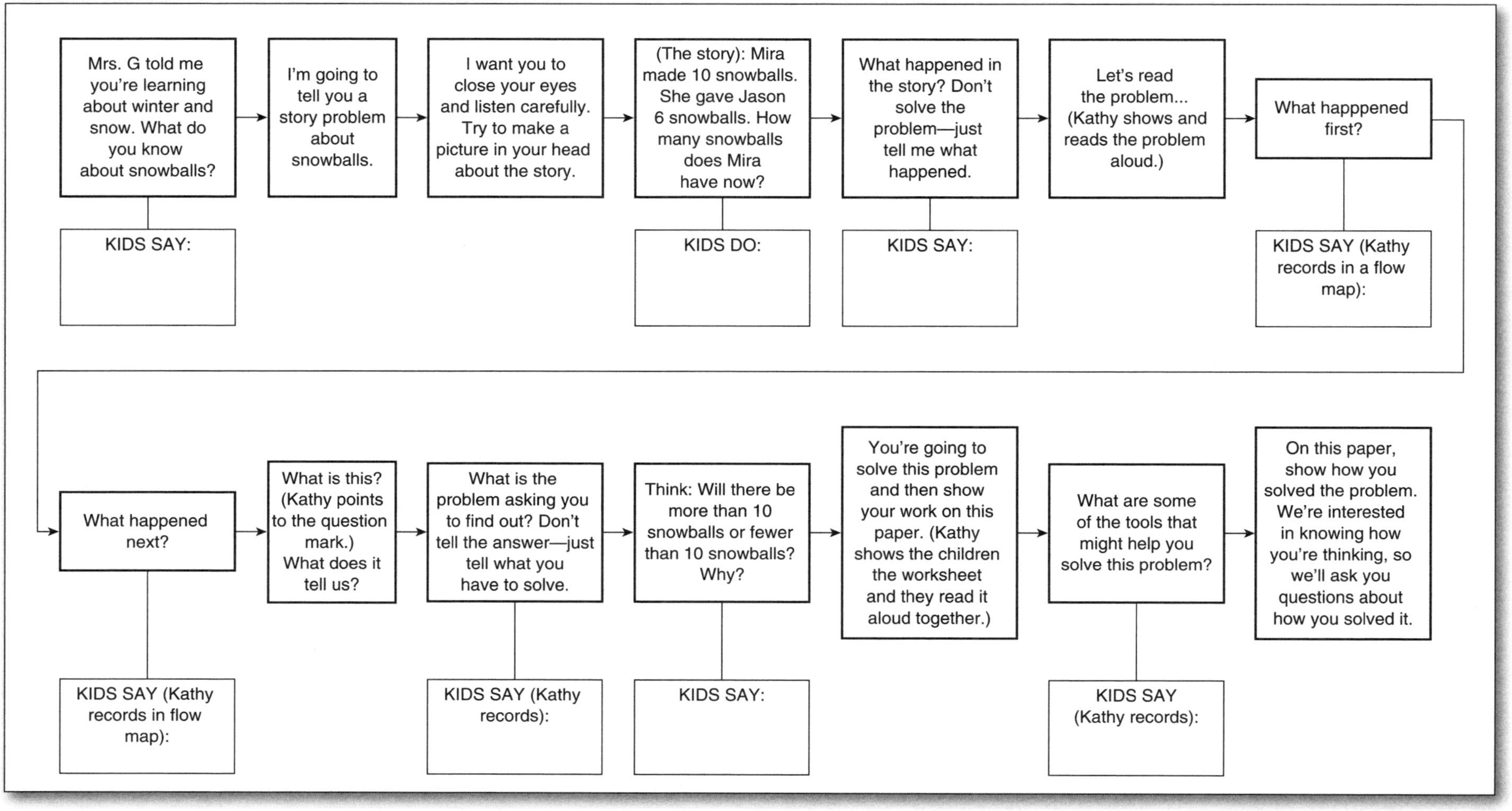

Mrs. G told me you're learning about winter and snow. What do you know about snowballs?

→ I'm going to tell you a story problem about snowballs.

→ I want you to close your eyes and listen carefully. Try to make a picture in your head about the story.

→ (The story): Mira made 10 snowballs. She gave Jason 6 snowballs. How many snowballs does Mira have now?

→ What happened in the story? Don't solve the problem—just tell me what happened.

→ Let's read the problem.... (Kathy shows and reads the problem aloud.)

→ What happened first?

KIDS SAY:

KIDS DO:

KIDS SAY:

KIDS SAY (Kathy records in a flow map):

What happened next?

→ What is this? (Kathy points to the question mark.) What does it tell us?

→ What is the problem asking you to find out? Don't tell the answer—just tell what you have to solve.

→ Think: Will there be more than 10 snowballs or fewer than 10 snowballs? Why?

→ You're going to solve this problem and then show your work on this paper. (Kathy shows the children the worksheet and they read it aloud together.)

→ What are some of the tools that might help you solve this problem?

→ On this paper, show how you solved the problem. We're interested in knowing how you're thinking, so we'll ask you questions about how you solved it.

KIDS SAY (Kathy records in flow map):

KIDS SAY (Kathy records):

KIDS SAY:

KIDS SAY:

KIDS SAY (Kathy records):

Figure 17.7 Tree Map: What is important to observe as children work on a removal subtraction story problem?

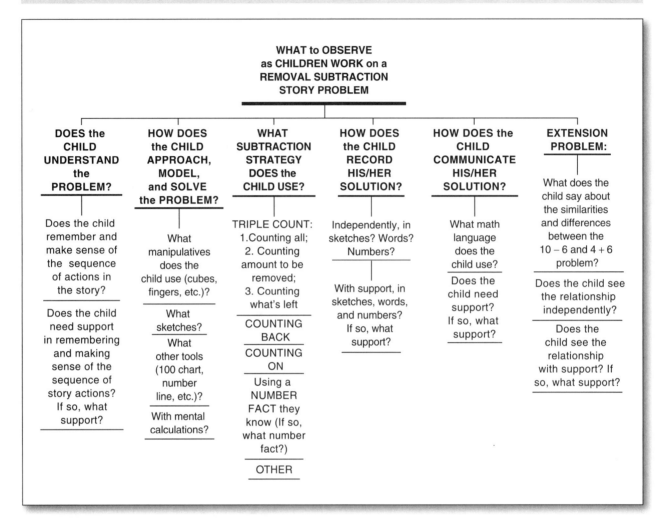

Part 4. Lesson Debriefing

In my version of lesson study, I structure the reflective conversation around the following questions:

1. What did we observe during the launch, workshop, and summary?

2. How can the lesson be improved?

3. What are next instructional steps for students?

4. What are some teaching takeaways?

We began our debriefing meeting with a collaborative retelling of the lesson launch. Referencing their observations written in sequence in their lesson Flow Maps, teachers readily retrieved and shared descriptive data about what children said and did in response to my prompts and to each other. As these observations were discussed, I charted them, for all to see, in the *Lesson Debrief* Tree Map (see Figure 17.8). Teachers noted how even students with limited English language proficiency had access to the problem because its context was meaningful

Figure 17.8 Tree Map: What is important to reflect on in our lesson debrief?

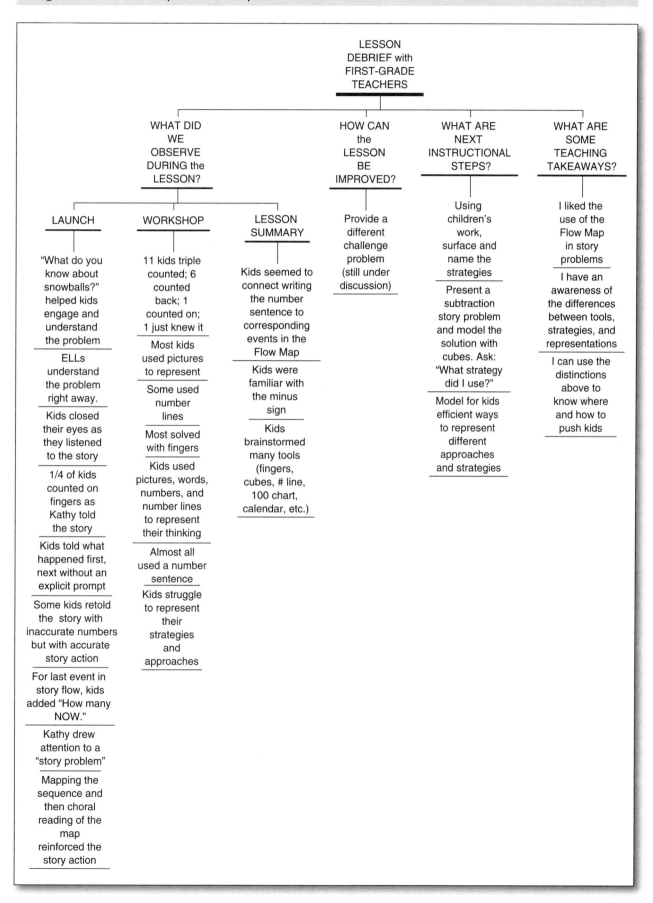

and the collaborative sequencing of events, charted in a visually clear Flow Map, enabled them to understand the problem. As teachers shared other observations about the launch, I added them to our Tree Map.

We then discussed our observations of children at work and sorted children's work samples according to the strategies they used. This process enabled us to readily identify, later in the lesson debrief, the next instructional interventions that were needed to support and advance the children's learning. Again, these observations were recorded in our *Lesson Debrief Tree Map* (see Figure 17.8).

Typically, by the time the teachers talk about what they noticed in the lesson summary, they have already surfaced aspects of the lesson that could be improved. This was the case with the team of first-grade teachers. They quickly identified the need to provide different challenge problems that would engage students in need of extensions. Although they had not yet decided on what problems would be more appropriate, they had a record of the problems that *didn't* advance student learning, so they were less likely to use them in this lesson in the future.

At the end of the lesson debrief, I asked teachers to reflect on what they took away from the lesson study process. There was general agreement that using a Tree Map to clarify the distinction among tools, strategies, and representations led to a deeper understanding of how they could improve the quality of their instruction to more effectively teach their students how to solve subtraction removal problems with *understanding* and how to represent their solutions *clearly and accurately*. In fact, the Tree Map had provided such visual clarity about these big ideas that the teachers constructed similar Tree Maps with their students, renaming the categories with kid-friendly language: "I used," "I did," and "I showed." The Tree Map provided students with a visual, metacognitive tool that enabled them to think about and access approaches, strategies, and representations in their problem-solving process.

CONCLUSION

Thinking Maps are essential tools for bringing explicitness, efficiency, and effectiveness to my work in supervising teachers and facilitating lesson study. As I discovered in my work with Milo, my use of the maps enabled me to facilitate a process in which the focus of the supervision postconference was on the *teaching*—not on the *teacher*. By providing a third point, the maps kept our eyes, questions, and analysis on the lesson data, shifting the power from *me* as supervisor to *us* as a collaborative team. This nonthreatening dynamic, essential to inquiry and learning, was also present in my work with the first-grade team of teachers throughout the lesson study process. Although I taught the lesson, we *all* were responsible for planning the lesson, writing our observations of the lesson experience, and analyzing and learning from the experience. The maps not only facilitated explicit thinking and learning throughout the process of our planning, observation, and debrief, but they served as visual imprints of the Habits of Mind that are inherent to what Linda Lambert (1998) asserts is the daily work of highly qualified teachers: reflection, dialogue, inquiry, and action. One quick glance at the maps constructed with the team of first-grade teachers gives the reader an explicit picture of the thinking and work throughout the lesson study process. This readily accessible documentation enables teachers to reflect on this work in the future.

As I continue to work with the team of first-grade teachers in lesson study, I will no longer teach the lessons—they will. They now have the tools and a process that enable them to establish the emotional safety essential to their collaborative inquiry and learning. I look forward to coaching them through a process in which *they* develop and sustain the capacity to keep the focus on the teaching and learning throughout their lesson studies—and to identify and implement actions that improve their teaching to meet the learning needs of their students.

REFERENCES

Fernandez, C., & Yoshida, M. (2004). *Lesson study: A Japanese approach to improving mathematics teaching and learning.* Mahwah, NJ: Lawrence Erlbaum Associates.

Jalongo, M. R., Rieg, S., & Helterbran, V. (2007). *Planning for learning: Collaborative approaches to lesson design and review.* New York: Teachers College Press.

Lambert, L. (1998). *Building leadership capacity in schools.* Alexandria, VA: Association for Supervision and Curriculum Development.

Lewis, C., Perry, R., & Hurd, J. (2004). A deeper look at lesson study. *Association for Supervision and Curriculum Development, 61*(5), 18–22.

National Council of Teachers of Mathematics. (2000). *Principles and standards for school mathematics.* Reston, VA: Author.

Stigler, J., & Hiebert, J. (1999). *The teaching gap: Best ideas from the world's teachers for improving education in the classroom.* New York: Free Press.

Watanabe, T. (2002). Learning from Japanese lesson study. *Association for Supervision and Curriculum Development, 59*(6), 36–39.

West, L., Hanlon, G., Tam, P., & Novelo, M. (2005). *Building coaching capacity through lesson study.* NCSM monographs.

Willis, S. (2002). Creating a knowledge base for teaching: A conversation with James Stigler. *Association for Supervision and Curriculum Development, 59*(6), 6–11.

18

Thinking Maps

A Language for Leading and Learning

Larry Alper, M.S.Ed.

KEY CONCEPTS

- Facilitating constructivist conversations and engagement across a whole school
- A Circle Map and Tree Map for creating a unified understanding and deeper communications within a faculty
- Linking leadership and learning using Thinking Maps® for school-wide transformation

FINDING OUR WAY

"The question I find most compelling is this: We can now understand our schools as they exist. And, we have an improving image of what sustainable schools look like, but how do we get there from here? How do we find our way to the sustainability we yearn for?"

—Linda Lambert (2007)

Finding our way. In New England it's not uncommon when asking for directions from one place to another to be answered matter-of-factly with the reply, "You can't get there from here." Indeed, there is rarely a straight path from here to there, and this is certainly true in our field of education, as well. The journey to a solution or decision can be quite complex and circuitous, with unexpected twists and turns. In fact, there may be multiple pathways and parallel processes at any one time, whose selection will be inspired as much by the multiple perspectives involved as by the nature of the challenges themselves. A central task of school leadership, then, is to enable educators to collectively and individually navigate these challenges and opportunities and develop a sustainable approach to engaging students in the learning process.

So, how do we "find our way," as Lambert (2007) wonders, through this complex landscape and not simply "get there" but do so in a manner that embraces the uncertainty of the journey and is inspired by the possibilities of the outcomes? How do we accomplish this in a way that is also sustaining of the organization, where, as East Syracuse-Minoa Superintendent of Schools Donna DeSiato says, it's not about power or position, but about understanding and being understood? As David Hyerle (2009) wrote, "Consider the impact on your school or system if everyone could navigate information, communicate options, and see solutions as fluidly as they can read a GPS [global positioning system] in their cars." What internal and collective compass can be used, then, to help people chart a course through this constantly changing and emerging educational environment? And how can such a tool, if it exists, be used to design pathways that engage all members of the school community deeply in the processes of discovery, learning, and actionable decision making along the way? These were among the essential challenges we sought to address as we transferred the work with Thinking Maps from the classroom to the context of the entire school community.

Over the past eight years we have been introducing school leaders—superintendents, principals, curriculum directors, teacher leaders, and so forth—to the use of Thinking Maps for the full range of leadership practices. Thinking Maps have been used for coaching professional practice (see Chapter 17, "Mentoring Mathematics Teaching and Learning"), facilitating school-wide investigations into changing instructional practices (see Chapter 16, "Inviting Explicit Thinking"), analyzing and applying data, engaging diverse stakeholders in essential conversations at the school and community level, and more. They have been used by teacher leaders and administrators to actualize the potential of professional learning communities by enabling all members of the school community to skillfully participate in and contribute to the processes associated with professional learning communities. We have been collecting data from these experiences and the subsequent work done with the maps in the field by a variety of practitioners. The research has primarily been in the form of surveys, site visits, and interviews. We have used these methods to uncover and articulate the degree to which this particular work with Thinking Maps, as a navigational tool for leading, has had an impact on the learning and decision making throughout the community of the school and system and, ultimately, on student achievement. Our findings, to be more fully documented in an upcoming publication (Alper & Hyerle, in press), have been compelling.

Several major themes have emerged from our research. Leaders consistently expressed enthusiasm for the degree of clarity their own use of Thinking Maps provided them with related to the complex issues they were addressing with their colleagues. Many described this notion as things "becoming clearer." And, as the issues came more into focus, leaders felt they had a deeper understanding and could work more effectively with others to improve the circumstances. Notice that the emphasis here was on clarity, the ability to see deeply and communicate precisely what they were thinking. The leaders did not mention finding or having the right answers themselves as a primary benefit of their work with the Thinking Maps. Instead, they focused on the clarity of thought they achieved through the use of the maps. This, they noted, enabled them to engage their colleagues in meaningful and productive processes through which they could collectively arrive at decisions. Veronica McDermott, a former superintendent of schools in New York, expressed this very point when she wrote in a reflection, "For me, the Thinking Maps have become my wonder tool of choice as I exercise my role as a leader. They have opened up the white space that I believe is needed in an organization for real dialogue to occur. I know they enable me to slowly shift from the go-to guy with the answers to the let's-explore-this-together instigator. Soon, I found myself more interested in finding ways to elicit deep questions and to provoke discussions than I was in providing answers neatly packaged and ready for adoption."

To effectively address the rich complexity and profound implications of our work, we need to have what Maxine Greene (1995) refers to as the "conversations that echo from somewhere else, some deep place." We need conversations that are rich in ideas, alive with uncertainty, and propelled by the anticipation of new learning and possibilities. With time and deliberate attention provided to open the space—the "white space," as McDermott described it—between and among people and the use of a common language for communicating ideas across multiple perspectives, these conversations can give full expression to people's thoughts and imaginings. As another superintendent expressed after having used the maps extensively with his leadership team and school board, "There is no topic I feel that I can't [use Thinking Maps to] lead a group through a constructive process in order to generate a sound decision. Regardless of the difficulty or sensitivity of the issue, I know my use of the maps will guide us successfully to a meaningful resolution." Courageous leadership, necessary to the individual and collective confidence of the organization, is achievable when supported by tools that are genuinely empowering.

In an unpublished reflective essay titled "Leadership Journey," Ken McGuire (2009), former principal of Bluebonnet Elementary School in Fort Worth, Texas, wrote about the effect his use of Thinking Maps had on his instructional program and on himself as a leader. In his reflection, McGuire described a process he guided his colleagues through using Thinking Maps to examine the topic of large group instruction. Using several different Thinking Maps, the faculty members surfaced their ideas about the topic. Some used a Circle Map to brainstorm all the possible settings where large group instruction would be the most appropriate choice, and others used a Tree Map to categorize other instructional strategies by content and setting. Commenting on the ensuing discussion after the groups shared their maps, McGuire observed, "The reflective dialogue about powerful instructional practices was one of the most insightful and passionate discussions we had experienced to that time." McGuire's use of questions and the visual representation of the thinking through the use of the maps totally engaged the faculty members and immersed them in the investigation and the conversation that followed. Commenting on the larger implications of this and subsequent experiences, he shared with the faculty members where Thinking Maps were used for their professional learning and decision making. McGuire wrote,

> Reflecting on our campus today, I would have to say that both Bluebonnet and I have been transformed. As far as my leadership, I continue to work to create effective communication and collaboration, help generate shared mission and vision, conduct meaningful and purposeful professional growth, direct problem-solving strategies, collect and analyze information, and manage the business of the campus. Thinking Maps have made me much more effective in each of these areas. I now have a set of tools that establish a common language and help the staff recognize the kind of thinking we are doing. The maps provide process and help define purpose in the work of our teams and committees. As an entire school community, we are learning to think!

The quality of engagement and the meaningfulness and relevance that McGuire (2009) and his colleagues achieved through their skillful application of Thinking Maps and, consequently, their thinking processes in these experiences have been supported by comments from other leaders we have interviewed and surveyed. In addition, they have described the cohesion and other significant benefits that sharing a common language brings to their interactions around matters of deep importance. Too often, meetings devolve into a competition of ideas, a closing of doors, rather than the creation of possibilities. People are sometimes quick to adopt and defend positions. They argue, debate, and ultimately defeat or are defeated by the ideas of others in the group. At best, under these conditions, outcomes are negotiated, and the results are more like settlements. In the end, there is very little enthusiasm for the results, and the process is simply done and the task completed.

Positional discussions are clearly inadequate for promoting the depth of thinking necessary to address the complex pedagogical, moral, and ethical dimensions of the decisions teachers and administrators must make in their work. Alternatively, propositional conversations invite people to offer their ideas for consideration, to open up thinking to be examined and enlarged upon. Such conversations demonstrate that ideas can be starting places for inquiry as opposed to end points for debate, defining school as a "home for the mind for all who dwell there" (Costa, 1991).

Our findings suggest that there is another path. The use of Thinking Maps has enabled rich, constructivist conversations to unfold in a variety of school settings. The collective and skillful use of the maps has enabled people to move beyond the borders of their individual ideas, beyond the centrality and certainty of their thinking and motivations. Multiple ways of knowing and seeing have been encouraged, and positions have given way to possibilities.

"Conversation," wrote Donald Schön (1987), "is collective improvisation." Like musicians, highly attuned to the sound and emotion coming from each other's instruments, people in constructivist conversations create ideas rich in texture, depth, and dimension. Collective improvisation or skillful participation, as Lambert (2007) might refer to it, is one of the hallmarks of sustainable schools. Empowering others through the use of Thinking Maps was another of the central themes to emerge from our research. As McDermott concluded, "What I discovered in the process was the latent strengths of the individuals I worked with and the combined power of the group." In essence, she found a way to get there.

THINKING MAPS: A LANGUAGE FOR LEADING AND LEARNING

Our school decided to commit to the use of a common language for teaching and learning that would extend to all curriculum areas and across all grade levels, having relevance in the multiple contexts that form the school experience. "Learning how to learn together" was stated as one of the central purposes of our school. It wasn't a prescription for teaching and learning we were after; it was a way to facilitate the fundamental thinking processes that were inherent to learning and vital to constructing knowledge and deepening understanding. Clearly, then, a common language, a way of talking about, forming, and representing each other's thinking, was essential to the foundation we were building to support us in this common purpose. We knew that words alone would be inadequate and not necessarily the most effective or democratic way to involve all members of the school community in this effort. Facility with language, something that challenged many of the children with whom we worked, might be a worthy educational goal, but it could not be the foundation for our school community. To enable every child to fully, authentically, and personally become engaged in the learning process, we needed a new language, a way to empower children as learners where learning is something they do rather than something that is done to them. We didn't state all of this explicitly, but as it turned out, we knew it when we saw it. What we didn't anticipate was how our own interactions as adult members of the community would be affected by the outcome of this search.

The language our school community decided to adopt as part of our foundation for learning was Thinking Maps. This work had immediate appeal, as it facilitated the use of language and the expression of ideas with visual forms and was designed to encourage the individual and collaborative construction of knowledge and understanding. Importantly, Thinking Maps were not prescriptive or task specific but could be applied to all areas of the curriculum and throughout the life of the school. We saw Thinking Maps as an opportunity to provide our students with tools that could help them reveal the full range and depth of their thinking. Disempowered in so many aspects of their lives outside of school and frustrated by the limitations of their language development and internal disorder, many of our students were in great need of concrete tools with which to be active and confident learners. Learning was, for many of them, an uncertain and discouraging journey. Thinking Maps, we believed, could enable them to navigate the unknown with greater excitement for the possibilities that learning represented and more certainty in their ability to succeed. Having read and discussed excerpts from *Visual Tools for Constructing Knowledge* (Hyerle, 1996), regular and special education teachers expressed equal enthusiasm for the work. It was obvious that all our students would benefit from access to these tools and the opportunity to enhance, extend, and apply their fundamental thinking processes to learning.

Our work with Thinking Maps began with a full day of training for the entire faculty. It was evident from the beginning that the impact was going to be not only on the students but on the staff as well. Not unlike our students, we also learn by patterning information and linking ideas. We are not always confident when facing ambiguity or comfortable expressing our thoughts or considering the ideas of others. As we worked to develop our facility with Thinking Maps during that first day and in subsequent training opportunities, we became fully engaged with each other's ideas and discoveries. The visual nature of the maps allowed us to externalize our thoughts, making it easier for us to be curious about each other's points of view, identify patterns, and discover and create structures from our thinking that would otherwise not have existed. Assuming the role of learners, we experienced the maps as we hoped our students would. Time was suspended as we were inspired by the activity of generating ideas together. Diane Zimmerman (1995) describes this infusion of energy into group dynamics in this way: "When group members become excited about the emerging relevance of the conversation, the group self-organizes around the emerging concepts." Clearly, Thinking Maps were facilitating this rich communication among us by creating a safe, noncombative way to build meaning together. Our connectedness was strengthened by the thinking we were doing in concert, as insights were made and as we moved beyond the boundaries of our initial ideas. Not surprisingly, we recognized the value of the maps to our work with each other and sought to apply them more deliberately to our own interactive processes.

EXAMINING OUR PRACTICES

The first major task we undertook using the maps as a tool to facilitate our thinking and decision making was the development of our writing program. Our Action Planning Team, which included teachers, parents, and administrators, had determined from state and local assessment data and teacher input that our students' level of performance in writing was not where we believed it could be. We acknowledged, too, that together we had not given enough attention to the area of writing and that our approach to teaching writing, across grades and in content areas, lacked coherence and connectedness. The recent introduction of Thinking Maps into our school reinforced our belief in common experiences upon which our students could construct new knowledge and develop their confidence and independence as learners. How, then, we asked, could we apply this to the area of writing? We decided to use Thinking Maps to guide this inquiry and to assist us in establishing a strong foundation upon which to design our program.

At a subsequent staff meeting, we used a Circle Map (see Figure 18.1), one of the Thinking Maps for defining things in context, to begin our process of responding to the question "What does a quality writing program look like?" People were asked to write five thoughts on individual pieces of paper that were then placed on a board with the question in the center. The group was invited to look at the collection of ideas before discussing them. Just as writing down the ideas before placing them in the Circle Map gave people a chance to formulate their ideas, this silent viewing gave each staff member an opportunity to consider the range of thinking before entering into conversation. Having the Circle Map to look at together gave us a common place to direct our attention and a central focus, the question, for our thinking. We followed this activity with an opportunity for people to ask questions of clarification, give fuller expression to their ideas, and share their individual frames of reference. Not only were staff members involved as regular and special educators, but several teachers in the group were writers themselves, adding another dimension to the reasons for their thinking. This aspect of the maps, the surfacing of multiple frames of reference, would continue to evolve for us as an important tool for looking beyond the surface of things to appreciate their full meaning and significance.

Figure 18.1 Quality Writing Program Circle Map

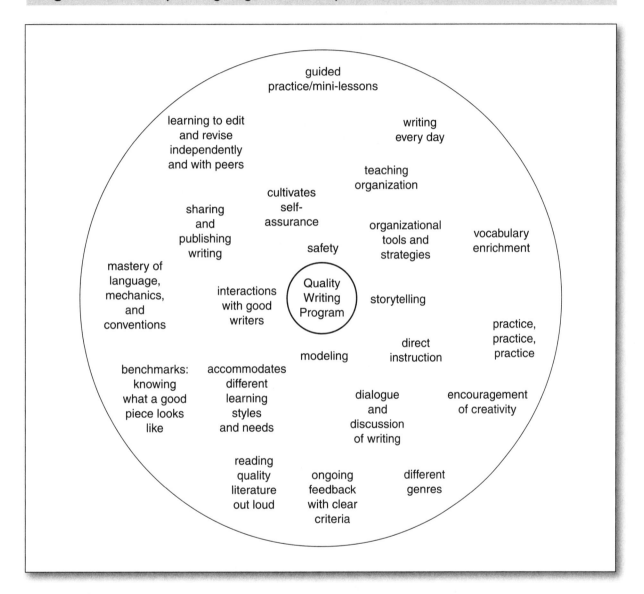

The next step in this process was to see the connections between and among the ideas we generated. We used a Tree Map to categorize and group the information and did so, again, initially without conversation. People were invited to move the papers on which individual ideas were written into clusters of related content. As they were formed, these clusters could be added to or changed as people made new connections and certain groupings became apparent. The discussion that followed gave us another opportunity to consider the information, this time in categories, to identify connections and add what might be missing. The Tree Map included items related to content and pedagogy, desired student performance outcomes, and qualities associated with being a writer. What we had created in this process was an agreed-upon set of criteria that we would use to evaluate various approaches to teaching writing.

Using the maps as a tool for how to think about this task gave us a way to see, understand, and value each other's ideas. From the beginning, the focus was as much on how we wanted to think about this topic as it was on what we thought about the topic. Consequently, people could remain comfortable with the formative nature of the conversation, knowing that we were building toward a common understanding and shared set of guiding principles for designing our school's approach to teaching writing.

Our use of the maps began to extend into other aspects of our work together and not always in response to major undertakings. They were useful in grade-level meetings, committee work, and, in general, any context where the facilitation of thinking could lead to richer, more meaningful, and productive interactions between and among the people in our school community. "How do we want to think about this?" became the leading question for many of the conversations we were having. In response, one or several of the maps would be identified as the appropriate tool to assist us in these conversations. Our library-media specialist, Andra Horton, observed, "Thinking Maps help us to harness ideas and put them together in powerful ways." As a result, we were able to enter these conversations knowing there was a way to get to the final destination without needing to know what that was from the start. "It's the difference," said Horton, "between seeing a pyramid and knowing how to build it."

Our school's capacity to respond to serious challenges was strengthened by our ability to effectively engage with each other in the face of difficult issues. No community is entirely free of problems or conflict, and this was true for our school as well. The character and, ultimately, the success of a community are often defined not by the issues themselves but by how the people within it, individually and collectively, respond to the challenges. As a group, our staff had always been inclined to confront our issues. We tried to view challenges as opportunities to strengthen our school and do better work with children. We also felt an obligation to model for our students the same personal and collective efficacy we wanted them to develop. "Freedom," wrote Greene (1978), "involves the capacity to assess situations in such a way that lacks can be defined, openings identified, and possibilities revealed." Taking constructive action requires having the tools to do so. We began to see Thinking Maps as an essential tool to draw upon in response to the complex and sometimes confounding issues we typically faced. Not only did we have the desire to respond, but now we had, in the maps, additional resources to help us do so more effectively.

SEEING OPENINGS AND OPPORTUNITIES

School communities are living organisms and exhibit the full range of emotions of the people within them. Stress is not only specific to the individuals within the community but can, in its many manifestations, begin to characterize the entire environment. Our school's Coordinating Committee, a representative group of staff members that meets weekly to guide the overall direction of our school, recognized that this was starting to happen in our school. With input from the staff, the Coordinating Committee determined that this issue needed to be addressed. These staff members realized that this was delicate territory we were entering, with the very real potential for things to get worse before they improved. Conversations about stress can provoke anxiety, exaggerate differences, and lead to finger-pointing. The committee members knew that we needed a thoughtfully designed process that would enable people to name and give definition to what they were experiencing. The process also needed to be restorative and transforming. We needed more than a group hug and certainly wanted to avoid adding to the existing tension.

Once again, we saw Thinking Maps as an ideal tool for helping us address this challenge. By providing a place for people to express the holism of their thinking, the maps locate ideas in each person's humanness. They provide people with a way of identifying where they are in their thought processes and a compass for navigating the journey ahead. As one staff member expressed, "Thinking Maps enable us to make the transition from the place we started to what we don't yet know." The ability of the maps to give people the confidence to go forward would prove to be especially important as we worked on an issue with such a high level of risk inherent in it.

We began the process with a question, as we try to do before entering any discussion or line of inquiry. "What are the land mines in the landscape of your professional work?" we asked. The imagery was purposely chosen to affirm the powerful component of people's feelings and to acknowledge the seriousness of the issue. After doing an individual Circle Map to define this for themselves and frame it within the context of their own experiences, people then joined small groups to share and combine their thoughts into a common Circle Map as shown in Figure 18.2. As these initial conversations unfolded, people became less guarded while giving each other support and recognizing similarities in their experiences. What evolved was a shared reality, a group narrative woven together from the feelings, thoughts, and events from each person's life. We had good reason to be hopeful that we could repair what had been damaged and, in Greene's (1978) words, "move through the openings, to try to pursue real possibilities." The maps effectively opened space between and among us, allowing us to see what was there and to imagine how it could be different.

Figure 18.2   Landscape of Stress Circle Map

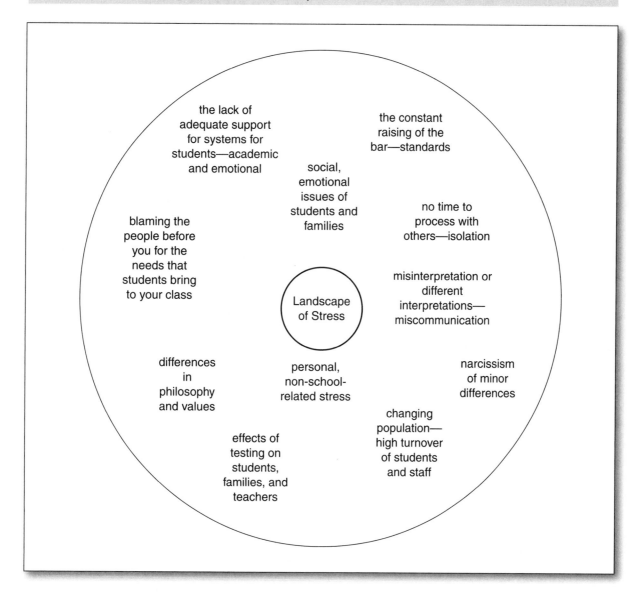

With the different Circle Maps displayed on the walls of the room, we talked about what we noticed and the ways in which our assumptions were being challenged. During the process our thinking about the problem changed, and our appreciation for each other deepened. Next, the Coordinating Committee took the Circle Maps and used a Tree Map (see Figure 18.3) to group the information into categories. The committee chose titles for the categories that represented the individual items and gave the staff a way to think about the actions people could take, individually and collectively, to strengthen our school community. In preparation for the next meeting, the committee sent a memo to staff members with the Tree Map attached. The memo concluded by saying,

> In preparation for our next combined staff meeting on Thursday, we ask that you give thought to the following two questions: In what way might I act, particularly in the Personal and Interpersonal categories, that can contribute to the strengthening of our school community? What concrete steps can we take to "repair" the lacks, particularly in the areas where we have the greatest degree of control—Personal, Interpersonal, and Systems? While we ask that you give equal weight to each of these questions, it is only the second that we will discuss at the meeting. It is our hope and expectation that your consideration of the first will be ongoing and that in doing so, each of us will be mindful of the impact our actions have on our collective ability to make real the possibilities we identify and the vision we have for our school community.

At the next meeting, we asked staff to respond to the Tree Map and tell us whether it accurately reflected the conversation we had at the previous meeting. We were then able to generate possible action steps and give further direction to the Coordinating Committee to develop a comprehensive plan for the staff to consider and, ultimately, to implement. It seemed that we had successfully taken charge of a difficult situation and could move ahead with a shared sense of purpose and a demonstrated commitment to the well-being of our school.

Having Thinking Maps as a tool to conduct these difficult conversations was reassuring and empowering to people. Deb Abbott, a third-grade teacher in our school, said, "By seeing your thinking, you can examine it, and you don't have to stop there." The reassurance comes, in part, from the maps' ability to help us formulate and capture our thinking and pursue the next level of thought beyond the familiar. "You're not going to forget it [your thoughts]," said Abbott. "You can reflect on it and build on it." When done collaboratively, the use of the maps can enable a group to build and strengthen its connections, even when confronted with issues that could easily pull it apart.

CONSTRUCTIVIST CONVERSATIONS

The ability of people to make meaning together, visualize the unknown, and formulate effective action is vital to the success of any organization. In today's school environment, where change is not an event but an ever-present reality, it is imperative that people develop the individual and collective capacity to process information, transform it into new understandings, and shape their futures. Constructivist conversations awaken people to possibilities and help them give shape to ideas not yet fully formed. The collaborative nature of these conversations helps organizations build an identity around a common purpose. Constructivist conversations provide a way for members of the learning community to share their individual frames of reference and develop trust and confidence in themselves and each other. The construction of knowledge and meaning is not solely an individual activity but is, more powerfully, a social one. In this way, groups of people interact to interpret, reflect upon,

Figure 18.3 Landscape of Professional Stress Tree Map

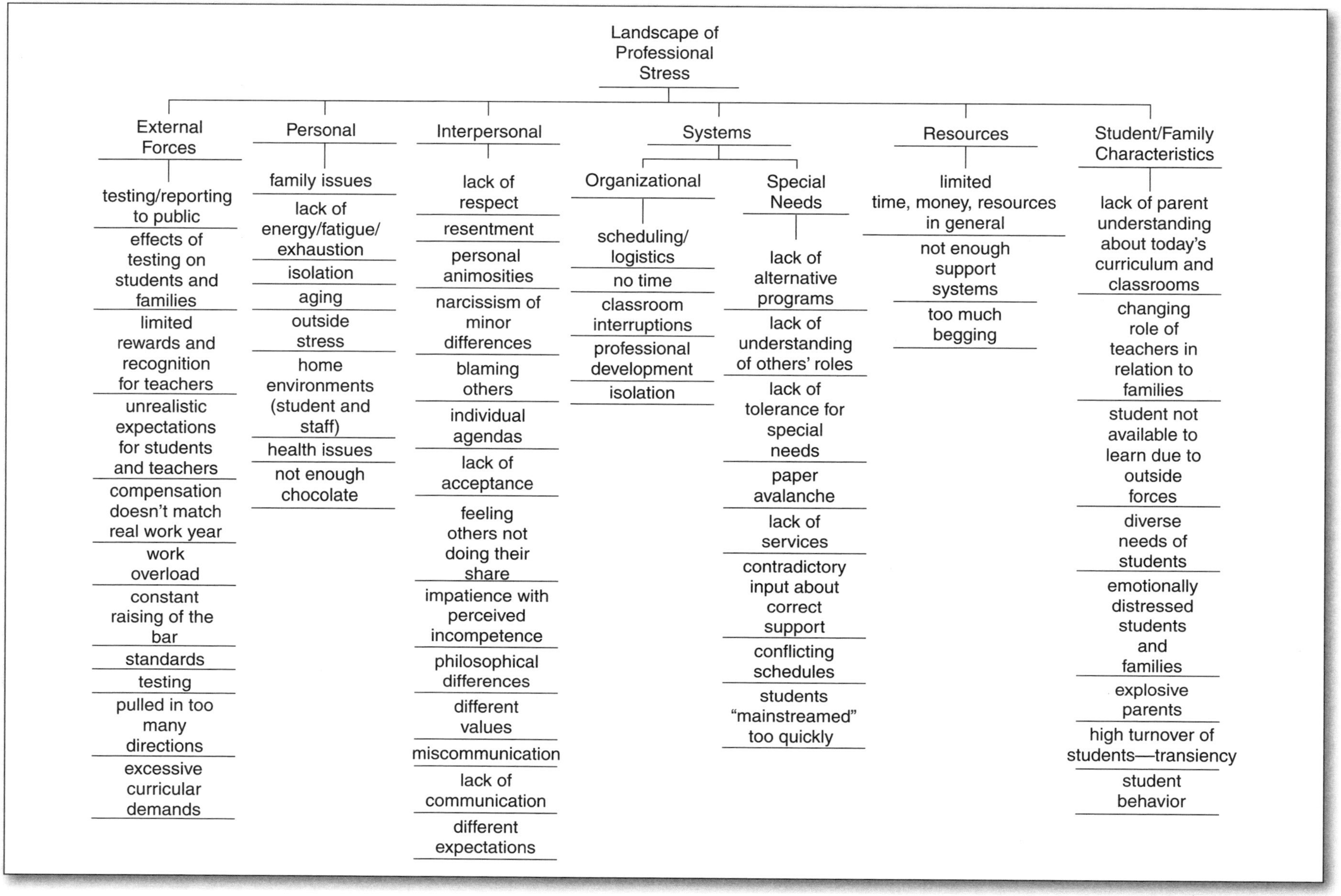

Landscape of Professional Stress

External Forces
- testing/reporting to public
- effects of testing on students and families
- limited rewards and recognition for teachers
- unrealistic expectations for students and teachers
- compensation doesn't match real work year
- work overload
- constant raising of the bar
- standards
- testing
- pulled in too many directions
- excessive curricular demands

Personal
- family issues
- lack of energy/fatigue/exhaustion
- isolation
- aging
- outside stress
- home environments (student and staff)
- health issues
- not enough chocolate

Interpersonal
- lack of respect
- resentment
- personal animosities
- narcissism of minor differences
- blaming others
- individual agendas
- lack of acceptance
- feeling others not doing their share
- impatience with perceived incompetence
- philosophical differences
- different values
- miscommunication
- lack of communication
- different expectations

Systems

Organizational
- scheduling/logistics
- no time
- classroom interruptions
- professional development
- isolation

Special Needs
- lack of alternative programs
- lack of understanding of others' roles
- lack of tolerance for special needs
- paper avalanche
- lack of services
- contradictory input about correct support
- conflicting schedules
- students "mainstreamed" too quickly

Resources
- limited time, money, resources in general
- not enough support systems
- too much begging

Student/Family Characteristics
- lack of parent understanding about today's curriculum and classrooms
- changing role of teachers in relation to families
- student not available to learn due to outside forces
- diverse needs of students
- emotionally distressed students and families
- explosive parents
- high turnover of students—transiency
- student behavior

and examine each other's ideas and experiences. As people experience uncertainty together in this context, ambiguity is embraced as the realm of possibility. Trust, respect, and colleagueship develop through collective engagement with compelling ideas and the collaborative meaning-making process.

Constructivist conversations, according to Lambert (1995), "serve as the medium for the reciprocal processes that enable participants in a school community to construct meaning toward a common purpose about teaching and learning." As a consequence of such a dynamic, members are more likely to feel proud of their association with the organization, be committed to its work, and become inspired to think beyond the familiar. In this way, the organization is transformed into a generative community, one in which new ways of thinking are encouraged and novel ideas are formed.

During the past year, well over 200 school leaders have participated in a two-day seminar using the text *Thinking Maps: Leading With a New Language* (Alper & Hyerle, in press). This seminar guides participants in the understanding and application of Thinking Maps as a 21st-century language for surfacing and communicating the breadth and depth of people's ideas and for building meaningful and sustainable solutions together. The story of one of these school leaders captures the transformational potential of Thinking Maps as she reflects, in an e-mail, on the impact that this work had on her leadership and the implications for the entire school community and, in particular, for the students:

> Well, I did it! Today was the test of using my plan to address issues around Professional Climate in our school! No, to be honest . . . I almost chickened out last night and then again this morning. In the end, though, I stuck with the original plan and I can't begin to tell you how powerful the experience was! My staff approached the tasks with honesty and openness. Using Thinking Maps we were able to get all the issues out on the table in a respectful manner. Some of the stuff was painful. I just kept going. By the end of the morning we had developed ideas and plans, people were sharing and working together, there were even tears! For the remainder of the day I have received positive feedback, praise, and thanks for my work. Even one person who came in unwilling to join our circled tables and sat isolated from the group ultimately pulled her chair in and ate lunch with us, worked with a team to solve a scheduling issue, and thanked me! . . . We are approaching our school year in a positive, can-do atmosphere and our students will only benefit.

This experience shows that constructivist conversations require leaders who have the tools to enlist people's participation. "Good leaders," said Horton, "are in control of keeping a constructive focus while keeping people engaged."

David Hawkins (1973) describes the importance of having "some third thing . . . in which they can join in outward projection" to move people beyond self-consciousness and the conventions of their thinking. This third thing can open the space for possibilities to exist and be jointly constructed. Thinking Maps become the third corner of Hawkins's "I-Thou-It" triangle and provide us with the "common engrossment for discussion." The use of Thinking Maps promotes curiosity, thinking in action, and collaboration. They give us the confidence to embrace complexity and deepen our appreciation for each other's ideas and experiences.

On the most fundamental level, Thinking Maps help us to have the conversations that truly make a difference in how we think and in what we are able to do with our ideas. In the context of the profusion of challenges we face as educators, these tools are essential to the pursuit of our collective ideals and aspirations. "All we can do," wrote Greene (1995), "is cultivate multiple ways of seeing and multiple dialogues in a world where nothing stays the same."

REFERENCES

Alper, L., & Hyerle, D. (in press). *Thinking Maps: Leading with a new language.* Raleigh, NC: Innovative Sciences.

Costa, A. L. (1991). *The school as a home for the mind.* Palatine, IL: IRI/SkyLight.

Greene, M. (1978). *Landscapes of learning.* New York: Teachers College Press.

Greene, M. (1995). *Releasing the imagination: Essays on education, the arts, and social change.* San Francisco: Jossey-Bass.

Hawkins, D. (1973). The triangular relationship of teacher, student, and materials. In C. E. Silberman (Ed.), *The open classroom reader.* New York: Vintage.

Hyerle, D. (1996). *Visual tools for constructing knowledge.* Alexandria, VA: Association for Supervision and Curriculum Development.

Hyerle, D. (2009). *Visual tools for transforming information into knowledge.* Thousand Oaks, CA: Corwin.

Lambert, L. (1995). Toward a theory of constructivist leadership: Constructing school change: Leading the conversations. In L. Lambert, D. Walker, D. P. Zimmerman, J. E. Cooper, M. D. Lambert, M. E. Gardner, et al. (Eds.), *The constructivist leader* (pp. 28–103). New York: Teachers College Press.

Lambert, L. (2007). Lasting leadership: Toward sustainable school improvement. *Journal of Educational Change, 8,* 311–322.

McGuire, K. (2009). *Leadership journey.* Unpublished manuscript.

Schön, D. A. (1987). *Educating the reflective practitioner.* San Francisco: Jossey-Bass.

Senge, P. M. (1990). *The fifth discipline.* New York: Currency Doubleday.

Zimmerman, D. (1995). The linguistics of leadership. In L. Lambert, D. Walker, D. P. Zimmerman, J. E. Cooper, M. D. Lambert, M. E. Gardner, et al. (Eds.), *The constructivist leader* (pp. 104–120). New York: Teachers College Press.

19

Bifocal Assessment in the Cognitive Age

Thinking Maps for Assessing Content Learning and Cognitive Processes

David Hyerle, Ed.D., and Kimberly M. Williams, Ph.D.

KEY CONCEPTS

- Bifocal assessment = assessment of content and cognition
- Reflective assessment
- Transfer

THE BIFOCAL LENS

Among his other revolutionary accomplishments, Benjamin Franklin invented bifocals to allow us to see things more clearly—that which is right before our eyes as well as that which typically requires closer inspection—with the same tool. The most effective revolutionary tools are elegant in their simplicity, leading to complex applications. Thinking Maps®, as a universal language of cognitive patterns as we have seen across this book, have shown promise as a model for informing and possibly transforming educational teaching, learning, and assessment. In the area of assessment, this set of visual tools allows teachers to see student content learning *and* thinking processes through the same bifocal lens—viewing the content at the surface and the normally invisible cognition with clarity—through the graphic form of students' independently created cognitive patterns. Thinking Maps offer visual representations of the "form" of thinking and thus a third way that bridges and breaks the traditional dichotomy of the "contents" and "processes" of learning.

The landscape of 21st-century learning is grounded in the focus on the direct facilitation of students' thinking and their capacities to transfer these cognitive processes into a wide variety of contexts. Our present "cognitive age" requires that our assessment tools keep pace with our new understanding about how the human brain learns (receives, stores, deletes, and accesses content) and how the mind processes information (see Chapter 2, "Why and How Thinking Maps Work"). As is often said, *we teach what we assess.* This means that until we tackle the complex and important area of actually assessing thinking processes as directly related to content learning, we may always step back into the comfortable silos of teaching and testing for content facts, "academic language" use.

This chapter will proceed from the "big picture" framework of Bloom's (1956) taxonomy and a short history of the use of visual tools for assessment to a refined look at how the development of students' *novice to expert* use of Thinking Maps is crucial for assessing learning and improving students' thinking abilities. Ultimately, Thinking Maps offer a language through which teachers *and* students determine not only *what* is learned but also *how* it is learned, so every student becomes a creative, analytic, metacognitive, self-assessing, lifelong learner.

A HIGHER ORDER: A NEW BLOOM
FOR LEARNING, TEACHING, AND ASSESSING

Back in the 1980s, educators were unabashed about promoting the need to ask students more "higher order" thinking questions based on Bloom's (1956) Taxonomy of Educational Objectives. Questions of analysis, synthesis, and evaluation were meant to drive learning, teaching, and assessment beyond factual content knowledge and toward deeper conceptual meaning. Ironically, at this time of high-stakes testing and an extraordinary focus on Adequate Yearly Progress (AYP) set by minimum standards of states under No Child Left Behind, the newly revised Bloom's taxonomy (Anderson & Krathwohl, 2001) has remained below the radar. The new taxonomy deepens and reframes the model of objectives developed 50 years before based on our understanding of the brain, the mind, and cognition. The six objectives (or "levels") that most of us know as the "cognitive dimension" have been retooled to meet our present knowledge in the field.

Under the original version of Bloom's (1956) taxonomy the progression from lower- to higher-order thinking objectives was as follows: *knowledge, comprehension, application, analysis, synthesis,* and *evaluation.* The new version keeps some of the components of the original but goes from low to high as follows: *remember, understand, apply, analyze, evaluate,* and *create* (see Figure 19.1). Note that these shifts in name and definition are related to how a teacher engages students' capacity to create new knowledge, not just evaluate what has been presented. Yet there is a deeper frame that has shifted in the new taxonomy toward an emphasis on the dimensions of different types of knowledge. In the revised taxonomy (Anderson & Krathwohl, 2001), the authors define areas of "knowledge dimensions": *factual, conceptual, procedural,* and *metacognitive.* This new four-by-six matrix dramatically deepens the original vision of learning objectives. At *every* level of Bloom's Taxonomy of Educational Objectives conceptualizing and metacognition are *essential* to teaching, learning, and assessment.

Unfortunately, this new Bloom (Anderson & Krathwohl, 2001) has barely flowered, especially in the area of assessing students' learning, creative thinking, and metacognition. The fundamental problem—which still has not been resolved—is that on a regular basis it is difficult for teachers to

Figure 19.1   New Bloom Grid

The Knowledge Dimension	The Cognitive Process Dimension					
	1. Remember	2. Understand	3. Apply	4. Analyze	5. Evaluate	6. Create
A. Factual Knowledge						
B. Conceptual Knowledge						
C. Procedural Knowledge						
D. Metacognitive Knowledge						

create and conduct meaningful formative *or* summative assessments of students' higher-order thinking processes. Why? Under the present constraints of high-stakes standardized testing, teachers focus formative and summative assessment on *content* learning rather than on thinking processes. Further complicating matters is the critical importance of differentiating instruction and assessment that ensures a high-quality education for every child—regardless of cognitive areas of strength. Isolated factual knowledge can be tested efficiently and effectively using verbal questioning, quick quizzes, short-answer responses, and worksheets. On the other hand, higher-order conceptualization—which embodies a range from factual to metacognitive knowledge to knowledge creation within every discipline—is complex, multidimensional, and nonlinear, and requires *independent and creative* thinking by students. The lacuna of education, the blind spot in our vision of learning and thus assessment, is the void in systematically mediating and assessing the evolving cognitive development of *every* student. So how can we create assessment strategies that allow us to determine not only what every child in every classroom has learned, but also *how* each and every student is thinking about what he or she has learned? This is a tall order.

If there is to be a breakthrough in formative and summative assessment, we must find valid, effective, *and* efficient instruments that enable students to show the complex, conceptual patterns that are grounded in the formation of content via thinking processes.

With this in mind, formative and summative assessments will need to *look* quite different as we fully transition into 21st-century learning and ask students to *think* differently. The most obvious reason is this: Most knowledge, thinking, and problem solving is *nonlinear* and thus not effectively represented in the linear representations of writing, speaking, and numerating. A second reason is dynamic knowledge creation: A widening array of digital sources, all transmitted across the range of global cultures, brings to the fingertips of our children (as digital natives) information that must be *transformed* into meaningful, useful knowledge. The dam will not hold: The shear mass of "content" knowledge accumulating and media access severely limits the 20th-century format of existing assessments. Thus the guiding question of this investigation becomes whether our assessments will continue to focus on "content" knowledge and skills or adapt to include feedback on how learners are "processing" and transforming information into knowledge. In light of neuroscience research, the dynamic networking-visual brain, and the inherent collaborative, visual nature of new technologies, we need to reframe our view presently bound within the limiting dichotomy between "content" and "process." We need to seek a theory and practice based on a synthesis of the two.

NONLINGUISTIC REPRESENTATIONS, VISUAL TOOLS, AND ASSESSMENT

How can teachers—and students as self-directed, self-assessing learners—look through a bifocal lens to determine what factual and conceptual content knowledge students have gained while *simultaneously* looking deeper at the thinking processes that are the drivers of higher-order learning? As we explore below, we may seek a unifying lens that draws together content and process through a third dimension: the "form" of knowledge represented using Thinking Maps. In *Concept-Based Curriculum and Instruction*, Lynn Erickson (2002) visually shows that many concepts are structured in the form of a hierarchical tree, with the guiding theory at the top of the tree, supported by generalizations, concepts, topics, and facts cascading down like branches to an isolated knowledge base. This reflects what actually happens when students draw out a Tree Map, one of the eight Thinking Maps: They simultaneously *show* their factual content knowledge, their process of either inductive or deductive categorization and conceptualizing, while also representing the visual form of the synthesis of contents and processes. As discussed in Chapter 2, an essential processing structure of the brain is *hierarchical*. Students are building content knowledge as conceptual understandings in these cascading general to specific categories, and are actively *forming* complex mental models grounded in complex visual patterns of thinking. When students create such visual models, teachers and students alike can scan quickly and *see deeply,* thus providing what all effective teachers need—an efficient, useful assessment tool that allows us to see both the content and the process through the same unified lens.

As noted in Chapter 1 ("Thinking Maps as a Transformational Language for Learning"), different types of visual tools—from brainstorming webs for creative thinking, to graphic organizers for analytical thinking, to thinking process maps for conceptual thinking—have been used extensively across classrooms over the past 30 years and are comprehensively documented in *Visual Tools for Transforming Information Into Knowledge* (Hyerle, 2009). In recent years comprehensive research has shown that "nonlinguistic representations" (Marzano & Pickering, 2005) are highly effective for improving instruction and learning, directly impacting comprehension and writing across *all* disciplines. Cognitive scientists, brain researchers, and learning theorists are now working off the same page: The brain networks and maps information, the unconscious mind builds schemata or linked associations about ideas and concepts, and fundamental cognitive processes enable all learners to transform static information into active, useful knowledge.

A rich history of "theory into practice" shows us how to use visual tools for learning, but applications for this wide range of tools for assessment purposes are scant. Attempts have been made to integrate simple graphic organizers into standardized tests and as scaffolds that students may use to respond to formal writing prompts. Some teachers now use ubiquitous graphic organizer templates and those included in structured reading programs and content area textbooks as handouts. But students don't need more handouts. They need tools they can use on their own when the teacher *isn't there.* Despite many of the hundreds of graphic organizers that may be helpful as tools for certain tasks of teaching, learning, and assessment, many of the prestructured boxes and ovals are merely replicating standardized worksheets that students "fill in" rather than allowing individual students to create their own maps of learning by hand and mind. Most of these graphic organizers have a glass ceiling, preventing students from *independently* going outside the box beyond preordained structures. This glass ceiling is also not clear enough to allow us as teachers to see the students' actual thinking at a higher level.

One of the most significant and well-researched mapping approaches, "concept mapping," was developed for integrating teaching, learning, and assessment and is detailed in a groundbreaking book, *Learning How to Learn* (Novak & Gowin, 1984). Teachers and students learn how to create hierarchical maps on a whiteboard and/or blank paper. Using simple ovals and curved lines for showing interrelated links between different levels of the maps, all students are trained in this model until they fluently create evolving visual representations of what and how they are *forming* their thinking about a concept. This is the heart of formative assessment: The teacher can walk around the room and look down at each student's map and, in the moment, question students based on three criteria: how they are expanding, clarifying, and assimilating new information and concepts into their new understandings. These independently created student maps are thus used as formative assessments as teachers check for any factual concerns and *misconceptions*. Early studies demonstrated how, at the end of a term, teachers and students score maps as summative assessments using the same criteria. The significance of this approach is that each student creates his or her own maps—there is no one correct map for any given concept—and the focus is on developing content knowledge, thinking processes, and ultimately the differentiated forms of unique concepts. Though well researched, dynamic, and highly effective, concept mapping may have theoretical and practical limitations preventing extensive use in classrooms. The model is based on a view that all knowledge is hierarchical, so all factual information and cognitive and metacognitive knowledge are subsumed within a highly complex, single map form. Again, as Kim Williams asserts in Chapter 2, the brain is much more than a hierarchical and sequential processor: Our brains are driven by a range of patterning structures, or what we could call *cognitive* structures.

A SYNTHESIS LANGUAGE OF VISUAL TOOLS BASED ON COGNITIVE PROCESSES FOR ASSESSMENT

The eight cognitive processes underlying, respectively, the eight Thinking Maps have been foundational to an understanding of human thinking from early developmental psychology through present-day neuroscience research. If you look back to early tests of cognition (and even early intelligence tests) through Jean Piaget's research, and to existing models of thinking skills, these cognitive processes are clearly identified.

Cognitive/neuroscientists and educators have understood and used these cognitive processes as *the* foundation for testing, mediation, tracking, and remediation. Unfortunately, rarely are these cognitive processes used explicitly in teaching, learning, and assessing in schools, but seen implicitly in curriculum and instruction. Thinking Maps are defined *visually* using eight unique graphic starters, or cognitive primitives. The discrete verbal and visual definitions of each tool, along with the extensive research on the eight types of cognitive processes, establish the internal validity of Thinking Maps as a strong theoretical model for thinking as well as a practical language for facilitating thinking, learning, instruction, and assessment.

Concretely, this means that students don't just talk about or write about how content information is classified or sequenced in a linear form; they *create* a Tree Map from a blank page that clearly shows the category structure that is driving *their* thinking. When used together as a language, the eight cognitive maps lead to more complex, higher-order thinking: problem solving involving evaluating, thinking systemically, thinking analogically, and creating new knowledge and understanding. Every learner is thus able to detect, construct, and communicate different patterns of thinking about content concepts and see into a reflective mirror of his or her own thinking patterns. Art Costa, creator of "Habits of Mind," has called this process "displayed metacognition." Every teacher can *see* these patterns and *assess* his or her own patterns of thinking.

FROM NOVICE TO EXPERT

As students move from novice to expert use of Thinking Maps with direct guidance from teachers, they are developing what Bloom (1956) called "automaticity" with the maps as a cognitive language for transfer to any learning task, not merely as isolated, static graphic organizers assigned by teachers for specific tasks. Once Thinking Maps are introduced, modeled, and reinforced over several years, students develop fluency with each map and uniquely combine these cognitive patterns as rich visual overlays of knowledge. They are also able to transfer multiple maps into each content area, becoming spontaneous in their ability to choose and use the maps for whatever content information and concept they are learning, for reading comprehension and a range of different forms of writing processes. How does this happen? The first step that teachers take after the initial professional development training is to teach each of the maps to students. This is done collaboratively and individually through very simple activities of applying each map to an object, such as an "apple," or guiding students to use each map for an autobiography. The next step is the assessment of students' basic fluency with each cognitive process and their abilities to apply each map in a specific content area.

After a basic level of fluency is established (within 8 weeks), teachers and students begin shifting toward more explicit transfer into content areas, most often through reading in the content areas. In Figures 19.2a–c we see excerpts from an activity based on using the maps for reading comprehension. In this example, students are given eight separate paragraphs about a boy named Marcus. Each paragraph is carefully constructed to reflect, respectively, a research-based text structure grounded in one of the eight cognitive patterns. In the area of reading comprehension, the research on text structures is conclusive: There are a limited number of basic structures that may be embedded in text, such as comparing and contrasting, main idea/details, problem/solution, and description. It should be no surprise that these text structures, respectively, are based on fundamental cognitive patterns: comparison, categorization, causality, and descriptive attributes.

In the three examples by a fifth-grade student who has developed fluency with the maps, we can see that he is able to correctly identify the thinking process and the map for each paragraph: the Double Bubble Map for comparing (see Figure 19.2a), the Multi-Flow Map for cause and effect reasoning (see Figure 19.2b), and the Bridge Map for building analogies (see Figure 19.2c). Remember, the purpose of this assessment is for both the students and their teacher to assess their abilities

Figure 19.2a Marcus Maps: Making Friends

Paragraph 2. Making Friends

You really have to make an effort to make friends. I think I made friends with Marcus mostly because we both like riding bikes. We like to talk about where we would travel if our bikes were airplanes! We also are both pretty shy people; we would rather be together than hanging out in a large group. Some people think it is strange that we are friends because we are also different in many ways. We do look a bit funny together. I am very tall and Marcus is very short. I would rather talk than write down ideas. I also really love to play sports. Marcus enjoys writing much more than playing sports—guess that is because Marcus can be a bit clumsy! But not with his hands! He is always making some sort of invention. I can't seem to make anything, but I can make a friend!

What Thinking Map? _Double Bubble Map_

What thinking skill? _Compare and Contrast_

(Continued)

(Continued)

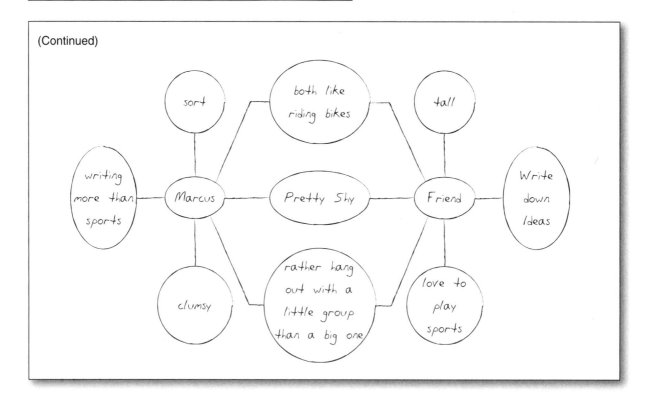

Figure 19.2b   Marcus Maps: Changing Your Mind

Paragraph 8. Changing Your Mind

Marcus and I became *best* friends when I helped him with a *big* problem. He is not very good at sports, but his dad is always watching sports on TV. Not Marcus. One day our teacher told us that the soccer team tryouts were coming up. At recess, two boys started teasing Marcus saying, "Hey, Marcus, why don't you try out for the team? Ha! You couldn't make it as the water boy!" Marcus was mad! After school he told the soccer coach, "Put my name on the list for the tryouts." I saw Marcus the next day and he looked very upset! He told me he was thinking about what made him sign up and about what might happen at the tryouts. I asked, "Do you really want to be on the soccer team?" After a few days he returned to the coach saying, "Please take my name off of the list. I was going to try out for the team for other people, like my dad, and not for myself."

What Thinking Map? *Multi—Flow Map*

What thinking skill? *Cause and Effect*

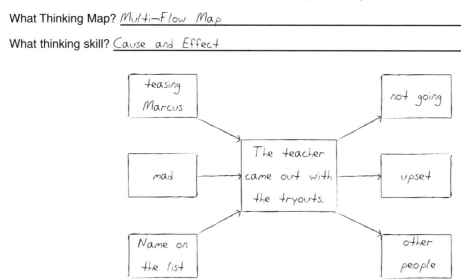

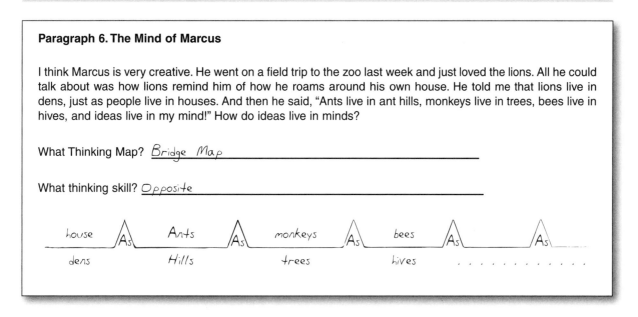

Figure 19.2c Marcus Maps: The Mind of Marcus

Paragraph 6. The Mind of Marcus

I think Marcus is very creative. He went on a field trip to the zoo last week and just loved the lions. All he could talk about was how lions remind him of how he roams around his own house. He told me that lions live in dens, just as people live in houses. And then he said, "Ants live in ant hills, monkeys live in trees, bees live in hives, and ideas live in my mind!" How do ideas live in minds?

What Thinking Map? _Bridge Map_

What thinking skill? _Opposite_

house /As\ Ants /As\ monkeys /As\ bees /As\ /As\
dens   Hills   trees   hives . . . .

to abstract an obvious cognitive pattern from the text, identify the thinking processes, and draw the map starting with the common graphic primitive for each map. This assessment has been piloted in schools and districts and has enabled teachers—across grade levels and disciplines—to make the concrete link between reading comprehension and cognitive patterns.

DEVELOPING TRANSFER OF THINKING FOR CONTENT LEARNING

While the fluency activity is focused on assessing basic use with each Thinking Map, the next step in the process is the use of the maps for learning and formative assessment. This is analogous to the way educators define the transition from "learning to read" to "reading to learn." Once students have learned to use Thinking Maps, they use the tools to think and learn and thus are able to see *their own* thinking patterns for self-assessment. They can also share their maps in paired discussion and combine them with peers in cooperative groups, while also offering an effective way for teachers to effectively assess individual and collaborative content knowledge learning and concepts. Teachers may ask students to use the map before, during, and after a lesson or unit of study.

For example, one student was asked to "think about" what she knows about the United Nations using a Circle Map (see Figure 19.3). From a blank page, the student created the concentric circles and defined the UN in the outside circle with what she considers to be important ideas (*help nations, bring harmony, stick together, democracy,* etc.).

The rectangle around the Circle Map is the "Frame of Reference," and it may be used around any of the eight maps to guide learners in critical reflection. This is an essential part of the Thinking Maps language. While each of the cognitive processes and respective visual patterns supports students as they draw out descriptions, comparisons, causes and effects, sequences, and so forth, a key dimension of thinking—as identified in the new Bloom's taxonomy (Anderson & Krathwohl, 2001)—goes beyond these cognitive processes toward a metacognitive perspective on what and how we all gather, organize, process, and reflect on the content we are learning. This is yet another level of Art Costa's concept of "displayed metacognition": As students look down at their maps, they see a snapshot reflection of their thinking, and with the Frame of Reference added to each cognitive map, students are

Figure 19.3   United Nations Circle Map

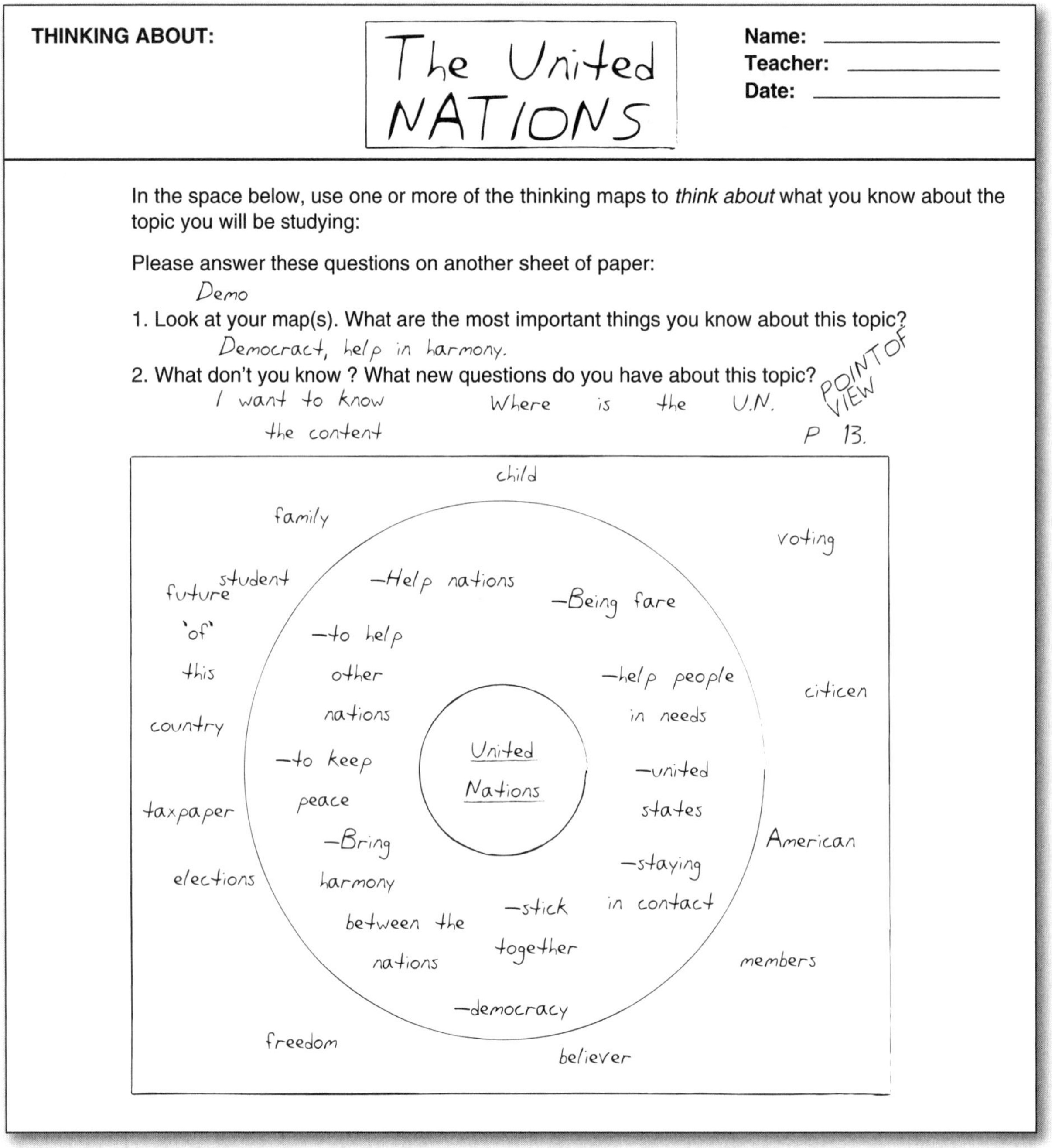

THINKING ABOUT:

The United NATIONS

Name: _____
Teacher: _____
Date: _____

In the space below, use one or more of the thinking maps to *think about* what you know about the topic you will be studying:

Please answer these questions on another sheet of paper:

Demo

1. Look at your map(s). What are the most important things you know about this topic?

   Democract, help in harmony.

2. What don't you know ? What new questions do you have about this topic? POINT OF VIEW

   I want to know   Where   is   the   U.N.

            the content   P 13.

child
family
voting
future student
'of'
—Help nations
—Being fare
this
—to help other nations
—help people in needs
citicen
country
—to keep peace
United Nations
—united states
taxpaper
—Bring harmony
—staying in contact
American
elections
between the nations
—stick together
freedom
—democracy
believer
members

concretely engaged in *explicit* metacognition. In this case, the student noted in the outside frame that there are many different frames influencing her knowledge base: that she is a *child,* the *future of this country, freedom,* being an *American,* and so forth. These are Frames of Reference that she identified as possible influences on her thinking and that directly affect her opinions and point of view about the United Nations.

This example shows the use of a single Thinking Map, which is often only a starting point for using multiple maps that reflect the pattern of content being taught through text or teacher. *No single cognitive map can hold the richness of any concept.* In Figure 19.4, after a short unit on "matter," a science teacher asked students to show what *and* how they know about this topic on one page. The student used four maps: the *Brace Map* for analyzing the physical parts of the whole atom, the *Bubble Map* for describing the properties of gold, the *Double Bubble Map* for comparing hydrogen and oxygen, and the *Circle Map* for generating examples of matter. This evidence shows that this student has moved beyond basic fluency with each map to a new level of being able to independently apply and transfer multiple Thinking Maps to show factual knowledge networked within conceptual displays. Importantly, all of the other students in the classroom are also able to select which Thinking Map(s) they wish to use for the content and processes embedded in the text, much like carpenters selecting multiple tools out of their toolbox according to the task at hand. To extend this analogy, a foreman on a construction job tells the master carpenters what they are supposed to build, but cannot be responsible for telling each worker which tools to use for the actual building of the final product. Once students gain basic mastery over Thinking Maps, the teacher can observe which kind of thinking the students choose to do, the tools they use, and the conceptual products they construct. The teacher, like the foreman, can thus see the products of work, observe student choices of tools, and assess the outcomes while looking at the formative development of thinking.

DEVELOPING REFLECTIVE ASSESSMENT OF CONTENT AND COGNITION

In the examples above, we looked at a sampling of student-generated Thinking Maps showing a progression from fluency to transfer. This happens over time, often over multiple years, and always within an understanding of the full variances of cognitive development in our student population from school age to graduation. When you walk into a school that has used the maps year after year, you see on the walls in hallways, in the classroom, in the teachers' planning books, and in student notebooks a wide array of applications that reveal that students are receiving an integrated approach to thinking and learning reflecting different learning styles.

In the examples above, we mostly looked at how teachers may use Thinking Maps for formative assessment on a daily basis. Once students are fluent with and can transfer the maps within and across disciplines (which can easily happen with 8-year-old students), teachers have an alternative way of structuring formative assessments. At the end of a unit of study, teachers may create assessments that ask students to draw comprehensive maps of the content they have learned. Often, content concepts are assessed by asking students to write down their answers in the form of multiple-choice questions, short-answer questions, essays, and reports. These traditional assessment formats are linear representations (our written code) of what are mostly nonlinear concepts, thus lacking congruency of *form*. What happens if a student is a very good thinker and a very poor writer? As noted by Stefanie Holzman (see Chapter 11, "First Language for Thinking in a Multilingual School"), Thinking Maps become a powerful set of tools for assessment of English language learners who do high-quality thinking while not fully fluent in a second language. How do we find out what they know? The outcome is exasperation by all: The teacher often knows that the student can do the conceptual work but cannot deliver on a test that requires the student to choose from multiple-choice options, fill in a word, or write out nonlinear concepts in the linear form of an essay. The student is frustrated as well.

MAPPER RUBRIC FOR SCORING EFFECTIVENESS

If Thinking Maps are used as formative and even summative assessments, how does one give value, or a grade, to the Thinking Maps created by students? Returning to Novak and Gowin's (1984) research on concepts and concept mapping, they defined three criteria for assessing and grading the student-generated maps: expanding, clarifying, and assimilating. As shown in Figure 19.5, the 5-point MAPPER rubric (Hyerle, 1996) offers a holistic framework for assessing Thinking Maps developed by students. The five dimensions across the top reflect the cognitive

Figure 19.4   Multiple Maps on "Matter"

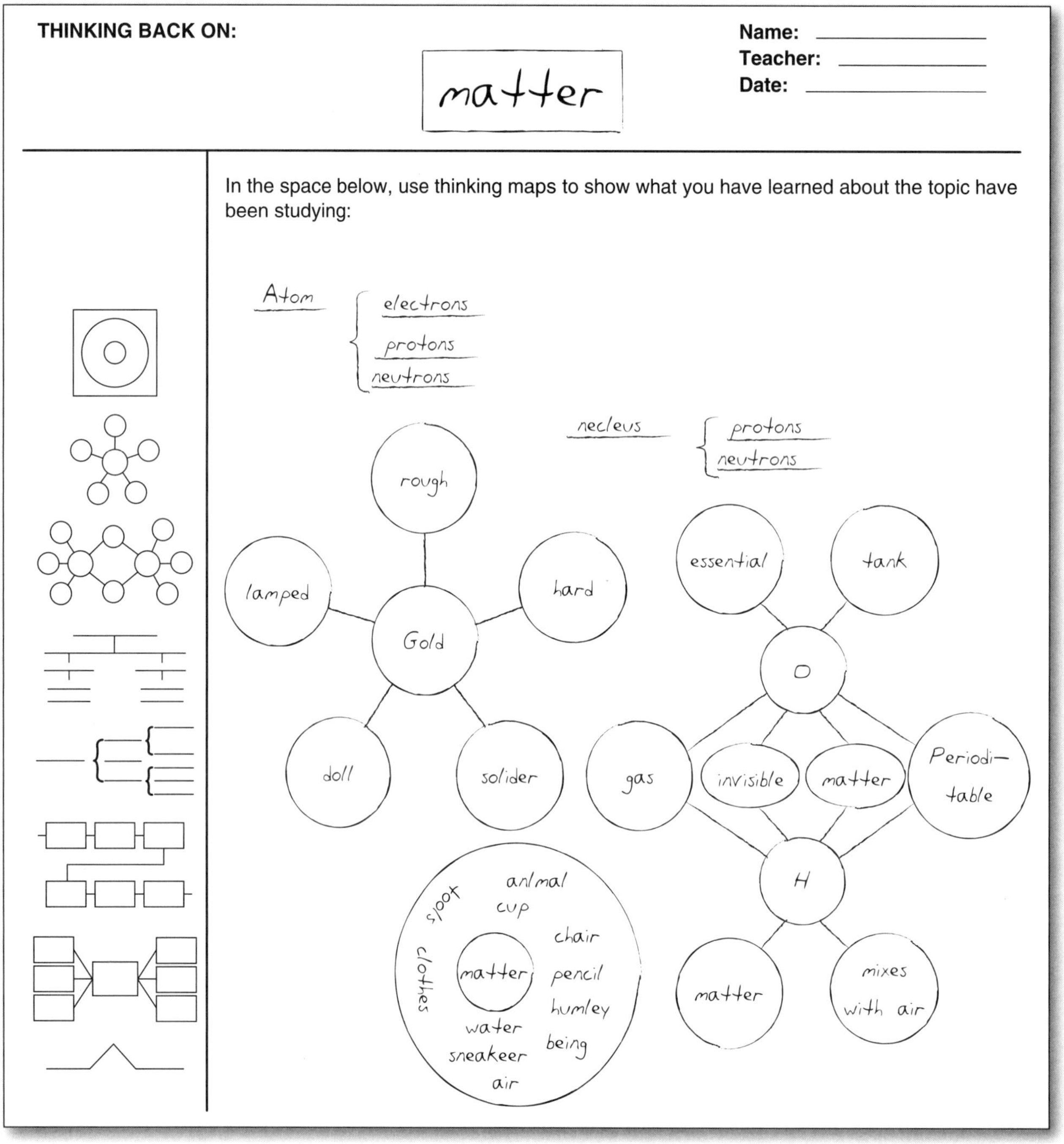

engagement of the student with content knowledge leading toward final products and a metacognitive, reflective stance. The three dimensions down the left side reflect the dynamic criteria for transforming information into useful knowledge established by Novak and Gowin. Note that the first cell at the top left of the three-by-five matrix is the minimum level: a student using only one map with very few connections. As you view this matrix, read across the cells and notice that as students are *expanding* the amount of information in the map, they must also work to *synthesize* the maps they create, as well as *clarifying* ideas by supporting general concepts with relevant details (see the center cell at *clarify* and *participating*). As an example of

Figure 19.5 MAPPER Rubric

	Minimum	Attending	Participating	Effective	Reflective
EXPAND	• Very few connections • Use of only one map	• Multiple connections • Few supporting details are shown	• Multiple concepts are shown with details • Multiple maps are used	• Thematic and interdisciplinary connections are shown	• Personal, interpersonal, and social implications are recorded
CLARIFY	• Bits of information are isolated, unorganized • Irrelevant information is included	• Different kinds of information are provided • Details are shown in relation to general concepts	• Patterns in maps are developed • Details are sorted • General concepts are fully supported with relevant details	• Connections are shown between multiple maps • Central ideas are highlighted for application	• Frame is used to establish point of view and value of map • Hypotheses are generated
ASSIMILATE	• One perspective or solution is shown • Rote repetition of information is presented	• Alternative way of presenting information is initiated • Points of confusion are highlighted	• Integration of prior knowledge and new information is shown • Fundamental misconceptions are resolved	• Several maps are coordinated for use in final product • Novel applications are created	• Multiple perspectives are shown • Limitations of map(s) are suggested • Self-assessment is initiated

	Minimum	Attending	Participating	Effective	Reflective
DESCRIPTION	The student is demonstrating a simplistic level of understanding of content and/or limited effort.	The student is attending to the task and demonstrates a basic grasp of content and information.	The student is actively engaged with thinking about content and is beginning to integrate and initiate new ideas.	The student is strategically synthesizing information with a focus on organizing central ideas and details for meaningful applications.	The student is seeking a deeper understanding of knowledge by recognizing multiple interpretations, implications, and limitations of work.
1	2	3	4	5	6

scoring, return to the "matter" example in Figure 19.4. Let's say that this student created only one map, a Circle Map, showing basic factual knowledge about matter. This student would probably receive a score of 1 as shown in the simple 5-point scale for holistic scoring. If the student completed the four maps as shown in Figure 19.4, then the score may rise to a level 2 or 3 as he has shown a basic grasp of knowledge and is actively integrating ideas together. This rubric is at this time a tool that may be used by teachers and students alike to reflect on and discuss the growing sophistication of not only their content knowledge but also their own growth as autonomous thinkers within and across disciplines.

SEEING THROUGH THE BIFOCAL LENS

When a teaching faculty as a learning community brings the Thinking Maps across the entire school, or a school system brings the maps across the feeder patterns from elementary to high school in its wider learning organization, a common visual language for thinking develops and the focus becomes trained on higher-order thinking, creative and analytic thinking, and supporting students in becoming autonomous, reflective learners. There is a transformation in the belief systems and expectations of teachers about what is possible to teach (Dweck, 2005), because they have a dynamic way of assessing students' thinking, connected to *and* with a different lens, apart from the content. The students have been offered a language that nurtures and facilitates continuous cognitive development, problem solving, and fundamental Habits of Mind (Costa & Kallick, 2008). Like any language, they have been given graphic starting points through which they creatively analyze content knowledge, spinning new patterns of thinking—consistent with how the brain learns. When given tools to show not only what they know, but how they know it, teachers can truly look through their integrated bifocal lens and determine both the content that students have learned and the thinking they used to process what they know. All can see the formative nature of thinking evolving before their eyes. And looking through this new lens a teacher may say to a student, with delight and depth, and with a reflective assessment that carries meaning for the student, "I see what you mean."

REFERENCES

Anderson, L. W., & Krathwohl, D. R. (Eds.). (2001). *A taxonomy for teaching, learning, and assessing.* New York: Addison Wesley Longman.

Bloom, B. S. (Ed.) (with Engelhart, M. D., Furst, E. J., Hill, W. H., & Krathwohl, D. R.). (1956). *Taxonomy of educational objectives: Handbook: Cognitive domain.* New York: David McKay.

Costa, A., & Kallick, B. (2008). *Learning and leading with Habits of Mind: 16 essential characteristics for success.* Alexandria, VA: Association for Supervision and Curriculum Development.

Dweck, C. S. (2005). *Competence and motivation: Competence as the core of achievement motivation.* New York: Guilford Press.

Erickson, L. H. (2002). *Concept-based curriculum and instruction.* Thousand Oaks, CA: Corwin.

Hyerle, D. (1996). *Visual tools for constructing knowledge.* Alexandria, VA: Association for Supervision and Curriculum Development.

Hyerle, D. (2009). *Visual tools for transforming information into knowledge.* Thousand Oaks, CA: Corwin.

Marzano, R. J., & Pickering, D. (2005). *Building academic vocabulary: Teacher's manual.* Alexandria, VA: Association for Supervision and Curriculum Development.

Novak, J. D., & Gowin, D. B. (1984). *Learning how to learn.* New York: Cambridge University Press.

Index

217

CORWIN
A SAGE Company

The Corwin logo—a raven striding across an open book—represents the union of courage and learning. Corwin is committed to improving education for all learners by publishing books and other professional development resources for those serving the field of PreK–12 education. By providing practical, hands-on materials, Corwin continues to carry out the promise of its motto: **"Helping Educators Do Their Work Better."**